A Jacana book

SOMETHING TO WRITE HOME ABOUT

EDITED BY
CLAUDE COLART AND SAHM VENTER

First published in 2004 by Jacana
5 St Peter Road
Bellevue
2198
South Africa

ISBN 1-919931-95-3

Cover design by Disturbance

Printed by Formeset Printers

See a complete list of Jacana titles at www.jacana.co.za

This book is dedicated to the memory of our friends and colleagues,

Ameen Akhalwaya
Miguel Gil Moreno
Chris Gutuza
Kerem Lawton
Aziz Tassiem
Myles Tierney

Gone too soon, always in our hearts

Contents

Acknowledgements

Thank you to all of you who contributed your work to this collection, despite the pressure of deadlines, memory lapses and emotional blocks. And also to those who for these and other reasons, could not put pen to paper. Gaby Neujahr and the Konrad Adenauer Stiftung jumped at the opportunity to offer their beautiful Johannesburg premises for the launch. We are also grateful to our dear friend, Maggie Davey for believing in this book enough to publish it; PR. Anderson poet extraordinaire and treasured voice of wisdom (when he answers his phone); Lavinia Browne for her endless patience, Ayesha Ismail and "Deedoo" – as always. To Brennan Linsley and Elida Ramadani for their photographs of Miguel and Kerem; and Elida for her amusing and touching words about Miguel and Kerem; Farida Akhalwaya and Zaytoon Akhalwaya-Abed for reminding us all of Ameen's sense of humour; Zenzile Khoisan for his tribute to Chris; Alistair Lyne for sharing some classic Myles moments; Shafiek Tassiem for his memories of his brother, Aziz and to John Lawton for his witness on behalf of his son, Kerem. For setting so many examples, our friend and hero, Ahmed Kathrada (who is about to publish his second book) and his researcher/ "boss" "Belinda" aka Kimberley Worthington.

And our heartfelt gratitude to Desmond Tutu, Archbishop Emeritus for his wonderful foreword and his inspiring acts of love and care.

Finally, to our families and friends and the loved ones of journalists all over the world, who worry, and are proud and wish they would get "proper" jobs, all in one breath.

Foreword by
Desmond Tutu Archbishop Emeritus

In recent days, the Fourth Estate has not had a good press. It has been thrust into the unwelcome glare of controversy because of the strange conduct of Jason Blair formerly of *The New York Times* and Jack Kelley formerly of *USA Today*. They have brought their profession into disrepute by plagiarising and making up stories that were sometimes prominently reported in their respective publications. This has fuelled a growing cynicism about the media. Some of the criticism has been entirely deserved when the public was served up unabashed jingoistic gruel, as in the runup to and during the Iraqi war when major US newspapers and TV networks kept dutifully spewing forth the disquisitions of his master's voice quite uncritically and almost as a matter of solemn duty. I never thought I would witness most of the US media so compliant and conformist, so ready to toe the Administration's line, for example not showing pictures of the body bags from Iraq. I had always imagined that the US really meant it when she spoke about freedom of speech until I discovered through sad personal experience that it was freedom of speech only if you said what was in accord with the official line. Anything critical of the White House was usually pilloried as anti-American and if it was uttered by a US citizen then such a person was branded as unpatriotic. Of course there were notable exceptions. As a South African, I experienced an awful *déjà vu*. That was what used to happen in apartheid South Africa. If you criticised the government of the day, rebuttals did not examine the validity or otherwise of your position. It was immediately castigated as unpatriotic, unSouth African. In the South Africa of those days the electronic media were unashamed propaganda agents for the apartheid regime. But not all journalists have been unprofessional or unethical. On the contrary, the opposite is the case. I want to use this opportunity to pay a very warm tribute to those journalists with whom I came into contact. Under very trying circumstances, having to contend with draconian legislation to control the media in South Africa, it is nothing short of miraculous that so many could tell the truth even as they were running a grave risk in doing so. It was no better under most other repressive dispensations. Our struggle would have been even longer had our story not got out to the outside world and alerted the international community to our plight and to our commitment to effect change nonviolently, despite what government propaganda said to the contrary. Foreign journalists were outstanding in this regard.

And during my public ministry I have met and become friends with many journalists, some of whom have contributed to this volume. I came to be really fond of them, knowing that they were people with hopes and fears, prejudices and beliefs. In short, they were ordinary human beings doing frequently extraordinary work that often exposed them to physical danger and death. I was touched by how those who reported on the proceedings of our Truth and Reconciliation Commission were frequently affected by the stories to which they were exposed. They helped immensely in the work of reconciliation in our land by publicising as widely as they did the traumas, the atrocities, the magnanimity and generosity of spirit of those who were willing to forgive and walk the path of reconciliation rather than that of retribution. The contribution of the media has been immense.

This anthology of deeply moving stories reveals that journalists are not callous, hardhearted cynical operatives moving like predators after their prey. They are wonderful sensitive human beings who laugh and cry, who love and hate, who are calm, who are frightened, who are brave and who are sometimes cowardly, but who are ultimately people who care about others and what is done to and for them. They care about our world and hope that they might help to make it a little more hospitable to love, compassion and laughter, and have given their services for free to honour their fallen comrades.

They are beautiful people and some of them have touched my life and I am a better person for that.

Vultures are human too

An introduction

Journalists are human beings who see things through human-being eyes and bring to their news coverage feelings, knowledge, bias, and experience from the rest of their human-being lives. Often labelled "vultures", they flit across the globe covering all manner of news during which they are faced with a range of feelings, from horror to occasional joy.

Usually left unexpressed, these feelings tend to emerge at unexpected and inappropriate times. Thoughtful accounts, if they emerge at all, are told to other journalists, sometimes to therapists and even more rarely, in published memoirs. These on-the-road moments and encounters hardly ever make it into reports, encouraged as journalists are to be "neutral and objective". What they encounter in the margins and on the sidelines of covering "the story" often remain on the back pages of their memories, triggered by the odd glimpse of private snapshots stuffed into boxes in the back of cupboards and minds.

Believing that all journalists have something to write home about, we wanted to create a space for these stories to show that these so-called vultures are human too. In so doing we want to honour our fallen friends and colleagues, whose loss to their loved ones and the profession has been enormous.

We were overwhelmed by the response from journalists throughout the world who jumped at the opportunity to express their emotions in this collective salute to colleagues who are no longer with us. Representing 25 countries, they have helped to create a mini-United Nations of writers, photographers, producers and camera operators. Drawing from their experiences in more than 40 countries, they write about the tragic, the sad, the poignant and sometimes the humorous, building a mosaic of emotions crowding the collective psyche of these witnesses to the world.

They have contributed their writing for free, knowing that all the royalties will benefit two very special funds, the Miguel Gil Moreno Foundation and the Kerem Lawton Fund. An award-winning international television cameraman, Miguel Gil Moreno was killed with Kurt Schork from Reuters, in an ambush in Sierra Leone, on 24 May 2000. Kerem Lawton, the husband of fellow journalist Elida Ramadani, was killed in a mortar attack on the Kosovo-Macedonia border on 29 March 2001, three months before the birth of their daughter, Tara.

The Miguel Gil Moreno Foundation has established an award which honours humanitarian journalism and is raising money to build a home for orphaned girls in Abidjan, Côte d'Ivoire, so they may attend school in the city Miguel called home for some time. Tara Lawton who lives with her mother in Pristina, Kosovo, will be almost three years old when this book is published. All the money collected by the Kerem Lawton Trust is earmarked for her education. It will keep alive that passion for discovery and communication that made her father get up every day to do his demanding and sometimes dangerous job [... even on the day he and Elida married, as she recounts in her contribution].

The devastating loss of Kerem and Miguel was felt not only in the hearts of their families and friends, but in the journalistic community across the globe. Described by his friend Susanne Ramirez as a "missionary with a camera", Miguel gave up a career as a corporate lawyer in Barcelona to offer his assistance to journalists in Sarajevo. He was driven by a profound faith to tell the story of the people whose plight inhabits the pages of newspapers and television screens around the world. "He felt he must bear witness to violence and give voice to the unspeakable. He felt the story must be told – even if the rest of the world was not paying attention," Susanne wrote of Miguel.

She describes the community of fearless and committed journalists with a moral vision as "a tribe". Another member of that tribe was Kerem Lawton, who was given the journalistic bug by his father John Lawton, a veteran journalist himself. Kerem loved being out there capturing history. Whether it was covering the end of German Chancellor Helmut Kohl's long political life or the fighting in the Balkans, he tackled it all with determination and good humour.

His friend and colleague Andy Stoneham remembered thinking "not another one" and feeling sick to the pit of his stomach when he got the message about Kerem's death. He also remembered being struck by the realisation that he had no idea what to say when he next spoke to Elida, suddenly a widow and pregnant with her first baby at the same time.

"Another one" indeed.

This book is also dedicated to Myles Tierney, Ameen Akhalwaya, Aziz Tassiem and Chris Gutuza, our friends and colleagues who left us much too early and whose humanity and journalistic work inspired us deeply.

Just over a year before his friend Miguel was killed on the roads of Sierra Leone, Myles Tierney was ambushed in the same country. Ironically he was shot while in a convoy in Freetown with that country's Information Minister who wanted to show the world that the capital was safe and in government control. Earlier on that fateful day – 10 January 2000 – the Associated Press trio was arguing about who would sit where in the car when Myles convinced his writer colleague Ian Stewart that he needed to sit at the window so he could point his camera. Myles smoothed the atmosphere by assuring Ian that his "fat body" would protect him from danger. Such New York-style wit was a Myles trademark and often lifted his colleagues' spirits on difficult assignments in Africa's hotspots. Ian later published "Freetown Ambush" which details his recovery after he was seriously critically injured in the same attack which killed Myles. Ian has offered a range of insights from his travels in this book.

Myles is also remembered in this collection by his close friend and colleague, Alistair Lyne, in his story "One day in Zaire". Based in Nairobi, Kenya, these friends worked as a well-oiled team of two, documenting news in many African countries. One of their many triumphs was being able to travel with Laurent Desiré Kabila and his soldiers as they trekked from the east to the west to unseat Mobutu Sese Seko from his throne in Zaire.

Aziz Tassiem lived to tell the world about news stories and died covering one in South Africa on 4 August 1991. His brother Shafiek, now a Reuters Television cameraman, writes of those early days when he wanted to be just like his big brother. Chris Gutuza was driven by a passion for journalism and for passing on his skills to those less fortunate. He is honoured in a poem by his friend and colleague Zenzile Khoisan. Chris, who passed away on 7 October 2001, followed in the footsteps of anti-apartheid scribes like Ameen Akhalwaya who, on his deathbed in Johannesburg in January 1998, was visited by the then President Nelson Mandela who thanked him for his contribution to ending apartheid. Ameen's fearless journalism was always marked by a keen sense of humour, which his widow Farida Akhalwaya and his daughter Zaytoon Akhalwaya-Abed remind us of in their contribution of one of Ameen's more humorous pieces.

All of these friends and colleagues are remembered in this collection, as are the hundreds of other journalists across the globe who have lost their lives in recent years. Their deaths continually remind us that this digital world which has given us the tools to cover stories anywhere, any time and faster than before, is also a more dangerous one. Their loss reminds us to be particularly vigilant, because as Stoneham reminds us: "I don't believe a story is worth people's lives".

Claude Colart and Sahm Venter
Johannesburg 2004

Walking in

Stuart Ramsay

"What do you mean they aren't bloody going in? What the fuck are we supposed to do? Walk?"

Stuart Ramsay of Sky News television was nursing a beer in the bar of the Nazran Hotel, a sort of journalist staging post a relatively safe distance from Grozny, the utterly destroyed capital of the would-be break-away republic of Chechnya.

It is August 1996, the eve of a potential cease-fire and indeed possible end to the first Chechen war, as it was known. It was also the eve of a final demand relayed by the Russian armed forces to the Chechen rebels – agree to a cease-fire or prepare for a blitz on the city that would leave nothing standing.

That's why Ramsay and his producer, Natasha Gorbacheva, were in town – hoping to cadge a lift in a Reuters TV armoured car to the centre of Grozny. But it wasn't going in – in fact they were planning to have the day off.

"I'm sorry Stuart there's nothing I can do, they just said no," whispered Natasha. She has that sort of theatrical James-Bond-tasty-Russian-spy accent that is quite endearing but, in noisy bars and whispered, is almost indecipherable.

"Orry Stuuuuaaaaarrt nee I cannndo idgez sezno," "What?", "Iz no", "For fuck's sake" – and so it went on – Ramsay disappearing into a bout of journalistic despair that usually results in a lot more beer and an argument with London desk or Wife, depending upon who answers the dodgy sat phone first.

There was no real choice; the pair elected to find a local taxi in the morning and head into Grozny in an ordinary car. The problem was finding a driver stupid enough to do it – but there is always one.

The key of course is that by definition the driver has to be stupid, mad or more likely very poor.

Ali was a driver with a rare and remarkable gift of combining all of these above traits into one fairly amenable bundle.

"No problem. We drive in – no problem, I know it very well, no problem," smiled Ali, counting a hundred US in tens.

Shortly before dawn with flak jackets onboard they set off in a convoy of two vehicles – the second carrying another pair of journalists, and driven by Ali's brother, an equally gifted individual.

The petrol gauge, almost needless to say in battered old Skodas, didn't work, prompting Ramsay to insist on a fuel stop – bunging Ali plenty of local to ensure a complete top-up.

In war zones the drive is often pleasant with few people on the road and an almost surreal sense of calm.

In the distance, fires from Grozny sent thick black clouds into the sky; the convoy slowly edging their way to the Russian lines surrounding the besieged city.

Russian soldiers seeing "TV" taped to the side of the cars waved the convoy through with dismissive gestures.

Helicopter gunships emerged from behind hills and buildings, hovering thirty or forty feet above the cars, tilting as if to fire before pulling away, causing a storm of rubble and vegetation and dust.

Ramsay and Gorbacheva were tense as they drove through the battered outskirts of the city – but not as tense as Ali. For about half an hour he'd been mumbling to himself.

Natasha asked him in Russian what the problem was.

"He says he didn't think it was like this," said Natasha.

"Hold on – don't tell me he's never fucking been here – he's the fucking guide."

"It's worse than that – he won't go any further. He says he'll wait if the firing doesn't start again. Sorry Stuart, we will have to walk in."

"Shit – this is a disaster, actually its worse than that, it's bloody useless," Ramsay watched his journalistic endeavours evaporating amidst burning rubble and a scorching Chechen sun.

London was expecting an end-of-the-war or total-destruction story by the evening.

By now Ali's brother had also refused to go further leaving the four journalists with a simple choice – go on by foot or go back.

They agreed on a short foray to check out the situation – then re-assess.

The foursome emerged into a makeshift market place and was quickly surrounded by groups of children and old women, many screaming hysterically about the fighting and the need for food.

The crowd hushed as an open-topped, flashy, American-made four-wheel-drive jeep turned the corner – on board five heavily armed Chechen gunmen led by an equally well-equipped woman freedom fighter dressed in designer camouflage gear, her waist-length hair tied in a pony-tail beneath a Che Guevara beret and sporting Ray Ban Aviator mirror shades.

A little boy tugged Natasha's hand, "They are trouble, they are looking for you. Go towards the front."

The front line was about 700 metres away on the edge of what looked like a football field. As they approached, the tell-tale whiz and pop of high-velocity rounds zinged around them. "They're trying to shoot us," Natasha pointed out.

As they beat a hasty retreat between bombed-out buildings the four turned a corner into the sights of four gunmen.

"We are British journalists covering the war from your side," said Ramsay, immediately falling into that well-trodden trench of being the best new mate of anyone pointing a gun at one's head.

It being Ramadan, the fighters were hungry and generally unhappy. At gunpoint they were frog-marched to the atrium of a burnt-out building. Inside, dozens of exhausted soldiers lay slumped against walls clutching their weapons – at first they were curious, then angry.

The Chechens were taking a beating on the front line – for an hour they screamed abuse, threatened to shoot and singled out the Russian Natasha for particular attention.

Slowly an ugly situation was getting really nasty. Brandishing his British passport, Ramsay finally turned back from the wall he'd been facing and in best British form addressed the soldiers.

"I am a British journalist. Natasha is an employee of Sky News and works as my translator. She is not a Russian spy and has covered the current conflict for two years – leave us alone. We now intend to leave."

Of course they didn't understand a word, but it did calm matters.

From the entranceway, dressed in black Armani jeans, black T-shirt and black loafers, a young man stepped forward.

"Shut up. I am in charge here. You shouldn't be here. Follow me."

Through a maze of buildings and alleyways the designer leader led the four, surrounded by his armed militia, to a flight of steps leading to a cellar.

"Down there," he pointed.

Ramsay at the front tentatively took the first steps down.

"Stuart, I don't like this," whispered Natasha.

As she spoke they froze, as the sickening sound of AK-47 gun bolts sliding across the breach of half a dozen weapons seemed deafeningly loud.

"Fuck," he replied. "Sorry Tash."

The door swung open revealing a pitch-black interior; the four ushered into the silence and darkness.

From behind them a match was struck and a lantern lit. As their eyes adjusted they could see dozens of bright eyes peering at them through the gloom. Women and children, whole families, sheltering from what they believed would be the imminent arrival of Russian fighter-bombers and helicopter gunships.

"Would you like some tea?" asked Mr Armani. "You must be very thirsty."

Beneath a bombed-out building the fighters and their guests were served tea and sticky buns by the women. Conversation drifted from the actual fight to the failure of the west to help the people of Chechnya.

"Why has nobody helped us so far – why are we forced to live like this?"

Treading a fine diplomatic line, Ramsay promised that reports like the one he was preparing would help expose the great suffering of the people.

"Actually that is quite the point," he explained. "We really need to be on our way if we are to make this evening's news."

Two hours later Mr Armani rose and offered to escort the journalists to their cars.

Clapping Ramsay on his back he promised a warm welcome whenever he returned.

"The British people are forever linked to the Chechens. You have been here for centuries, and I know your army will come to support us. Good luck."

They didn't speak much until they got to their cars.

"Tash, I can't tell if we were really in the shit then or whether it was never that bad."

"Fucking hell, Stuart – you should have heard what they were saying to me in Russian. Ali get us home."

Half an hour into their drive – Ali ran out of petrol.

"OK, this is just about fucking it. We are in the middle of nowhere, it's dark, the Russians are going to wipe Grozny out and Ali the idiot has run out of bleeding petrol. DOES ANYONE HAVE A CLUE WHAT WE ARE GOING TO DO?"

"Calm down Stuart, we'll borrow petrol from Ali's brother, and we'll get back and file."

So playing a ludicrous game of mechanical leap frog, Ali would borrow some petrol, drive until it ran out, borrow some more and so on.

In the distance the lights of Nazran began to twinkle. Mobile phone range finally reached. But it was late — very late to cut and feed a piece for news that evening — but still there was time.

Five goes on the mobile — then through at last!

"Hello Foreign."

"Mate, its Stuart. We are safe. Sorry we're late. Very weird day but got some good stuff — when can we file? Will you book a feed?"

"Hello mate — we are very busy, nothing needed – where are you anyway?"

"Forget it."

Stuart Ramsay is currently the Sky News Africa correspondent. Previous postings include Washington, Russia and Ireland. He has worked in hot-spots around the globe for Sky News for the past 11 years. In 2003 he spent three months as an embedded journalist with the United States Army in Iraq before returning to his current beat. He is married with three children, three dogs, three fish and a cat.

Bosnia, April 1993

Christiane Amanpour

It was a terrible time in Bosnia, the war was at its height and it seemed every day uncovered a new atrocity. In the spring of that year the Bosnian Serbs had launched a devastating artillery attack on the tiny village they had besieged, Srebrenica in Eastern Bosnia. It was clear a calamity was unfolding with scraps of news emerging about men women and children being killed and wounded.

At the time the Serbs allowed no journalists in, and no relief workers either. But finally after long negotiations the UN worked out a deal with the Serbs whereby they would go in with trucks to evacuate the women and children and old men from the village. The only way for us journalists to cover this story was to go to Tuzla, the nearest big city, and wait for the truck to cross into Bosnian territory.

Eventually, as night fell, we spotted the first UN truck; there were many of them and most went directly to Tuzla's big sports stadium where these new war refugees were to be sheltered and fed. Most of the journalists followed those first trucks, but one turned off in another direction and by some instinct my crew and I followed. The hospital was its destination.

We prepared to take pictures as those inside were being unloaded, but nothing prepared us for what we saw: inside were children, bloodied, bandaged and crying in pain and fear. I remember the few journalists there let out a gasp of horror, even though many of us had covered so much suffering before. One little boy was carried off first; he was about five years old, badly injured and terrified. I will always remember someone repeating over and over again, "don't be afraid, you are free now".

The picture of that little boy went around the world and defined the horror of the war that spring in Bosnia. Little did we know that much worse was to come for Srebrenica. Two years later, the Serbs overran the little village and carried out an orgy of mass murder. To this day about 8,000 Bosnian men and boys from Srebrenica are still missing and presumed dead. To this day what happened in Srebrenica remains the single worst atrocity in Europe since World War Two and will be seared on the conscience of the world forever.

Christiane Amanpour is CNN's chief international correspondent based in London. Amanpour has reported on most crises from many of the world's war zones. For her reporting from the Balkans, Amanpour received a News and Documentary Emmy and the Dupont, Polk and Peabody awards. Amanpour began her CNN career in 1983 as an assistant on the international desk in Atlanta. She is also a contributor to CBS News' 60 Minutes.

When the sun kisses the dew, drought makes love to the future

Vukile Pokwana

A large and shapeless woman emerges from the circular mud house. Over her dirty black dress she wears tattered pullovers, each of a different colour. Flies are dancing around her making round and snake-like formations. A bare-bottomed infant crawls just outside the hut. The dried up mucus paints his face in grotesque shapes. He is unkempt and soaked in dirt.

As we draw closer to the kraal, a short, stocky man clad in a black pin-striped suit (that has seen better days) and an American pork pie hat, holding a *knobkerrie*, is looking at us with curiosity. True to the tradition of the Eastern Cape manner of exchanging pleasantries, I start with a polite "*Molo*" followed by a heap of my ancestral imprecations. A broad smile slithers out from his wrinkled face and he commands that we sit.

Other curious onlookers give us quick appraising glances, and dogs at surrounding homesteads bark feverishly as if to announce our arrival. The old man who prefers to be only known as Tshawe, is a descendant of the Xhosa King Hinsta, who was killed and beheaded during a battle between the Xhosa and the British in 1835. He shuffles his legs nervously before agreeing to the interview and quickly asks if we will pay him. The woman who is now humming a long, drawn-out, sad song of life joins us.

The old man clears his throat and shoots from the mouth: "We are scavenging not for bread or meat but for pity and human kindness. We are helpless and waiting for hope. We have been terribly let down by our government. We have lost our pride and dignity due to the grinding poverty. It is sad … very sad."

His wife, Nomathembu, without being provoked, charges in a high-pitched voice: "Our children are the hardest hit. We live on the brink of hunger and death." Death and poverty are synonymous here. She continues: "We have nowhere to go. If you are an illiterate person, where do you start with this government of the educated people?"

The child who has been crawling close by begins to wail, as if confirming the mother's statement. We are in Embewuleni, "place of harvest" and just a stone's throw away from where we are conducting the interview is the Mbeki homestead near the main road, occasionally covered in dust caused by the speeding bakkies that double up as taxis.

This poverty, the hopelessness etched on the people's faces coupled with corrupting fear is a relic of the past. In part it is an economic condition calculated by the erstwhile government. Conversely, our new democratic government has failed to rescue the locals from the abyss of poverty. The government has been unable to demonstrate an urgent commitment to eradicating poverty in the rural communities.

It is no wonder that the Eastern Cape is the poorest province in South Africa in terms of average monthly expenditure – followed by the Free State and then Limpopo, based on the Statistics South Africa report "Measuring Poverty in South Africa". The Eastern Cape is rich with history and a fertile ground for studies in culture and anthropology.

It is here that the great Xhosa warriors fought nine frontier wars over 100 years from 1779–1879. It was 100 years of intermittent bloody warfare ending in resettlement, pain and anger. The Frontier Wars – or as they are fondly known by the previous regime as the Kaffir Wars – were some of the longest battles fought by Africans against European intrusion.

The Eastern Cape is the third largest province in the country. Its people speak mainly Xhosa, English and Afrikaans. Hedonists, bohemians and others tell tangy tales of its marijuana plantations. It is a land of undulating hills, endless sweeps of sandy beaches, majestic mountains and emerald-green forests.

It is not the beauty of the Eastern Cape and the prospects of breathing clear air that fascinate me. Back at the homestead, new faces have gathered around eager to participate in the conversation. Asked whether the locals are not being too hard on the government for which they knowingly voted in 1994 and continued to do so in more recent local government elections, Tshawe shrugged.

An air of quietness settled around the kraal as he cocked his head to one side in a deprecating gesture peculiar of the locals. "What do you expect? We are the lost, poor and forgotten children. We have been reduced to beggars with no pride or shame. Our government needs to do something favourable."

In 1994, the ANC promised the masses that attacking poverty and deprivation would be the first priority of a democratic government. The extent of poverty in the Eastern Cape is so glaring and scary that one is left helpless, angry and filled with pity. Such is the nature of a place that produced politicians of the calibre of Nelson Mandela and the late Govan Mbeki. On the other side of the Indian Ocean, Utah Pradesh, which has produced stellar folks in politics, business and other fields, is also faced with monumental poverty.

South Africa has been praised in many quarters as having the most liberal constitution in the world. The same constitution is against poverty and establishes rights to access adequate housing, health care, water, land, education and social security.

It dawned on me after this self-sponsored three-day trip that people are not only bitter about the widening gulf between the haves and have-nots but also feel let down by the policies devised by government. Undeniably, white values continue to permeate our country despite the mantra of the new South Africa, the African Renaissance, which embraces *Ubuntu* – humanity. The saying "Every man for himself" slithers out in the daily human exchange. Worse, the RDP and Gear (Growth, Employment and Redistribution policy) are regarded only as jargon with no meaning for rural communities.

They need the government to listen to them. The voice of the rural poor is inaudible, and the government continues to be sluggish when it comes to delivering basic services. Hardest hit by poverty are children. When Gear was announced, it was widely referred to as "market friendly". But the truth soon dawned on the masses that it was a mere wish-list aimed at appeasing investors, containing little hope for the poor and impoverished masses.

The government, although it continues to defend Gear as a policy, knows that the alleviation of poverty can never be resolved by the markets alone. The poor need to be heard, and not through some neo-liberal framework that leaves them reeling from hunger and deprivation. A fundamental restructuring of the economy needs to take place in order for programmes that deal with poverty alleviation to be put into practice. Government needs to rethink and make substantial changes in the distribution of income, wealth and economic power.

What is really needed is for the government to listen to the poor through rural forums. "This is our government. We will continue to vote for it. But they have to get the simple rule of democracy clear – to step down from their ivory towers and get close to the people, smell and feel the texture of poverty. If this is not done, our children will be wiped out by poverty and history will judge the ANC badly," argues Tshawe.

As we bid farewell and exchange telephone numbers, a willowy fellow who has been listening attentively arrests my attention with his hoarse voice as he calls out my clan name. "It's still a rich man's world for the poor. We live on the edge of death here. It is the white man's rope around our necks that is causing all this suffering and poverty. Every day it tightens a bit."

Born and raised in Cape Town, Vukile Smanky Pokwana worked for a range of newspapers including as Showbiz Editor for South Africa's *City Press*, a widely circulated Sunday newspaper. He is the Strategic Director for Vutha Advertising and Marketing and Vutha Entertainment, a socially conscious communications and entertainment company. He is also a poet and a budding screenplay writer.

African children

Jimi Matthews

It's always a race.

"What time is the bird? What have the opposition got?"

"Bodies? How many? How many do you have?"

"No, don't bother. There's no interest. Maybe if you had some bodies."

I had some bodies yesterday, but there was a train crash in Germany. There's always more interest in dead Germans than in (barely) living Somalis. Dead Somalis competing for the headlines with dead Germans? No contest!

"How quickly can you get from Cairo to Dakar? Some Italian tourists have gone missing, maybe kidnapped."

"Well, I'd have to fly to Paris and get a flight from there to Dakar."

That was the nature of my daily conversations with the newsroom in London.

I was not at home much as my son was growing up. I was always on the road, chasing headlines. And when at home, consumed by the demons lurking in my subconscious, I lash out at those who care. The emotional gunge corked deep down.

We do not give a toss. We are just there to record the stuff. Too many years, too many images. No breaks. The places and people morph into one horror show. Too few pretty pictures to ease the discomfort.

And, through it all, is the little boy in Baidoa. Sunken dark eyes. The contours of his skull barely disguised by his pallid skin. He sits quietly next to his mother. She is dying. He holds her hand. He has nothing else to hold on to.

I do my routine. Tripod out, white-balance the camera and check out where the light is coming from.

I frame her face. There are flies perching on her eyelids. Her lips are dry. Her shallow breath emits a rasping sound. I pan from her face to her hand. The hand that he holds so gently. And then up to his face. To those dark, sunken eyes. He stares directly into the lens. Not a sound. Just a hopeless look.

I move back. Get the tripod. Get the wide shot. I move around trying to find the right angle. He does not move. Only his eyes slowly track my movements. I squeeze the tit on the lens. Done.

I remove the camera and gather up the tripod. It is time to move on. I do not look at the boy (or his mother). I try not to walk away too quickly. I feel his eyes on my back. I can't look back. Just get the shots. Do the pieces. Feed the pictures to London. That is my job. (They did not want the pictures. Maybe if his mother died on that brown raffia mat. Maybe if I had recorded her dying. Maybe then they would have taken the pictures in London).

Just sitting there. Next to his mother. Those sunken eyes clinging to me. Coming back to me at the oddest times, in the oddest places.

There are other stories. In other places. Child soldiers doing the bidding of their elders. Erupting volcanoes wiping out entire towns. Tyrants being toppled. Small revolutions. A decade of stuff. And always it is the women and the children.

In my country I recorded the happiness of liberation. The darkness of racial oppression giving way to the inauguration of Nelson Mandela. The toads of the apartheid state now pledging their allegiance to the new order. State pensions secured, they try to convince us that there was no malice intended.

But it is the children that we have to thank. Those brave wonderful ones, the ones who ate the teargas and felt the whips. Ten-year-olds locked up and tortured. Some crippled, others dead. The jails filled with those who were brave enough to scream, "No!" It's the price that history extracts.

Archbishop Tutu reminds us that the fascists are also God's children.

I have a son – born free of the horrors of apartheid oppression. Gentle, intelligent and with all the possibilities that life has to offer. An African child. His large dark eyes curious right from the beginning.

He enjoys reading and travelling. He is interested in the world. He has stood in the shadow of the great pyramids of Giza. He enjoyed Marakesh and Mombassa. In Malta we swam together, in clear blue waters, marvelling at the multi-coloured fish. We share stories. He seems interested in my work. Sometimes I want to tell him of the boy in Baidoa or the child soldiers in Sierra Leone. But I don't. Not yet. He is a child of Africa.

A veteran South African journalist, Jimi Matthews is a writer, stills photographer, editor, cameraman and producer. Former head of eTV News, he is now Head of TV News and Current Affairs for the SABC.

Montezuma's revenge

Fergal Keane

The stomach moves in mysterious ways. After 25 years on the road I think I've experienced every nasty bug imaginable. The worst was a bout of amoebic dysentery in West Africa, which kept me out of work for weeks and left me a much thinner man.

The rice I ate had been boiled in water contaminated by a dead animal. I truly wanted to die. Unluckily the illness coincided with a visit by my in-laws. To this day they believe I feigned illness in order to avoid them. In Africa, the Balkans, Afghanistan, Papua New Guinea and a few places in between, I have felt that terrible churning deep in the guts ... and galloped to the nearest safe haven.

Ask any foreign correspondent, photographer, producer and they will surely agree: bullets and bombs can be faced with equanimity but nothing taxes the soul like a dose of Montezuma's revenge. My answer a lot of the time is to volunteer to do the cooking for our small tribe. In Iraq at the end of a day covering war I would settle down in front of our portable stove and cook up a desert storm. It wasn't exactly a case of happy, eager faces around the campfire, more a collection of slavering wolves who would have eaten anything I produced.

But there are occasions when local hospitality demands you set your fears to one side. In Afghanistan a local warlord invited us to a feast of fatty mutton one evening and was reduced to hysterical laughter when I said I was a vegetarian. I am not of course, but the warlord simply couldn't imagine a man who didn't eat meat. I was forced to swallow the sticky globules to an accompaniment of rousing cheers. The warlord felt he'd performed an important conversion. Later that night in a dark hovel crawling with scorpions I was violently sick.

But none of the aforementioned can possibly compete with the story of the lunch, the minister and the Angolan toilet. It began with the best of intentions. I had travelled to the Angolan capital Luanda with the Canadian writer and radio producer Noah Richler. Noah thought it would be a good idea to get me to travel around Africa reporting on the putative African renaissance. That was in the mid 1990s when people still believed in the idea. Our first port of call was Angola where war, corruption and poverty seemed to present an insurmountable challenge to the reform-minded.

On our first day in Luanda we were due to interview the Minister of Mines. We checked into my old haunt the Tivoli Hotel and headed for lunch at an old Portuguese-owned restaurant somewhere in the warren of streets behind the port. Starved after the long flight down from London via Johannesburg I ate heartily. Suitably energised I headed off with Noah for the office of the Minister of Mines. He was a genial if somewhat formal fellow. My first hint of worry came as we climbed the stairs to his office (the lifts were out thanks to one of the regular power cuts.) A curious tingling feeling was starting in the pit of my stomach. We had only just started the interview when the tingle became a churn and that quickly became a swirl and that all too swiftly became a violent whirlpool. "Excuse me sir, do you have a toilet?" I squeaked.

The minister looked frightened. He was looking into my eyes and did not like what he saw. He pointed quickly to a door in the corner of the room. I sprang towards it and made the toilet within seconds of disaster. There followed a period of discomfort quite astonishing in its variety and force. Heaven knows what the minister and Noah, sitting just outside, made of it all. When the storm had subsided I looked around for some toilet paper. There was none. I whimpered to myself "Oh God, oh God, please, please help me." God being temporarily unavailable I called out to Noah. "Mate, please, pass me a few sheets of notepaper." Being the perfect producer Noah shoved several sheets of the BBC's finest notepaper under the door. It was sharp and uncomfortable but it was paper. I rose and turned to flush the toilet. But there was no water, only a wretched clanking noise. There was nothing to be done. I slithered out and took my place once more in front of the minister. Noah looked mortified. The minister was mystified. I smiled, pressed the record button and got on with the job.

The writer is a Special Correspondent with the BBC.

Hectic and dangerous, crazy and funny

Elida Ramadani

A story about two different people and two different experiences to illustrate just how hectic and dangerous, crazy and funny, covering wars can be.

It was the winter of 1998 when Miguel and I were tipped off to go to the northwestern part of Kosovo to cover an operation undertaken by the young, 20-year-old enthusiasts of the Kosovo Liberation Army, the guerrilla force that started the armed insurgency against former Yugoslav President Slobodan Milosevic in Kosovo.

The trip meant going to the KLA local headquarters in a muddy village tucked between forested hills, where young Kosovo Albanians were scattered, holding their weapons, which were mainly rust-stricken AK-47s. It meant going and talking to the local commander and his staff. It meant drinking lots of strong Turkish tea, made with God knows what water, and spending hours talking about the most important issues of those days and the little details that were important to them.

Those conversations would last for hours and would make you an expert on local football teams, but would also make you drunk and dizzy from the strong tea. Your eyes would itch from the fog created by the hundreds of cigarettes smoked - a fog one could cut with a knife.

Still, the local commander didn't change his mind. We could not convince him to let us meet his people who were going to take armed action against Serb forces without his consent.

But, we were convinced the attack was going to happen and, being very curious, we wanted to be there to film it. So, there was no way we would give up so easily.

We said good night to the local commander and instead of driving back to our offices in Pristina, we turned around and went to meet the guys in action, who were at a house-turned-guerrilla-shelter. As we entered the houses, I spotted around 11 or 12 very young guys, bracing for a fight: they helped each other put on scarves to cover their hair, placing their ammunition around their waist and picking up their guns. They were all set and ready for action, and so were we.

As we drove along the long track of dirt that night, Miguel and I were following the guerrillas and discussing how to film without our lights on and other technical issues we had to deal with. We had no clue how close we were to the Serb positions, until one of the armed guys with his finger on his mouth told us to stop our loud conversation. It was only then that we could hear very clearly what the Serb police were saying – that's how close we were.

I felt that my heart stopped beating. But, Miguel had a more urgent issue. He turned to me and said, "Please translate, but don't laugh loud. Can you tell them to stop [before they take the action] because I have to go to shit."

The armed guys could not believe it. I couldn't either. I turned around to look for a spot but there were no trees – only small bushes – none that could offer privacy. But a man's gotta do, what a man's gotta do!

One of the guys offered to be Miguel's shield. And he was. After a few minutes, Miguel came back and we could not stop laughing. We almost stopped an action for a very bizarre reason. Later, we referred to it as our small "shitty" mission.

My wedding day

Elida Ramadani

Kerem and I, both of us being journalists, agreed that we would have our wedding party in Pristina. At the same time, judging by our characters and our dedication to our work, it meant that we would work that day. It was a nice Sunday in mid-December 2000, the happiest day in my life. I had already chosen my wedding dress and the shoes to go with it. We had invited our families and friends.

But, the contrast between regular brides and myself was startling. I have been to friends' weddings several times. They usually start with an early wake-up – as early as 5 a.m. – when close family relatives come to help you get your final things packed and give finishing touches to the mascara that has been tested and worn a thousand times, and all the shampoos and gels that go with the "bride".

I too woke up early that morning – but not to put on my mascara, eyeliner or lipstick. I wore my muddy Timberland boots and my yellow, waterproof jacket to head to northern Kosovo, the city of Mitrovica, where a rally–turned–riot was taking place.

Ethnic tensions between Serbs and Albanians were running high in the city divided by a river and thousands of peacekeepers. On the previous day, people had been injured in those riots and peacekeepers were attacked by a stone-throwing crowd. We provided footage all day long. Both Kerem and I each made some five trips between Pristina and Mitrovica that day so we could satellite feed the material that showed what was going on.

I hoped Sunday would be calmer. But, it wasn't. While there, I was saying, "Nothing can happen to us, because I am getting married today." I left for Mitrovica only to return at 6 p.m. so I could put on my wedding dress. The party was scheduled to start at 8 p.m. I had two hours to look like a bride. On the way from Mitrovica to our office in Pristina, I was reporting what I had filmed and forgot to check the driving speed. I was only reminded when a UN police officer stopped me to show me the radar and fine me.

I really had no time to stop. I had to make it to the hairdresser. I had to put some make-up on. I had no choice, but to explain to the officer that I was getting married in two hours. That seemed like an interesting lie to him. I bet he didn't hear anything like that before.

I had to give him some evidence. I opened the door and showed him my boots. You could not notice they were boots - they were covered in mud. The police officer laughed hard. He told me, "go and get ready, you crazy bride".

Appearing to Kerem covered in mud was a tough cookie. He expected to see me differently dressed – with nice, white, clean shoes and a dress. And if he was lucky, a hairstyle too. He was shocked to see me nowhere close to that. He threw me out of the office, and pushed me to go to the hairdresser, saying I could not move from the chair of the salon until I was ready. We had a wedding to attend.

TO KEREM: You will always live with us. Love always, Elida and Tara

Elida Ramadani Lawton has been working as a producer with Associated Press Television News since 1998, when the war in Kosovo began. She was married to Kerem Lawton, the British producer who was killed during the Macedonian conflict. They have a daughter, Tara.

In memory of Adam Chris Gutuza

Zenzile Khoisan

Brother,
Your cigar, your quiet background manner,
   your easy way with people
   and your ability to listen
   has left a gaping hole
in this crazy metropolis of Cape Town.

Even now, Long Street is left bereft
   of a brother who walked tall.
   Your plotting smile,
your desk in the corner of a large office
   your wish that it be better for all.

In a week of bombings and double speak,
   mixed messages from the matrix,
   simple ones are now wondering,
   trying to decipher messages,
in those cards that you held so close to your chest.
In your worldly-wise smile and steel-trapped mind
   you gave the damned a voice,
gave hope to the doomed and dignity to the despised.

   Friday, with the scent of the soil
   of your simple grave still in our nostrils
we survey the mountain of your final resting place.
   On we march soldiers, sailors, troubadours,
   workers of the world,
renovating a stonehouse you built for us all.

Zenzile Khoisan is a South African freelance journalist. Born on the Cape Flats, he experienced the hardships of apartheid, which led him into exile as a teenager in the 1980s. He writes for his friend and colleague Chris Gutuza, a journalist who lived for the end of apartheid, and then to train young, previously disadvantaged women and men in the craft about which he was so passionate. He died on 7 October 2001 leaving his wife, journalist Ayesha Ismail, and their two daughters, Zahra and Mira.

Tiny pieces of paper

Walter Marwizi

A friend from Bindura town, a small agricultural town, about 100 km south of Harare, had called me in the afternoon the previous day.

"They are coming," she said in a terrified voice. "Be careful what you do when you go about covering tomorrow's final push. We do not want to hear something bad has occurred to you," she said before she quickly hung up the phone. I had to call her back trying to figure out what she meant by that.

"They (Zanu PF) have hired two buses to ferry their terror gangs from Mashonaland provinces. They are coming to help police and the army crush the final push. They have been told that British Prime Minister Tony Blair and the British-sponsored press have ganged up to remove President Mugabe from office and their mission is to see that none of that occurs," she said.

I needed no further explanation. Like any other Zimbabwean, I was well aware that the opposition party, Movement for Democratic Change (MDC), had planned a nationwide action, which they had dubbed the Final Push, to force President Robert Mugabe out of office starting from 2 June 2003. After holding a series of successful mass job boycotts, which crippled industry and commerce, the opposition party decided the time had come for the masses to rise up in the streets and claim their freedom from the dictatorial regime of Robert Mugabe.

The plan had been to have a mass of people march on State House, Mugabe's official residence, and somehow manage to push the veteran statesman-turned-dictator out of power. We all knew it was a tall order, what with the heavy security wall that surrounds the state house, watched over by Mugabe's menacing 24-hour armed guard, but many people were determined to create a piece of history.

An hour later, after the call, I spotted a packed government bus, covered in dust, making its way towards the Zanu PF headquarters, which are, ironically, less than ten metres from our office, located at 1 Kwame Nkrumah Avenue in Harare.

Peeping through the office curtain, I saw young men and women, some of them barefoot, disembarking from the bus. They appeared clearly overawed by the sight of the Zanu PF headquarters, an imposing building constructed by a Yugoslav company close to the ruling party, just after independence. You could see some of them rubbing their eyes so as to get a clearer view of the building. Some of them appeared mesmerised by the glittering five-star hotel about a hundred metres from the Zanu PF headquarters. Surely this was a spectacle for anyone coming from the impoverished rural areas, where pole and *dagga* huts characterise the landscape.

Five minutes later, yet another dusty bus arrived, this time carrying mostly elderly women. Silently, the two groups quickly moved into the headquarters' conference centre where they were to spend the night. Knowing that there was little I could see from outside, I went home anxious, but fully aware that action would start tomorrow. The following morning I woke up very early and asked my brother to accompany me into town. I didn't want to take chances alone, in case something occurred to me without anyone knowing about it. In Zimbabwe, journalists working for private media routinely get harassed, beaten or arrested while on assignments.

"We need to watch the activities of Zanu PF supporters who have been bussed from the rural areas," I told my brother, as we got off a bus about two hundred metres away from the Zanu PF headquarters around 6 a.m. We did not have to wait for long before the action started. They started coming out in groups of four, pretending to be just like urban workers on their way to work. Their appearance however betrayed them. The youths wore worn-out, dirty clothing, unwittingly sending strong messages about the kind of life they led in the drought-wrecked rural areas. Some of them also wore crude homemade rubber sandals, commonly found in the rural areas, on their chapped feet. The elderly women did not resemble urbanites either: they looked strange in tattered old multi-coloured doeks. Worse still, they were carrying suspicious-looking bags.

Curious, we followed one of the groups down Kwame Nkrumah. Two hundred metres down the road, the group stopped at a news stand near a busy downtown street, where there were heaps of early morning copies of the *Daily News*, Zimbabwe's only independent daily newspaper, which had been a target of government attacks since its formation in 1999.

Apart from making my heart bleed, what I saw clearly made me realise the extent to which unpopular regimes, desperate to cling on to power against all odds, will go to suppress the free flow of information. Without provocation, the youths pounced on the hapless newspaper vendor: beating him up with clenched fists and stones, taken from those same suspicious-looking bags. By some act of God, the vendor managed to escape from the marauding vigilante youths and ran for dear life. The youths then started tearing up all the copies of the paper. In less than two minutes, a whole heap of newspapers which carried a story on the Final Push, had been reduced to tiny pieces of paper, effectively denying Zimbabweans an alternative voice on a crucial day.

And the "triumphant" group went down the street carrying out their mission. Horrified by such a crude attack on the press in broad daylight, I did not have the strength to confront them as they went about their business of silencing a critical alternative voice in the face of a sustained propaganda onslaught by an increasingly repressive Zanu PF regime. By 6.30 a.m., several thousand copies of the *Daily News* had been torn, burnt and destroyed across various centres in Harare. The enemies of a free press, with no visible support in the urban areas, had bussed in obviously brainwashed rural folk to come and destroy newspapers in open defiance of the law.

At the end of the day when the Final Push had been made impossible by the heavy presence of a brutal army, police, the dreaded secret operatives and war veterans, the "victorious" rural folk trooped back to the Zanu PF headquarters where a feast was held into the early morning. I then remembered what Jesus said as he died on the cross: "Forgive them Father, for they know not what they do." And now, it appears, they might not have another opportunity to hold another all-night party at the Zanu PF headquarters. The *Daily News* is no more. It was shut down by armed government agents on September 11, ironically, the day now synonymous with terrorism worldwide.

Note: As this book was going to the print the owners of the *Daily News* were still battling to get the paper back on the streets.

Walter Marwizi is a Zimbabwean journalist working as news editor for *The Standard*. He is winner of the 2003 CNN African Journalist of the Year Free Press Africa award. You can contact Walter on waltermarwizi@yahoo.com, just in case someone might want some news about the trials and tribulations he and his fellow journalists and compatriots are facing in Zimbabwe.

One day in Zaire

Alistair Lyne

The gods had treated us to another glorious morning – overcast skies giving way to bright saturating sunshine and thick white clouds punching holes in the deep blue African sky. It was April of 1997 and civil war in Zaire had kept Mother Africa on the global news map for the better part of five months – one of the more complex and unpredictable conflicts on the continent at the time.

Myles Tierney (APTV producer), Adil Bradlow (AP photos), Liz Gilbert (photographer) and I (APTV cameraman) left Hotel Zongia in Kisangani, rushed down to the Congo River and loaded our motorbikes as usual into a *pirogue*. Those huge hollowed-out tree trunks are used as river taxis, plying goods and people from the town, across to the poverty-stricken villages and recently established UN refugee camps on the other side.

The noise of the outboard engine and the bubble, surge and flow of the mighty Congo River drowned out the voices of the frantically waving Reuters team crossing upstream. We gave little comment, as they were headed in the opposite direction back to town and we were keen to cover the familiar 21 kilometre journey from the river to the first refugee camp to confirm some killings.

The refugees were Rwandan Hutus who had fled their own country after perpetrating genocide there in 1994. They butchered nearly a million people in three bloody months before fleeing into exile – UN protection in camps in Zaire. Two-and-a half years later the rebel war uprooted these camps in the East. Most of them picked up their bundles and walked back home to an uncertain future in Rwanda.

Zairean emotion had again been fuelled by the arrival of some 100 000 refugees near Kisangani. They were well looked after by the international community while locals were left to endure their own poverty.

I'd been following the refugee story for the last two years and these camps were home to what was left of a hard-core bunch of killers – even by African standards. They refused at any cost to return to Rwanda, and fled the rebel advance. Trekking thousands of kilometres through thick jungle, fighting the Zairean uprising along the way. These men, known as the *interahamwe* or "those who hunt together", had used their own women and children as human shields in a firefight. Some of the *baddest* motherfuckers you could meet anywhere.

That morning the high-speed bush telegraph told of a commotion in the jungle: looting of UN food supply stores and stoning of staff and vehicles. UN personnel pulled back across the river to Kisangani after being prevented access to the jungle by angry and violent Zaireans. The jungle was in turmoil.

From the river we had run the gauntlet through the villages, getting abused and feeling all too exposed on the bikes. Angry men were lining the track armed with machetes, clubs, stones, even the odd knife. "Here we go again," I thought. We passed the umpteenth stash of looted UN food bags piled next to the track and with the help of a local calming the mob, managed to get through safely to the murder site – a neat little hutted village in a clearing. Our temporary safety in that village was not due to our profession, but to the respect the locals had for the dead lying there.

Late the previous night unknown gunmen opened fire with automatic weapons, killing seven Zaireans. No witnesses. No wounded. The villagers blamed the "refugee situation". The killers could have been anyone: *interahamwe*, Zairean rebels, or even the Rwandan RPF Army –"allies" of the rebels. This time only the jungle would claim the killings.

We were allowed to work freely and film their story – likely to be the only outsiders to take any notice. The villagers treated it like a crime scene, drawing lines on the ground, sealing off huts where the corpses were and making circles around spent AK-47 shells in the hot white sand.

A bone-chilling wail came from the small hut we were ushered into: on the bed, the body of a young dead boy with a bullet hole in his chest. Under the window in a ray of light, his grief-stricken grandmother. Naked but for a small loincloth, she had torn her clothes off after hearing of her only grandson's death. Flailing her arms in despair. Tears streaming. Heaving and sweating with effort and sorrow. I don't even know that she noticed us. Powerful pictures. I still remember her sad, continual cry.

Another hut – two young brothers, shot dead in their beds. Their mother had run off into the jungle and not yet returned. Keep rolling tape. Show some compassion, apologise for interrupting, say goodbye gently.

We had a really strong piece, knew the competition were nowhere near and so decided against going into the refugee camps – even though we were so close – not wanting to be seen as showing any solidarity with the refugees. We brace ourselves for the return trip and bolt.

On our way back you could see from a distance the men blocking the road. They were agitated. They had chosen their location well; we'd have to slow down to pass. No choice but to stop and try negotiate our safety. I felt like being swallowed by that jungle right then – or swept away by the Congo – or something. Anything but being right here right now.

Myles, Adil and I stay seated and keep the bikes idling. Moments later Lizzie and her driver, who had fallen behind, come breezing through the checkpoint and the mob nail them, pulling the bike down into the sand. Lizzie on her feet and she's on the back with Adil. He's had his watch ripped off his arm and been punched in the side of the head – the mob all over us now.

Sunglasses snatched off my face and I drop my chin after a sucker punch in the forehead, hoping to take the next blow on the top of my head. My eyes streaming. Adil bolts – taking off in a spray of sand, huddled low with Lizzie trying to shield his head from the missiles raining down: stones, sticks, half bricks, machete, a lead pipe – we're rocking in the jungle here.

Amazing. They disappear safely into the sweaty jungle. "Our turn," I think – the Betacam still OK, strapped around my neck and the camera resting on my knees – my bike being yanked from side-to-side as the villagers fight for my bag of batteries and microphones – fuck it. Fighting to keep the handlebars mine – a smack in the kidneys and its time to get the hell out. I snatch a glance at Myles – on his feet over the bike – *sans* baseball cap. At 6.4 and around 100 kg, with two Brooklyn-grown hammers on the ends of his arms, he's got the locals to back the *fuck* off. He looks hard at me and flicks his head towards the jungle – no flash of teeth from Big MT for once. He'll follow me.

Rev and drop the clutch – back wheel digging in as I try to huddle over the rig and keep it from bouncing against the petrol tank at the same time. Picking up speed – trying to escape the missiles. Hanging on, slipping and sliding at last into the shade of freedom. Pull over next to Adil and Lizzie and turn to see Myles' fine frame filling the light circle at the end of the jungle tunnel.

Adil gives Lizzie a wad of Zairean banknotes and she throws liberal handfuls into the air whenever the pissed off Zaireans run close to our bikes. It's hairy. Machetes and knives in angry hands. Too close. We stop for nothing now and slow down only where the dirt track meets up with the railway line. *Fuck.* Incredibly, a train blasts out of the vegetation into the clearing and it's swamped in heavily armed uniformed troops – even on the engine. Rebels or RPF. Their surprise is as big as ours. They open fire on us and we *fuck off* at high speed.

Miraculously we make it to the river, unscathed but for a gash on Myles' neck from a long metal pipe. Lizzie even manages to shoot a frame of the three of us grinning with relief in our *pirogue*. Memories of special moments.

Rest in peace Myles.

Alistair Lyne joined the TV news business in 1993 and got hooked capturing history: one take, one chance, no repeats. He travelled extensively around Africa to capture grim reality. After the death of his friend Myles Tierney in Sierra Leone in 1999 he took a break from news and shot a wildlife series for a US network. It also fuelled his passion to photograph birds. Since then Alistair has been on and off shooting news and taking his wife and three kids on long trips through southern Africa.

Rory's diaries: letters home

Rory Peck, and contributed by Juliet Crawley Peck

Here are some extracts from Rory's diary when he travelled to Afghanistan in December 1991. Rory was travelling with Peter Jouvenal and Vladimir Snegerev, a Russian reporter for Pravda, who had covered the Afghan war from the Soviet side, whilst Rory had been filming on the side of the Mujahideen. They went together to meet some Russian POWs held by the Tajik Commander Ahmad Shah Massoud.

Rory wrote this diary as a letter to his wife who was in Northern Ireland awaiting the imminent birth of their daughter.

1st December 1991
My darling Juliet
We are finally across the border with good prospects for moving on soon. Yesterday we left Dushanbe by helicopter courtesy of the KGB to the border base at Ishkishm. They signalled the local muj leader Issatullah, and I made the one and a half hour walk up to his base. Where, by extraordinary coincidence, I met Colin Boyle and an English cameraman; both on good form, they were just leaving for Pakistan.

The commander of course knew nothing of our arrival, and said Peter and I could cross but not Vladimir. He did however agree to send a message to Najimudin the senior commander at Barak, and I agreed to come back the following morning. Very pleasant hot springs on Tadjik side – probably last bath for some time. Endless toasts over dinner with KGB Colonel and Captain – all very merry. I went to the border again this morning to be met by Ismatullah who said we could cross so back to the guest house for the others while the muj marshalled some donkeys. Just as we were crossing the KGB border, guards forbade the Tajik interpreter to cross as he had no passport. So, my darling, we will have to rely on the one or two words I can string together.

3rd December, Baharak
We set off at 8.30 this morning. There is quite a lot of snow and large ice flows on the river – very cold my love, not for you. When we turned north from Zebok the river narrowed and the road became somewhat

dangerous. Imagine our surprise when we felt the car tilt towards the edge, dragging furiously until we came to a halt, and bouncing merrily down the side of the mountain went the back wheel, jumping sometimes 20–30 feet through the air. That was the end of the ride until several hours later when the small truck we had left in the morning arrived and they gave us a lift. There were 34 of us on board which eventually damaged the rear right wheel to the point where we had to stop every 15 minutes to tighten the nub.

11th December

We finally got permission to meet Massoud and drove up this morning. Very wet all day, just like Ireland. Vladimir ecstatic. When we arrived at the cultural committee office there were a few muj around, including a Ukrainian who is a bodyguard of Massoud. Very amusing watching him circle around Vladimir, each time getting nearer. Like a fox closing on a chicken. They finally spoke. The Ukrainian, Islamaudin, does not want to return and has not answered any of his parents' letters.

Massoud appeared for dinner and preceded to question Vladimir on Soviet politics and history of war like a professional journalist taking copious notes. V. waxing lyrical. They all sat up watching a film on the Gulf War which Peter brought.

12th December

Have seen Massoud again. He received Vladimir and has been his usual hospitable self. Agreed to our film and we are off tomorrow to Takhar to film the Russians.

16th December

We came here this morning in a last effort to find Nik Mohammad whose parents we visited in the Ukraine. A UN flight flew over Taloqan yesterday from Kabul. I was walking through a field when I heard it. A ploughman abandoned his oxen and ran; people everywhere dashing for cover while the Muj opened up with Dashakas and Zikuyaks. Fortunately it was very cloudy with a lowish mist. At any rate the plane landed intact and, according to Dr. Abdullah, the delegation were unaware of any shooting. I had seen Dr. Hyder earlier who told of the proposed visit which he is organising. Very badly obviously. Not satisfied with their marksmanship the muj let off again as the flight departed. Very glad, darling, you are not working for the UN here.

Market day in Taloqan, very noisy and crowded, all sorts of merchants lining the pavement, one old man had a slide viewer with circular slides of various European countries. With a fine patter he pretended to show me some of Monaco. The oceanographic museum he explained was the "BBC markaz," soldiers guarding the castle were "Askari BBC Londoni". A wedding shot of Prince Rainier and Princess Grace was the "King and Queen of England". Then, with a sidelong glance, he described a river scene in England, and before my eyes appeared a reclining Hindi actress. A not very titillating dirty peep show on one of those old viewers I remember as a child.

16th December

We crossed the river on makeshift rafts. Two inflatable cowskins and some half-filled tyres in driving sleet. Very wet and cold. Two muj making flailing movements with their legs finally propelled us to the other side. A longish walk to within sight of a border guard post where we parted with our muj. Peter watching the guard through bios. Eventually as we started walking towards the post, someone spotted us and a salvo went off, and some ten minutes later a jeep appeared and, in good Soviet fashion, out hopped solders who proceeded to arrest us despite Vladimir's protests in good Moscow Russian. We were trussed and hustled into a jeep. V. explaining to the officer in loud protesting terms eventually brought them to their senses and they untied us but kept us in the jeep in case we see any state secrets at their border guard post. V. thinks the officer is dazzled by visions of promotions, transfer to cushy post, medals etc. for arresting British spies and a Soviet dissident. Thank God there is a prospect of a bath tomorrow.

The film that Rory, Peter and Vladimir made on Soviet POWs in Afghanistan helped raise the issue of their plight in the Soviet Union. Rory and Peter continued to promote their stories and, before Rory was killed in Moscow in October 1993, he was delighted to entertain two of these POWs in his dacha at Peredelkino.

Showing the true story

Sam Cole

"We need to tell the factual story – good or bad – before others seed the media with disinformation and distortions, as they most certainly will continue to do."
– US government guidelines for embedded media

"Man overboard! Man overboard!" yelled a voice on the intercom system of the USS Constellation, where I was embedded for one month. We all rushed to get our cameras, tripods and notepads and hastened towards the flight deck, only to be met by a frantic Public Affairs Officer (PAO) who herded us into the Commanding Officer's reception room, where we were told to wait. A plane had slipped off the flight deck and into the sea; the two pilots had ejected themselves and were fine. Only when the pilots had been fished out of the sea did they allow us to film and interview the rescuers. A several hundred thousand-dollar cock-up (the plane was lost) became a story of courage and success. We all wondered what sort of coverage we would have been allowed to do if the pilots had died. In the event of a real news story, like an attack on the ship, would we again be locked in a room and released only when it was all over?

When we started our stint as embedded journos, we were asked to sign ground rules. They told us that we were there as professionals to report on what we see, whether good or bad, but that some information would have to be retained for security reasons. We were free to wander around the *Connie* but were warned that all communication to and from the ship would be monitored randomly and anyone caught breaching security would be sent home. One reporter made the mistake of mentioning a poster on the wall in a pilot's "Ready Room". He referred to "a bikini-clad woman". This was not considered the right message to portray and the reporter was sent off the ship. We all tried to work out where the security breach lay and concluded that she must have been a secret map of Iraq with bikini-denoted areas under US control. They always manage to get the best parts.

Rarely did anything of any interest happen onboard the *Connie*. We spent our days trying to rest and our nights filming endless lives of planes taking off and landing. The highlight of the week was alcohol-free beer on Fridays. Things livened up when the captain, during his morning pep talk over the intercom system, congratulated the crew on their successful night's bombing. He announced with glee that they had destroyed Saddam's luxury yacht in Um Quasr port. All the print journalists were delighted, they finally had something with which to spice up their reports. Just as they were about to transmit, an embarrassed PAO officer told us that the information was classified. The gratuitous use of a 200-pound bomb was obviously not the image the military were aiming to convey.

Once we were asked to attend a special briefing by Lieutenant Gormley, a New York fireman and ex-fighter pilot who re-enlisted after 9/11. He made a tear-jerking presentation of slides showing the devastation and the amazing courage of the firemen. He explained that attacking Iraq was in direct response to 9/11 and made no distinction between Al-Qaeda and Saddam Hussein. Before the slide show, an F-18 pilot showed his self-made video, shot with lipstick cameras inside the cockpit, of beautiful, sexy shots of fighter jets silhouetted by sunsets. The final shot showed their logo: "Kill them all." I was politely asked not to film this as it could have been misinterpreted.

As "Shock and Awe" bombing started up, videophone lives of ground troops advancing were replaced with red-coloured planes taking off, juxtaposed against green night-vision shots, as explosions rocked Baghdad's skyline. If it weren't for journalists in Baghdad the coverage would have continued to show a sterile war with casualties you could imagine but not see. Images of injured civilians, bombed residential areas, overrun hospitals and maimed children came from non-embedded journalists.

Quite a lot took place on the US military base at Kandahar Airport where I was embedded for a month in February 2002, but we were not allowed to cover any of it. Kandahar Airport was the centre for Special Operation activities but we were warned not to film, mention or even refer to their nationalities. It was the stop-over for prisoners on their way to Guantanamo, but it was forbidden to even point the camera in the direction of their compound. The only time we could mention the prisoners was during Eid when we were invited to interview the US cook who had prepared lamb in the traditional way. After great persuasion, we were also permitted to film a tight-shot of a barbed wire fence. The message we were putting across was how well the US treat their POWs, even to the point of respecting their religious celebrations. We had no idea what was really going on. When you are embedded it is like being in a cocoon, and you don't know what is happening on a larger scale.

Once, the airport perimeter was attacked and breached. We were only informed after the news had been released from Washington, two days later. At the time we complained, claiming that embedded journalists should by definition get better access. During the Iraq war, news or press statements came out of Central Command or the Pentagon, and often those on the scene were the last to know. We were merely adding colour to the picture.

Apart from daily briefings, we were encouraged to do the odd "soft" story, like US Muslim soldiers praying in the airport's derelict mosque, Christian masses for soldiers, Valentine's Day celebrations, the occasional perimeter foot patrol and some Mad Max style dune-buggies rippling with guns. We even got to ride on them.

I spent most of my time in Kandahar with Taras Protsyuk, a Reuters cameraman. Taras was a lovely guy who was tragically killed in Baghdad when a US soldier fired a shell from a tank into the Palestine Hotel. Everyone in the world knew it was the hotel where journalists were staying except, it would seem, the US soldiers on the ground. Taras was 35 years old, and married, with an 8-year-old son.

When asked about the deaths of Taras and Spanish cameraman Jose Couso, also killed during the attack on the Palestine Hotel, Pentagon Spokeswoman Victoria Clark said, "a war zone is a dangerous place. We continue to warn news organisations ... you should not be there." Ironically, Clark was one of the main promotors of the embedding programme for journalists in war zones, so presumably her warning was directed only to those journalists not under US supervision. When a journalist is embedded it is clear that he or she is showing just one side of the story. This is fine if someone else is able to show the other side. Comprehensive coverage of war inevitably has to be a team effort between embedded and non-embedded journalists. On the same day that Taras and Jose were killed, Al Jazeera's journalist Tareq Ayyoub was killed when their offices in Baghdad were shelled and the Abu Dhabi TV office was bombed. In light of these events, Clark's warning to non-embedded journalists to keep out of war zones suddenly becomes more sinister.

After the war, General Richard Myers spoke of the success of the embedding programme as a "showcase of our great men and women". Victoria Clark, in her outrageous warning to news editors to withdraw their journalists from war zones, was obviously worried that the showcase might be tarnished by reality.

At the time of writing Sam Cole (cameraman/producer) had left APTN, where he had worked since 1999, to go back to freelancing. He lives in Rome, Italy and loves travelling.

Hostile environments

Eya Doumeng

Working in a hostile environment does not only mean facing dangerous situations, it also means having to deal with personal challenges.

This is what I had to learn after I had been sent to the West African country, Ivory Coast, to cover a story on the activities of the Chinese.

I was to film the story myself and arrived at the designated location, ready to shoot. I immediately noticed an unusual amount of animation. I asked our translator what was going on, and was surprised to discover that we were considered guests of honour. A special meal was being prepared just for us.

I have to say that, in normal circumstances, I love Chinese food and was looking forward to enjoying the famous meal.

If only I knew what was cooking!

In short, folks, I hate snakes. I can't even stand to watch them on TV or even look at them on a picture. I find snakes exceptionally repulsive. Those long, sticky reptiles with little yellow hateful eyes, ready to bite you at any moment.

Well, the object of some of my most memorable nightmares had been served on a plate — for us to eat.

That is how, that unforgettable day, I had to learn to eat a snake, and negotiate a truce with my worst enemy!

This is sometimes what we have to learn in the field. *N'est ce pas Clotaire?*

Eya Doumeng, the Togolese-born TV producer has worked with international television news agencies. She lives on the island of Reunion where she produces documentaries. Email: edoumeng@hotmail.com

Humanising experiences

Asha Krishnakumar

Covering deprivation for the last 13 years has broadened my understanding of reality immensely. The exposure has made me modest, sharpened my sensitivity and heightened my empathy and concern for the wretched of the earth. It has enhanced my ability to listen. On balance I think I am a better person for it – something those trying to create a better world strive for all the time.

Whether child labour or bonded workers, starvation deaths or hunger-induced suicides, kidney sales or trafficking in girls, female infanticide or foeticide, they are all rooted in socio-economic changes brought about by the development policy of governments, which have stopped making even a pretence of protecting the weak and the vulnerable.

Each story of deprivation follows the same pattern more or less – of narrowing options, weakening coping mechanisms, intensifying despair and inevitable death.

But some experiences remain etched in your consciousness forever, reminding you of the harsh realities of life and the unfairness of this world towards the downtrodden.

Two of the most striking stories of helplessness and despair will live with me forever. I can never bring myself to erase them from my memory as they keep me firmly rooted in reality and have made me a more sensitive and caring human being.

It was less than a year after I joined the profession. The assignment was to study the situation of child workers. For the first time in my life, I was setting foot in a match factory in Tamil Nadu's Vellore district.

In an eight by six foot room, sitting knee-to-knee, were 20 girls aged between six and 14, busy lining up sticks in a box. The wage being on a piece rate system, the girls worked very fast, almost like high-speed robots, making quick, economical movements. Only then could they earn the maximum wage of 30 rupees a day, which comes to just over half a US dollar.

I had been in the room for over 40 minutes while the manager explained the process of match manufacture. I realised that while most girls looked at me now and then – perhaps the only distraction in an otherwise dreary day

– four small girls did not raise their heads at all. I tried to get their attention, but anything I did was in vain. They just would not lift their heads. After the manager left the room, I began to talk to the girls. To my shock, I found that the four girls were undergoing punishment for talking to one another in the morning. And the punishment for the five-year-olds was that they should hold between their chin and their collarbones, a match box – through the day, for a whole week – even as they continued working. If they dropped the matchbox they would be beaten – not at all uncommon at the factory.

Here were four little children, and, perhaps, millions like them throughout India, who had no idea what play or school meant. Their world began and ended with work and punishment. This was my first close encounter with the harsh realities of the world. It affected me especially deeply as my daughter was seven years old at the time.

It is 11 years since I visited the match unit. Yet, nothing has changed. If anything, things have become worse.

• • •

In the summer of 2001, I was in the South Indian State of Andhra Pradesh, where, unable to face starvation due to loss of employment, some 80 weavers had committed suicide.

In Sircilla town, 70-year-old Mallava was inconsolable. Her 36-year-old son, Nagula Ravinder, had committed suicide just the day before. She and her son's family – his wife and two children – had been surviving for the last 17 years on the 200 rupees (about four dollars) the family got every week from weaving coarse handloom cloth. But in 1997, the Union government's policy of intensified liberalisation, globalisation and structural adjustment, had sent costs skyrocketing and the price of cloth nose-diving.

By the end of 2000 the industry situation had worsened such that there was no work for the family. Even the supply of subsidised food grains through the public distribution system had stopped. The government's structural adjustment policy, in a feverish attempt to reduce fiscal deficits and usher in a free market system, was cutting subsidies given to the poor. Mallava's family started to borrow from local moneylenders at usurious interest rates (credit to the poor was choked by the government's reforms in the financial sector that reduced priority sector lending given to the poor and the vulnerable).

The family's debt began to mount. With no work in sight, they were unable the pay the exorbitant interest, and soon moneylenders stopped advancing any sums. With no money, the family began to starve.

Unable to bear the hunger cries of her grandchildren, Mallava sent her daughter-in-law, along with her children, to her parents' place in the hope that they would be able to eat at least once a day. Mallava and her son Ravinder desperately looked for some work. After 10 days, when they had barely eaten anything, Ravinder became so weak that he could not even come out of their hovel. But Mallava, pushed by her love for her son, continued to look for work.

Hearing that a cotton farm, 15 kilometres from her home, was hiring hands, she willed herself to walk, possibly deriving strength from the thought of taking home some food with the 40 rupees she would get by the end of the day. After toiling till sunset, weak in body but happy that she was taking home some food, she all but ran home. Only to find Ravinder hanging from the beam of the pit loom that had provided him and his family with a living for the past 17 years.

After intense media attention things have improved for the Sircilla weavers. But tragedy continues to stalk the handloom industry with weavers continuing to end their lives elsewhere in the country as the thread of hope runs out for them.

Dr Asha Krishnakumar is Special Correspondent with *Frontline*, **the socio-political fortnightly from the publishers of** *The Hindu*, **Chennai, India. With the magazine since 1991, after a PhD in Economics, she won the 2003 Kurt Schork Award in International Journalism (given by the Columbia School of Journalism, Reuters and the Kurt Schork Fund) in the local reporting category for her stories on child bondage, kidney trade and weavers' distress. She is also the recipient of the 2002 Lorenzo Natali Prize in International Journalism from the Asia Pacific Region for her story "Starvation Deaths Among Handloom Weavers in Andhra Pradesh". This award was instituted by the European Union and administered by the International Federation of Journalists.**

The day Mandela voted –
from the darkness into the light

Sydney Duval

Dawn on 27 April 1994 was a moment of rising, both real and symbolic, for millions of South Africans. Their country was having its first democratic election unfettered by racial exclusion, and they would be voting for the first time.

I had little idea as I set off for Durban in the early hours of that morning that the election was to take me back to my childhood roots and some undimmed memories with a strong African sun lighting the way to the polling stations and the landscape of the past, and redefining hope. A black woman standing outside a polling station would be inspired to say: "For the first time in this country, black people are being recognised as human beings."

Two assignments had brought me to Durban. One was to report on the election for Vatican Radio; the other to report on the election for *UmAFRIKA*, a weekly Zulu newspaper published by the Mariannhill missionaries which first appeared as *Izwi Labantu* (Voice of the People) in 1888. Under Cyril Madlala's editorship *UmAFRIKA* had been a courageous voice in alternative press coverage of the liberation struggle and its attendant violence in the 1980s and 1990s. There were other voices that spoke of the struggle – the *Weekly Mail* (now *Mail & Guardian*), *SOUTH* and *SAAMSTAAN*. These papers had worked conscientiously under difficult and dangerous circumstances to fill the gap caused by the closure of the *Rand Daily Mail* on 15 April 1985.

I left the Monastery at Mariannhill at 4.30 a.m. on election day to be at the Durban headquarters of the African National Congress in St George's Street by 5 a.m. The ANC had told journalists they would have to take a special media bus if they wanted to witness Nelson Mandela casting his vote at the undisclosed venue chosen for that historic moment.

Durban was still shrouded in darkness as the convoy of three buses and several ANC cars set off up Berea Road, entered the N3 to Johannesburg and then veered off on the ring road to the North Coast. The journalists on board were from a variety of local and foreign newspapers and agencies, their chatter about the election and the political violence competing with the roar of the diesel engine. A few days before, on 24 April, militant right-wingers attempting to sabotage the election had set off a car bomb that had killed nine people and injured 92 in central Johannesburg, a block away from the offices of the ANC and Pan African Congress.

Possible destinations were also part of the chatter. My intuition had narrowed it down to two: a symbolic journey to the home of the late ANC leader and Nobel laureate Albert Luthuli at Groutville, near Umhlali; or a journey of reconciliation to Inanda where election campaigning had plunged ANC and Inkatha supporters into violent confrontation. Inanda seemed to be the more likely destination, being closer and having greater immediacy because of the bloodshed tearing the surrounding community apart.

Among those on board was Peter Magubane, a robust personality now tinged with grey, who had been dubbed the black cavalier of press photographers. We had worked together on the *Rand Daily Mail* in the 1970s. After his unbanning in October 1975, Peter and I had been assigned to "shoot up Johannesburg in words and pictures" to mark the occasion. At the end of a long frustrating day, with little to inspire his camera, Peter had bought a basket of fruit and vegetables and taken me to meet Winnie Mandela, who was under restriction orders. She took the basket with a thankful smile.

The next time I saw her in the flesh was on the Parade in Cape Town on 2 February 1990 when FW de Klerk announced the unbanning of the ANC and other organisations. She was sitting on the back of a lorry with UDF leaders and Peter was photographing her. The next weekend, on 11 February, Nelson Mandela walked out of Victor Verster Prison a free man.

In 1976 *Sunday Express* reporter Carol Lazar and I had visited Peter at Modder B prison, Boksburg, where he and many others were being detained following the Soweto riots. After his release Benjamin Pogrund had asked me to write a profile of Peter for an exhibition of his work at Durban which was being organised by Fatima Meer, who was herself to endure banning and restriction. In 1978 Don Nelson published Peter's brilliant photographic essay on Soweto with text by Marshall Lee, who was also on the *Mail*.

I had bumped into Peter on various assignments over the years, at struggle actions, and at the protest against apartheid signs on Durban's South Beach. And now we were on a bus going past the Quarry shack settlement. I called out: "Hey, Magubane." His face shot round and I snapped him, wanting a souvenir of an extraordinary man who had survived those very rough days for English-language journalism. So much of our past was etched indelibly in that handsome head with a story to tell about police and batons and teargas and prisons.

I thought of the many journalists from the English-language press who had supported the struggle for a democratic, non-racial South Africa during the long hard years of political profligacy. They could have filled a bus on their own, headed by Laurence Gandar of the *Rand Daily Mail*. I recalled his damning commentary written in the early 1960s and entitled "The Nation That Lost Its Way." And now the nation was finding it again.

Soon we were crossing the Umgeni, a river I had crossed a hundred times in childhood and youth by train, car and bus over the Connaught, Athlone and Leo Boyd bridges. Encroachment from industrial landfill had squeezed the Umgeni into a slur of sluggish brown water. Effingham appeared and disappeared and then it was Avoca, with its iron railway bridge where we had stood in shorts and barefoot in the 1940s to drop fishing lines into the little stream below.

The convoy veered left and I knew we were heading for Inanda, past KwaMashu, Ntuzuma and Bhambayi, an informal settlement convulsed by successive acts of violent reprisal. On the right on a little rise was the original Phoenix ashram where Mahatma Gandhi had tried out his theories on self-sufficiency and collective effort, where he explored the efficacy of *satyagraha* – and forged the spirit of passive resistance. Hills and valleys that years ago had been covered with bush and sugar cane and patches of millet, were now glimmering with lights from a thousand dwellings, heartbeats that pulsed with apprehension and celebration. First light was appearing on the horizon to the east as we climbed a long, last hill to Ohlange Institute, the burial place of Dr John Dube, founding president of the ANC. And there was his tombstone and its message for all Africa: "Out of the darkness into the glorious light."

We were at the end of the road we had walked and talked and cycled as young boys – childhood friends ligatured together by roads that rose and dipped to the next hill and the next. This was the kind of road altar boys thought of at early morning mass which began with the old introit: "I will go up unto the altar of God; to God who gives joy to my youth." Little did we know then that just a year later, in May 1948, the dark spectre of apartheid would rise up to snuff out the light of the world around us. And now the road was changing forever.

In 1947, we were just children with sturdy, heavy, squeaky and clumsy bicycles, so hard to move on bad roads, our young dreams giddy from smoking pawpaw leaves in a giant of a wild fig tree that looked out to the world at the rim of our experience, to the hills rolling on to Inanda. And the war that took our fathers and uncles to battlefields in North Africa and Italy was a fading sound of trampling boots, drumbeats and bugle calls.

Early one winter morning Roger Gallet, Fabian Lassak, my younger brother Denis and I set off from our village on the edge of the sugar plantations north of Durban to find the Inanda Falls which Skwebane the old grass-cutter had told us about. We pushed and cranked and sweated most of that day on a road of some 30 km that was hard and hilly and full of *dongas*, dust, stone and gravel. We cycled past thatched huts and fields the colour of rust and yellow and ochre. Erythrina petals burned red along the way. We exchanged greetings with men in the fields. *"Sakubona!"* we yelled.

Deep into the afternoon, heartened by rock buns and lemonade, we found ourselves peering over the edge of the Inanda Falls, which are among the highest in the land. This was Shembe country for ritual bathing in long white robes. Far below, two young black bulls were locked in mock battle, their horns twisting and turning, their heads butting each other at the end of a charge. I never forgot that day or the two bulls. They seemed to me to have been a sign of things to come beyond the understanding of childhood.

There were no bulls at the bottom of Inanda Falls the day I returned there in 1989. The bulls were raging elsewhere against the system that humiliated them – in the ghettos on the edge of white cities, in the schools designed to subjugate them, in the valleys which the Comrades and Inkatha were turning into killing fields.

It was now about 6.15 a.m. on 27 April when Angela King, chief of the United Nations Observer Mission, addressed some 100 journalists and photographers assembled outside the hall at Ohlange. She wanted no misunderstanding about protocol and procedure. She said Mandela would be casting his ballot at the table specially set up on the *stoep* of the hall – and a rope would be used to help the media keep its distance. There was an immediate stampede as journalists and photographers, some with stepladders, jostled one another for the best spot as the rope was put in place.

I had other ideas: the rope would never hold once Mandela appeared; there would be a knee-jerk scramble for the centre spot; standing to the left at the very end of the rope would give me the quickest path to the *stoep*. Happily for me this proved to be the case.

A little after 7 a.m. Mandela appeared on the *stoep*, jubilant and smiling and with some words for the media: "This Wednesday, as you expect, is for all South Africa an unforgettable occasion. It is the realisation of hopes and dreams that we have cherished over decades. It is the beginning of a new era ..."

Mandela moved towards the ballot box. Journalists and cameramen reacted as one irresistible surge of bodies, cameras, video cameras, tape recorders and notebooks. I simply ducked under the rope and ran towards the *stoep*, missing the traffic jam to the right. At 7.10 a.m. Mandela was standing right above me as he dropped a slip of paper into the ballot box and I was able to catch that consummate moment in 35 mm black and white for *UmAFRIKA*.

I ended the journey to Inanda with a broadcast on Vatican Radio that included these words: "In the autumn of 1994, a little under 46 years later, it took four days of hectic and passionate electoral ritual to bury apartheid under a mountain of votes. The system the world had judged a crime against humanity, was finally in its grave ... Mandela showed, in that brief illuminating moment, that the best way to have a democracy is to use it."

Sydney Duval has worked on South Africa's *Rand Daily Mail* as special writer, film and theatre critic; on *The Star* as special writer; on the *Sunday Express* as chief sub-editor; on the *Cape Argus* as columnist; on the *Pretoria News* as journalist; on *The World* as sub-editor; and at Vatican Radio as broadcaster.

Ameen's article

Farida Akhalwaya and Zaytoon Akhalwaya Abed

When we were asked to write an article about my late husband, Ameen Akhalwaya, our daughter Zaytoon and I thought "what aspect of his character has not been exposed to its fullest extent?"

It then hit us; it was his wonderful sense of humour, wit and satire.

The following article written by Ameen appeared in the August 1998 issue of The Indicator, *the alternative anti-apartheid newspaper that Ameen launched in 1985.*

I was stumped, bowled over – what more can one say about a man who fought courageously for his beliefs and for justice with nothing more than a pen? How do I describe the wonderful loving father figure who dealt with everything with humour, love and tact? This story written by my father explains him best; his wit and satire shone through some of the darkest times in South Africa's history. Instead of my mum and me telling the story maybe it's best you hear it from him in his own words …

If music be the food of love, get your kicks elsewhere!

Ameen Akhalwaya

The phone rang. "You are invited," said the caller, "to a small tea party on Saturday for friends of the Mandela family."

"It's a private little party, so please we don't want any publicity. There'll just be some food, music and a soccer game."

She gave directions to the venue, a smallholding near Honeydew. "By the way," she added, "bring your soccer gear along. You'll be playing for a team of journalists".

"Against whom?" I asked.

"The main match," she replied, "is between the Mandela XI and the Delmas Dazzlers, the guys who are on trial in Delmas. The journalists are going to play against the losers."

I didn't dispute this insult to the footballing ability of journalists, since in private I would concede that we play even worse than we write. There was a little problem though. I'd hung up my football boots 15 or 16 years ago, and they had probably faded like biltong. I had long since outgrown my football shorts, and my soccer socks had years ago been discarded and used to clean cars. My red-and-white Fordsburg Shepherds jersey had also vanished long ago.

Now it is true that I had played in a soccer match of sorts about seven years ago in the United States. I was in a team of over-aged and over-weight foreign journalists pitted against a team of American journalists. The Yankee team comprised mainly women, and since the Americans don't know much about soccer, they kept confusing the game, picking up the ball, running towards the posts and yelling: "Touchdown!"

It is also true that on the morning of the match in Honeydew, I took part in a street procession held by the Association for the Physically Disabled in Lenasia, but I bowed out after about 100 m because I couldn't keep up with the five year olds. And, the only thing I had tried to kick in the last five years was the smoking habit, but missed. With such preparation, I was ready to play ball. I decided that my kit would consist of faded denim jeans with air vents in them, takkies and a T-shirt sporting the legend "Mwasa 1981".

I was going to insist that our team of journalists be called 'Media Terrorists' in keeping with Stoffel Botha's wishes, though I was prepared to answer to "Media Guerrillas" if need be. I needed music to cheer me on, so I took my Beatles and Elvis tapes along. On the way to Honeydew, I worked out my game plan, tactics and strategy, since a massive crowd of between 150 and 200 people would witness the spectacle. Since I wouldn't last longer than five minutes, I had to work out how to make a quick, speedy exit from the match before anyone could call me a puffed-out coward and heap further disgrace on the journalistic fraternity. I decided to go in for an early, hard tackle, feign mortal injury as I have seen Italian stars do on TV, and be carried off to mutters of sympathy and equally sympathetic applause.

Or, I would go into a tackle so hard that the ref would have to send me off. That was the plan.

On the dirt road near the smallholding, I spotted a group of men around some fine cars. Aha, I thought, these must be the trendy northern suburbs radicals waiting to get into the party house ... until I saw one of them talking into what looked like a two-way radio. Just then, Roger Harris, owner of the smallholding and with his wife Miranda, host of the party/match, stopped me and said ruefully that the occasion had been banned.

"A tea party and soccer match banned?" I said incredulously. "You must be joking."

"No," he said, "a magistrate banned it. We went to the Supreme Court, but the return date is on August 9." (The case had been postponed.)

The police had asked a Roodepoort district magistrate for the ban. In his notice signed under the *Internal Security Act*, the magistrate said he had "reason to apprehend that the public peace would be seriously endangered by the sport occasion (football) and provision of food and music and/or such a gathering which has a connection with Nelson Mandela".

Music banned? I thought long and hard. The Beatles did sing a couple of political songs like "Revolution", but, led by peacenik John Lennon, they were anti-war. Perhaps Elvis songs like "Jailhouse Rock" and "I Want to be Free" might be regarded as a reference to political prisoners. But Elvis was said to have been on the right of the political spectrum. Could it be the food? Perhaps the cops suspected that someone might sabotage the biscuits with the spicy, devastating laxative called *jamal*. About 200 people simultaneously making a beeline for a couple of toilets might have endangered the peace.

64

But somehow, I doubted if the cops knew about *jamal*. So it had to be the soccer match. Perhaps the sight of my paunch and hairy legs through the vents in my denims might have sparked adverse comments and caused spectators to riot. Perhaps the cops had got wind of the fact that all my colleagues wanted to play as strikers, and that might have been regarded as illegal industrial action.

Then the answer struck me like a Ruud Gullit free kick. Since Ruud, captain of European Nations Champs Holland, had dedicated his European Footballer of the Year award to Nelson Mandela, it was clear that soccer had become a plot to free the ANC leader. Added to that, the cops might have discovered, by telepathy, my plan to call our team "Media Terrorists", to kick my opponents and get sent off.

Not for nothing did the *Golden City Post* tag my team "Dirty Shepherds", for we enjoyed nothing more than the sight of our opponents hobbling to work on crutches every Monday morning. Yes, the cops reasoned, this guy was going to be a threat to the peace. The ref would have to deal with such hooliganism, but he might just feel intimidated. He would first have to show me the cautionary yellow card – and spectators would obviously see this as support for the Chinese communists.

Then he'd have to show me the red card. That would be a devastatingly devilish communist ploy. The red card would be a subliminal message of support for the Communist Party.

Now I understood why the cops were so concerned, and was about to tell Roger Harris that when he said quietly: "You can still come to my house for a cup of tea and a snack before driving home."

"No thanks," I said.

I didn't have the heart to tell him that hungry as I was, I wasn't about to break the law – by eating banned food.

Ameen Akhalwaya a journalist in South African for more than three decades, was a Nieman Fellow and newspaper editor. He died of cancer on 2 February 1998, days after Nelson Mandela visited him and thanked him for his role in the fight against apartheid.

"What's that noise?"

Mort Rosenblum

I started out as a foreign correspondent about the same time Joseph-Desiré Mobutu started out as a ruthless tyrant, in the mid-sixties, and both of us were in the Congo. Happily enough, I was back in Kinshasa when Mobutu Sese Seko – the same durable dictator – finally beat it out of town.

Though normally as unflappable as cities come, Kinshasa went bananas that morning. Mobutu's troops fled every which way, spraying gunfire behind them. Joseph Kabila's ragtag army marched to the centre of town in flip-flops and laceless boots, with an eerie discipline. Well-armed, they blasted away at anything appearing to be resistance.

In the meantime, joyous citizens dug any sort of gun they could find out of hiding places and fired into the air just for the hell of it.

When I first worked in Kinshasa, filing copy could take hours, or days, at recalcitrant telex machines in a smelly corner of the main post office. This time around, I could dial New York direct on a cell phone. Crouching behind a flimsy tin partition in the market by the Memling Hotel, I dialled my desk to dictate a story.

Kabila's forward elements were hot on the heels of Mobutu's laggards. Lead flew in every direction, and spent bullets dropped from the sky. There was plenty to say, but, for safety's sake, I tried to say it quickly. An eager young desk editor in New York was determined to get it right. He kept asking me to spell things, repeat details and add lengthy background. I asked him to hurry.

"What's that noise in the background?" he finally asked.

"Gunfire," I told him.

"Gee," he replied, conversationally, "Isn't that dangerous?"

"Not for you," I told him, finally losing it. "Just take down the damned copy."

Mort Rosenblum, special correspondent for the Associated Press, first reported from the Congo in 1967 and later covered the Biafra war. Now based in Paris, he is former editor of the *International Herald Tribune* and author of 12 books, including *Squandering Eden: Africa at the edge*.

66

EU summit trail offers goodies galore

Paul Ames

After more than 10 years covering European summits, it's with not a little shame that I confess to still feeling a little tremor of excitement at the handing out of the goodie bags.

These are the packages of treasures that EU governments offer to the multitudes of journalists that flock to such events. The quality and quantity of the goodies inside varies from bumper hampers of gastronomic specialties to humble souvenir ballpoints.

Contents can be surprising, but unlike life and Forrest Gump's box of chocolates, there is a pretty good way of knowing what you're going to get, and it depends largely on the location of the meeting. Southerners tend to see the presence of thousands of international journalists as an opportunity to promote their edible attractions. Thus the Italians who held the EU presidency through the second half of 2003 sent the press home with bottles of grappa, sparkling Prosecco wine, Extra Virgin Olive Oil, pungent cheeses, along with a CD of crooned *canzoni d'amore*, supposedly favourites of Prime Minister Silvio Berlusconi.

Nordics like to highlight design and culture. The trendy black kitchen apron was a lasting souvenir of the 2001 Goteborg summit; Copenhagen the following year yielded a CD-ROM on the works of Hans Christian Anderson, and press types were able to toast the success of Helsinki 1999 with a pair of slender-stemmed Champagne glasses, although French-inspired EU rules prevented the Finns from using the much protected "C" word when describing the surprisingly drinkable arctic berry bubbly that came with the glasses.

The British take a more practical and austere approach. The highlight of the Cardiff summit goodies back in 1988 was a computer disk illustrating the attractions of Wales to international investors. In contrast, the ever-hospitable Irish enjoy a reputation as the most generous suppliers of media bounty. The 1996 Dublin summit was a cornucopia of smoked salmon, aged whiskey, richly illustrated books of poetry and folk music discs ...

Visitors from across the Atlantic often view such largesse as an illustration of Old World impropriety. At an earlier Dublin meeting, one worthy American scribbler was patiently trying to explain to a puzzled Irish official why she couldn't possibly accept a side of salmon the size of a small torpedo, when a Belgian photographer intervened with a "don't worry I'll take hers too". Of course, the lady from the US has a point. Granted, it's unlikely that coverage of the 2001 Ghent summit got any rosier because of the garden gnomes handed out to journalists by the Belgian government or that Austria's stint at the EU's helm got a warmer write-up after they passed round tee-shirts emblazoned "Fitness for Europe". But the whole business does carry the unsavory whiff of payola.

Government officials argue that the goodie bag is an innocent PR exercise to present the attractions of their countries to influential foreign visitors, particularly when the summit showcases some backwoods city or region grateful for some international exposure.

Journalists can claim that they just can't say "no" since the gifts usually come as part of genuinely useful press kits providing vital summit information, from the location of toilets to the correctly spelt names of the Greek defense minister or Luxembourg's central bank governor.

However it can be hard to ignore the incongruity of the lavish offerings at some meetings. Take the recent gathering of finance ministers in the beautiful Italian lakeside resort of Stresa, where the main issue was the importance of restraining government spending during the continent's economic slump. Somehow the money was found to provide the hundreds of attending journalists with a hunk of Parmigiano-Reggiano with the weight and dimensions of a building brick expensively wrapped in the ribbons of Milan's choicest grocer.

The 1995 summit, in the French Riviera resort of Cannes, marked the debut of President Jacques Chirac, at which the press was given a particularly sumptuous reception. In the shadow of the famed film festival menu, a vast marquee was set up on the beach lapped by the Mediterranean. In typically French fashion, the catering was of the highest standing; hundreds of pressmen and women were served course after gourmet course for lunch and dinner. The deboned quail stuffed with morille mushrooms doused in Armagnac sauce lingers as a mini miracle. Of course, we weren't the only ones enjoying such delights; with massed ranks of bureaucrats and diplomats and support staff, several thousand were tucking in at the banquets.

At least somebody managed to tear himself or herself away from the top notch nosh to look in on the leaders' debate, which was deadlocked on a dispute between France and Germany over how much EU aid should go to

Africa. Gradually the word spread round the dinner tables that disagreements between the two camps on the sums to be spent on several African nations – that these actually amounted to less than what had been invested in the summit catering.

It was enough to make even a hardened hack choke on his deboned quail. Perhaps, fittingly, the leaders were back on the Cote d'Azur five years later for a meeting in Nice that may well have killed off the goodie bags and all that summit haute cuisine.

In a back-room compromise designed to rewrite the EU's rule book, Belgium was brought on board by an offer to end the travelling circus of summits, bringing all such meetings to a drab EU headquarters building in Brussels, where the press room is a converted basement garage, the only presents are copies of the EU's draft constitutional treaty and journalists even have to pay for their wine.

Paul Ames, a native of Ipswich, England, has covered European affairs since 1992 as an Associated Press correspondent based in Brussels.

"Yeltsin is breathing"
(or The heart of the matter)

Sahm Venter

"Parteee!" trilled the impossibly young Air France steward as he deposited champagne into the glasses at the end of our desperate, outstretched arms.

He was not to know that Yves had not touched alchohol in years, but having heard of our expulsion from Zaire after several bizarre days of violence, intrigue and suspicion, he welcomed our presence on his Paris-bound 747.

Even the waiter on the crammed ferry to Brazzaville who brushed away the money we offered for two Cokes and a Primus beer when he heard of our plight was happy for us. It seemed that everyone was on our side. Well, everyone except the "Snip" or Zairean Security Police who had slowly beat out our *L'Invitation a quitter le pays* on a portable typewriter in their lime-green offices. They were "inviting" us to leave the country.

Nice of them to do that.

It was early November as we thundered across African skies toward a winter morning in Paris where our sweaty T-shirts and shooting vests would be totally inadequate. But warmth was the last thing on our minds.

It was only a few days since Joao and Yves had been beaten up by "students" at the University of Kinshasa and had their camera gear stolen. Part of the capital's confused reaction to an uprising in the east, which, in less than a year, would end Mobutu Sese Seko's rapacious rule.

We hadn't intended on staying long in Kinshasa. We were going to be out of there as soon as we got our official accreditation to cover the story of more than a million Rwandan refugees caught in the region's conflict.

Our daily pilgrimages to the Ministry of Information seeking this authorisation involved travelling in a darkened elevator where a man, whose job it was to push the buttons, sat almost completely invisible in the corner. A hopeless routine. The lights had long gone out in the lift but the man still sat there, pushing buttons while war loomed.

Finally it came.

Permission from Deputy Prime Minister and Minister of the Interior Gerard Kamanda wa Kamanda, to cover news in Kinshasa and Kivu, as long as we didn't stray into telecommunication installations, military camps or airports. Interesting to see what happens when we fly out of Kinshasa to Goma Airport.

Nevertheless we were thrilled at receiving the two worthless pieces of paper. For US $350 each to the Interior Ministry and $500 to the Information Ministry, they were ours and a prize for our patience. An extra $175 was for Julie the secretary-gatekeeper who did nothing. Sweet Julie who drank coke and ate buns for breakfast while we waited and smiled and watched the upholstery patterns dance all over the sofas.

The accreditation and the official protection it afforded were theoretical. We never got to Kivu and the authority to cover news in Kinshasa didn't mean a thing. Yves and Joao were assaulted and robbed of all their equipment.

To make matters worse the story was being pushed off the map by Boris Yeltsin who had just undergone heart surgery.

"Yeltsin is breathing," announced the CNN anchor from my Memling Hotel window on what is important in the world (depending on what else is happening at the time). The same could not be said for all the refugees we were trying to reach. A blow-by-blow account and analysis of the Russian President's successful "Seven-Hour, Multiple-Bypass Heart Operation" was the type of headline that journalists dread. It wiped Central Africa from the headlines.

"After slicing open the skin over Mr. Yeltsin's upper chest, Dr. Akchurin's team split the president's breast bone with a saw," said Michael Specter's front-page article in the *International Herald Tribune*.

We were frantically trying to trace our cameras. Who had them? Would they be returned?

"Then they used a metal retractor to lift the rib cage while Dr. Akchurin removed an internal mammary artery from Mr. Yeltsin's chest."

Calls to the Ministry of Information, the very people who had kept us waiting days for our precious pieces of paper, resulted in feigned concern and little else.

"Meanwhile, other surgeons removed one of the superficial, or saphenous, veins from his leg."

Our well-connected driver John hustled us into his old Mercedes Benz for an exploratory visit to another government information office. The desperation of more hours of waiting for nothing to happen hurled us from our seats to leap about madly in a welcome sudden tropical downpour.

"As they continued, the surgeons fashioned the arteries and veins to construct five grafts to revamp the blood supply to Mr. Yeltsin's heart, Dr. DeBakey said."

"Who are those important-looking men in suits," we drowned rats wondered as a posse of them loped into the government office.

"They are going to deport you," whispered John.

A-ha, some progress.

Our hotel rooms are searched as SNIP officers watch us pack. Some colleagues quickly get a message to the South African embassy.

"Dr. DeBakey said the surgeons sewed an internal mammary artery to the left anterior descending artery on Mr. Yeltsin's heart."

No time to calculate the accuracy of a $10 000 hotel bill, I paid it and asked SNIP for permission to go to the bathroom where I created a Zairean-Wonderbra by stuffing $2 000 under my T-shirt.

"They also made four grafts from the leg vein. Two were used to bypass blockages in the obtuse artery, one for the right coronary artery and the fourth for the diagonal artery."

The words: "Filming a nuclear installation without permission," jumped off the page of our invitation to leave, just as Bob made his knight-in-shining-armour appearance. Our saviour from the South African Embassy was there to make sure we left the country in one piece.

"Until the circulation was repaired, the arteries on Mr. Yeltsin's left chamber were nourishing that side and much of the right side."

In addition to the $20 each for ferry tickets to Brazzaville, another 25 000 Nouveau Zaire found its way to the SNIP "for photocopying" our passports.

Close your eyes at the port, and the gateway between Zaire and the Republic of Congo and the thronging, pushing and shoving masses with desperate eyes, becomes soothing, promising.

"Stopping a heart for 68 minutes during a bypass operation is 'not unusually long' for such a procedure, Dr. DeBakey said."

So, Yeltsin was breathing in Russia, people were dying in eastern Zaire, miraculously-recovered camera equipment was thrust into our arms on the ferry and within seven months the rebels would march into Kinshasa and declare victory.

And in two weeks I would be back in Kinshasa and welcomed back into the country with no blot against my name.

Sahm Venter is a freelance journalist based in South Africa who has covered events in Africa for local and international print, radio and television organisations.

The hostage

Ravi Nessman

I lay curled over on my side on the bench seat, my arms wrapped around my stomach, writhing with the searing, churning pain of a potently evil intestinal bug I have never been able to identify.

My struggle to take deep breaths and fight back yet another bout of nausea nearly turned into a hyperventilating pant. I shivered from fever and sweat. Only occasionally was I able to focus beyond my miserable physical nightmare and realise the larger nightmare of my situation: I had been kidnapped by the greatest athletic legend in Kenyan history.

I had been sent to the central Kenyan town of Eldoret to do a story on camps that major international sneaker companies were holding for promising young runners. I had dreams of spending a few days there, maybe going for a jog with the kids and coming out with a nice story.

My guide was to be Kipchoge Keino, whose legs carried him to a gold and silver at the 1968 Olympics and another gold and silver four years later. Kenyans adore and revere him. Not only was he the centre of an international Coca-Cola campaign, but he runs an orphanage out of his house. I, and a photographer whose complicity in this nightmare forced me to keep his name out of this, took a taxi for five hours over barely paved streets during massive rain storms, with the driver chewing the narcotic Qat plant the entire way, until we reached the Eldoret Country Club, where we were to meet Kip.

We arrived at night, and were told Kip was not there but would return in the morning to pick us up. We had booked rooms at the club, which reeked of seedy colonial nostalgia, a shoddy effort by the town's black elite to imitate the upper-class airs of the British colonists who once ruled here. It was the kind of place where all the men wore dark suits, though they were threadbare, ill-fitting and often stained.

The guest rooms smelled of mildew and the blankets had cigarette-burn holes in them, but you could not eat in the restaurant without a jacket and tie, so my jeans and T-shirt were a horror. We were sequestered in the lobby, where they deigned to bring me my tilapia. Only the next morning, when dull exhaustion began to seep through my muscles and sweat drenched the sheets did I remember those warnings that fishermen in Lake Victoria had found a new tool for reeling in tilapia – poison.

While I worked to ignore the illness incubating in my gut, Kip seemed to spend the entire next day evading us. He did not come to pick us up at the club when he said he would. When we went to his farm, we were told he was out and would meet us at the club. The club sent us back to his house. Back and forth, back and forth, until we finally found him that night – having wasted a whole day – having dinner with the orphans and a small group of elite African runners he was training. He said that he would take us to the running camps the next day, as promised.

That night the cruel fish truly began to do its work. Nausea, vomiting, repeated runs to the bathroom. Sleep was a delusional swirl.

"*Mizungu*, you don't look so good," Kip said – essentially calling me "whitey" in Swahili – the next morning when he came to pick us up, finally, for our visit to the running camps.

As we headed to the camps, Kip, long, lean and amiable, laughed and chatted with the photographer, while I sat pale and still in the back seat, praying I would survive the day. But before the camps, Kip said, wouldn't we like to see the school he helped build? Not really, but my weakness took with it my ability to resist. The principal gave us a lovely tour of the concrete compound, showing us the new construction and praising Kip for all his help.

Then we headed to the camps.

"Where are they exactly?" I asked.

"Well, we shouldn't go straight to the camps because no-one will be there right now. They'll all be out running," Kip said.

So he drove us through the lush green hills of his native Nandiland, pointing out the area where he grew up, the hills he used to train on and the rest of his autobiographical road map.

"They usually run right here," he said perplexed as we drove past an empty field. Over the next hill, by coincidence, we came to the Nandi Bears Country Club. As Kip walked in, everyone in the nearly empty building ran over to worship him. I hobbled to the bathroom hoping to rid myself of a little bit more of my illness.

"I'm going to wait in the car," I told him a few minutes later, and fell asleep, shivering in the backseat.

"*MIZUNGU!* Wake up. You look cold," he laughed and then threw an olive green sweater vest embossed with the Nandi Bears logo – a bear – on top of me.

"Can we please find the camp?" I begged.

And we were on our way. But first, Kip wanted to show us the tea plantations scattered throughout the hills. He owns a tea plantation, you know.

Here, a few words should be said about the photographer, a man I thought was my journalistic ally, my teammate, who would pick up the slack for his dying comrade. But this man, a Kenyan, confronted by his hero, was in a daze of idol worship.

"Sure Kip, I'll take some file photos of tea," he said, as I groaned pathetically in the back seat.

Next stop, a tea factory. No runners there; but there was a toxic outhouse I made desperate use of.

With time running out to find the runners I made one last plea.

"Patience, *mizungu*, we'll find them," he laughed.

And then he drove us up a winding country driveway.

"This is my vacation home," he said proudly.

He gave us a tour. I was only interested in the bathroom. He showed off the new solar panels he had installed on the roof. The last ones had been stolen by thieves, you know. He climbed into a passion fruit tree and plucked us two of the painfully acidic fruits, an act I prefer to see as simply unthinking rather than intentionally evil.

"Beautiful home, Kip," the photographer said. And I wanted to kill him.

The sun had set, we went back to the club and I begged the photographer to please, please, stand up for us the next day if I still did not have the strength.

Overnight, I began to feel a little better, and the next morning, with a small fraction of my strength restored, I demanded that Kip stop screwing around and take us to the runners. And then he drove us to a track, maybe a mile away, where scores of the young athletes were stretching on the side, jogging on the infield and sprinting right before our eyes.

"How often do you train here?" I asked one runner. "Every day," he said.

I was shocked and ashamed. They had been so close the entire time and I never knew it. I turned to Kip, maybe to tell him, maybe to yell at him, but he was already gone.

Then again, he had probably always known where they were: right here on this track, square in the middle of Kipchoge Keino Stadium.

Ravi Nessman has covered southern and eastern Africa and the conflicts in Iraq and Afghanistan as a foreign correspondent. He is currently The AP's Jerusalem correspondent.

"Look, pygmies!"

Chris Tomlinson

I was a ten-cent-a-word stringer for the Associated Press in late 1996, based in Rwanda and was assigned to cover the rebellion in the country then known as Zaire.

The rebellion, war, invasion or whatever it was, had only started a few weeks earlier, but already the soldiers who now called themselves the Allied Democratic Front for the Liberation of Congo, had advanced 210 kilometres from the Lake Tanganyika town of Uvira, to just past Goma, on the north end of Lake Kivu.

In the early days of the war, who was fighting whom and why, was hard to divine from the stories told by the self-proclaimed rebel leaders and the Rwandan Tutsi soldiers we'd seen on the front lines. Despite claims that the rebellion was indigenous, the fighters were certainly not. There was no doubt, though, that the mysterious troops were forcing more than 500 000 Rwandan Hutu refugees from their camps in Zaire. Rebel troops were also marching north as soldiers from Zairian dictator Mobutu Sese Seko's army – with Hutu extremists mixed in – fled ahead of them.

When the rebels captured Goma, most of the refugees returned home to Rwanda. We wanted to cover the rebel advance, but the rebels had set up a checkpoint on the only road going north and they wouldn't let us pass.

The AP was rotating crews through Goma. Photographer Ricardo Mazalan returned to Africa from his new post in Bogota and AP television sent Miguel Gil Moreno, whom I met for the first time. I had also hired my regular translator, Norbert, whose last name I am ashamed to admit I cannot remember.

I thought I could convince rebel leader Laurent Kabila to give me a pass. Day after day I would go to Kabila's headquarters. Bodyguards in their early teens would make me wait until I gave up. I could usually find a rebel commander who would make claims of victories on the northern front, but he would do nothing to help me witness them.

During their forays for images, Miguel and Ricardo had discovered a road around the rebel checkpoint. Miguel suggested that we should take the road and see what we could find. Ricardo and I thought we'd just encounter another checkpoint. But Miguel, having run out of stories and not wanting to waste time with Kabila, saw no harm in trying. So we decided that Miguel would see how far he could get, and I would try one more time to get a permission slip.

The next morning, Miguel headed north. By the time the sun had set, Miguel wasn't back and Ricardo and I were alone in our apartment at the La Frontiera Hotel, so named because it was built with money that an immigration officer had extorted from journalists over the years.

When Miguel did not return the next day, we knew he had been successful. So the next day we set off to follow him, loading our two four-wheel-drive vehicles with food and fuel, without any idea whether our journey would last hours, days or weeks.

Our drivers manoeuvered the vehicles through the banana plantations north of Goma, taking paths better suited for the farmers' handcarts than our Toyota Land Cruisers. The dirt road twisted and turned through the trees and past farmers' huts, where barefoot children dressed in rags waved at us. Eventually, we came to the road leading north.

The road passed through Volcanoes National Park and the shadowy, dark-green forest was eerie as we drove by destroyed tanks and army trucks, some with dead bodies next to them. The forest then gave way to open plains, where black rock filled the valleys between the green, dormant volcanoes and we saw deserted camps where refugees had lived for years before the Congolese rebels – and Rwandan soldiers masquerading as Congolese – violently forced them home.

We came across another rebel checkpoint, but we adopted the imperious airs that so often serve white journalists well when confronted by African functionaries. We told the rebel soldiers we were entitled to pass and they let us drive on.

None of us had been this far north along this road. The rolling hills and picturesque villages of thatched mud huts was stunningly beautiful compared to the filthy, ramshackle concrete cities further south. In these villages there was no sign of war, only idyllic agrarian life.

When we pulled into the town of Butembo, we saw Miguel on the side of the road, taking down the antenna of his satellite phone. He saw us driving toward him and gave us a wry smile as if he was wondering what had taken us so long.

Typically, African hotels are little more than brick rooms with a bed made from scrap lumber and a three-inch-thick mattress. I expected nothing else behind the steel gate and brick walls surrounding the Auberge du Butembo.

Instead we found an island of colonial civility unimaginable in the dusty and decaying town. The lawns were carefully manicured and the majestic wood, brick and stucco buildings were surrounded by tropical flowers and palm trees.

We were greeted by a bellman dressed in a uniform – a double-breasted red jacket, black trousers and white gloves – usually found only at old-fashioned hotels. Despite a decade of under-employment and a civil war raging around them, the staff had maintained the standard of service set by the Belgian founders 50 years earlier. That night we watched Miguel's tapes being broadcast on satellite television.

Butembo was teeming with rebel soldiers and hundreds of child militia known as *Mayi-Mayi*, voodoo warriors who believed that their shamans' magic made them invincible and invisible in battle. We also learned that the rebels' grandiose claims of victory were complete fantasy. Mobutu's men were fleeing, but there had been a battle for Beni, an hour's drive north, and Bunia, the last major town in the east, had yet to fall.

The next day we descended from Congo's eastern mountains into the rainforest that covers most of the country. We found Beni brutalised by war, everything of value or nourishment looted and most of the women and girls raped or kidnapped.

Our goal was to catch up with the front line, so we drove further north and discovered the real reason for the slow advance. The road to Bunia was deeply rutted and the rains had flooded much of it. The rebels were slowly cutting bypasses through the forest. We followed the new road to the end and found a Rwandan officer with 30 soldiers. He told us everything north of him was no-man's land.

We were ill equipped to stay, even if they had allowed us, so we turned back for the night. Along the way Miguel wanted to call AP's television headquarters in London, so we stopped at an opening in the forest. As Miguel set up his phone, a group of young men dressed in scraps of cloth, some carrying small spears and none of them more than 150 cm tall, emerged to watch us.

"Look, Pygmies!" Norbert shouted in excitement. Even for a man who'd spent his life in Congo, he'd never seen Pygmies before.

Behind them in the forest, we could barely make out their tree houses. Norbert tried to speak to them, but the Pygmies didn't react. They kept their distance and just stared.

For the first time I thought about what we must look like to them. An American with blue eyes, an extraordinarily tall Argentinean and a wiry

Spaniard, all driving new trucks and setting up a strange box and talking into it. To the Ituri Forest Pygmies, we must have seemed like aliens from outer space.

I was reminded that what I knew of Congo and its people was immeasurably small and that the war I was covering, though at the moment the top story of the day, was just another short episode in Congo's long, violent history.

I looked into the forest, and knowing that it stretched for thousands of kilometres to the Atlantic Ocean, I realised that it was full of mysteries. I also wondered how many enclaves, like the Auberge du Butembo, existed behind high walls in other towns.

When we drove away, I suddenly longed to sit at the Pygmies' fire and hear their stories and their version of history, which I knew would be radically different from anything that I knew.

Alas, I never got the chance, but their silent gaze remains with me.

Chris Tomlinson is a correspondent for The Associated Press based in Nairobi, Kenya. A resolute Texan, he has covered wars and disasters across Africa, the Middle East and Central Asia.

How an African nation falls

Greg Barrow

The border guard's fat fingers worry the edge of a dog-eared pad, the top sheet separated by carbon paper the texture of wrinkled black skin. A ballpoint pen, chewed at the end and down to its last inch of ink, but still precious in this northern outpost of Zambia, stands poised above the immigration form.

It is early April, 1997, and we find ourselves here on a balmy evening, punctuated by the cries of cicadas and the buzz of malarial mosquitoes, waiting to cross the border at Kasumbalesa, the entry point into south-eastern Zaire.

It doesn't look hopeful. The border guard is irritable and tired. His khaki uniform is stained by the sweat of a day's toil in a thankless job at an insignificant border crossing that has rarely, if ever, attracted the attention of the international media. Outside, the pounding of maize, and the cry of children as they are put to bed, signals the distant prospect of dinner. Night is falling, and he wants us to go away.

A hen squawks and rushes behind the customs building. It is enough to spur the border-guard into action.

"Ladies and gentleman, we are closed for business," he says, carefully sliding his ball-point pen into a pocket marked by a bluish leak from a previous occupant.

"You come back tomorrow, and then we will see."

The protests are loud and impatient. We have all travelled a day to get here, only to be blocked at this final, and seemingly insurmountable hurdle. Voices cracked by too many cheap cigarettes and not enough water plead with the guard, but he will not budge. Then the wallets open. A little money to grease the wheels of bureaucracy. It is a fatal move. The border guard is deeply offended that we could imagine he might possibly bend to this kind of persuasion.

"We Zambians are not like our brothers over there in Zaire," he hisses, "Now, you go home."

Somewhere down the road, beyond this hot breeze-block cell where the immigration official works, something is happening. We have heard the occasional shot, but we cannot see or report what is going on, because we cannot get across the border. All we know is that the rebel advance is proceeding, and just north of here, up the road, is Zaire's second city of Lubumbashi. If it falls, Zaire, and its corrupt leader, Mobutu Sese Seko, are for the taking.

With dawn, we are back again. The orange light peeks over the horizon, silhouetting the elephant grass, and illuminating the chorus of sleepy cattle and energetic birds. The customs office is closed, and the guard does not arrive until almost nine o'clock. In his absence two Zambian soldiers, hung-over from the night before, keep us in check with battered rifles that look incapable of firing a shot.

"So, you are here again," our friend says when he eventually arrives. His ballpoint pen pokes out of the top of his pocket, as yet unsheathed.

"There is a small, small problem," he says, "We have lost communication with our friends over there in Zaire, and until we know they are at their border post, we cannot let you through. I suggest you wait."

So we wait, while the fresh morning transforms into a brutally hot day. The hours pass, the birds fall silent, the shade under the trees diminishes as the sun reaches its zenith. Then, as we are about to fall into a stupor, there is activity. A dusty Land Rover pulls up, carrying a senior Zambian police officer, and his staff. He has gold braid on his shoulders and he carries an ebony walking stick with a metal tip. It is enough to impress the border guard, who springs to attention.

After a short conversation the Land Rover and its occupants leave. As our guard plods back to his desk, he reaches up and pulls out the ballpoint pen. An hour later our passports are stamped. Now, we are standing in front of a horizontal, hollow metal pole with a cement block on one end, counterbalanced by the hand of a Zambian soldier at the other. When he is ready, he will let go, the pole will rise, and we will walk into Zaire.

But something is stopping him.

"You must wait some more," he says, "There is something happening over there." His tone is understated and unrushed. There are things that do not need explaining, some that cannot ever be explained.

Half an hour passes, and there is more activity, this time in the no-man's land between Zambia and its northern neighbour. Somebody shouts from the Zambian side, and the customs officer comes out to join us at the barrier.

Emerging from the bush in front of us is a short man in camouflage fatigues that look as if they have been barely worn. Loping behind him are ten very tall, very thin soldiers carrying beautifully maintained AK-47 assault rifles, and shining, rocket-propelled grenade launchers.

They look like Tutsis, the dominant minority in Rwanda, the foreign ally of the rebel movement. Their brand new boots look tight and uncomfortable. They are hardly soiled by the ubiquitous red African mud.

They ignore us, and instead shake hands with the customs official, with whom they confer quietly before walking back the way they have come, and disappearing from sight again.

"They are the new ones," the customs officer says, "They took over last night, and came today to explain who they are. That small one, he is Joseph Kabila, he is the son of the man who is chasing Mobutu away. Now you can go and see."

We walk the short distance across no-man's land, dragging our equipment with us, and praying there will be cars on the other side. There are no customs officials waiting for us at the Zairean border crossing. Instead, they are lying dead outside, with fat, black flies buzzing around their bloody wounds. All have had their trousers and undergarments pulled down, exposing their genitalia for all to see. It looks like a final humiliation for the corrupt workers of a crumbling regime.

Lubumbashi waits, a half-hour drive away. A man with a sorry looking Toyota Corolla is offering a ride. We negotiate and get on our way.

Greg Barrow worked in Africa from 1994 to 2001, first in Nairobi and then in Johannesburg as the BBC's Southern Africa Correspondent. At the time of writing he lived in New York and was the BBC's United Nations Correspondent.

Thoughts

Ian Stewart

From early 1993 until January 1999 Ian Stewart worked as a bureau chief and correspondent for United Press International and The Associated Press. The following is a selection of excerpts from his personal journals while he worked in the Far East, Indochina, the Indian Sub-continent and West Africa. These are the thoughts and emotions that never made it into his dispatches, but reflect the story behind the story:

• • •

July 1, 1993 (Beijing): This decrepit old train has been rumbling its way through the Chinese countryside for close to 18 hours now. For the most part I've recovered from one of the most serious bouts of vomiting I've ever encountered (damn rotten eggs). This comes on the heels of diarrhoea and a fever – I'm concerned that this may be a bit more serious than a simple case of traveller's sickness. Throughout this trip, my eyes have been almost involuntarily drawn to the peasants in the fields; they slave over their land, land that looks spent – a very tired, parched brown. And still, with a hoe and a lifetime's worth of patience, China's classless and somehow forgotten rural people set to work.

I'm brought to wonder about their lives, hopes and dreams – their fears and visions. What's beyond the fields? If nothing, what's in the fields? Then, I suppose I wonder about my own life and make a very unfair comparison. I'm a very lucky person, or perhaps "fortunate" is the better word.

I watch an old man (40-something, but already old). Alone in a vast, exhausted field he strains against the earth, tugging at a massive plough better suited for an ox. Using the force of his legs, and walking in reverse he painstakingly, agonisingly carves a single row in his field. Alone, he'll make another.

• • •

October 23, 1994 (New Delhi): *"Sahib"* she says, hands clasped together in gesture of prayer, or begging – what's the difference? *"Sahib."* I continue to walk. She scampers, barefoot, to keep pace. Filthy, tiny hands grasp my arm and stroke the hair. I've given her ten rupees (a pittance) and she knows very well I have plenty more to give, but where does it stop? She'll take the money and have to hand it over to a gang leader. A few rice husks and maybe a swallow of unpasteurised milk are her reward.

I've seen her before on every street corner of New Delhi and Calcutta and Bombay. At stoplights, she's digging through the putrid trash in an overflowing dump.

Her hair, which should be thick, silky and black in pigtails with red flowered berets, is brown and orange. Malnutrition steals her childhood. Her eyes, deep, rich brown, will never read. The sadness, so striking, has become a tool of her trade. There is no record of her birth; there will be no record of her death. She's a little girl in India, and that's a shame.

• • •

October 26, 1994 (New Delhi):
I saw a ghost tonight,
his body black and parched;
his eyes fixed and piercing.
I looked away too slowly.
He's with me now.

I saw a ghost tonight,
the rags that he wore tattered and high
with the stench of the gutter.
I looked away.
He didn't move, but he followed me home.
He's with me now.

Distant eyes stare blank at the night.
Flames and smoke dance at his knees.
He sits, he stares.
His life drags on in pain and hunger.

I saw a ghost tonight in the gutter on a street.
He followed me home to haunt my dreams.

And in the morning, the ghost was gone.
He's with me now.

I saw a ghost tonight.

• • •

January 9, 1996 (Peshawar, Pakistan): It's a brilliant sunny day in the rugged Northwest Frontier Province. The air is cool, but the sun warms. There's a clatter and rattle along the city's main Sadder Road. The traffic is a constant drone; roadside merchants hawk their goods with shouts to passersby. At the right time, the loudspeakers at the local mosque crackle to electric life and the Mullah beckons the faithful to prayer.

The small auto-rickshaws zip through traffic like tiny bugs between blades of grass, making a stinging buzz as they pass. It's hard to believe that this bustling market street was crippled just a few weeks ago. It was a car bomb that did the damage – levelled a building, killing at least 38 people in the blink of an eye. Life tinkers along in Pakistan, interrupted by horrendous acts of violence and bloodshed: terrorism. As fast as it seems to be halted by death, life seeps back into the streets and bazaars. I love this place. I hate this place. I'll never look at things in the same way after this place.

When a suicide bomber plowed his pickup truck into the Egyptian Embassy in Islamabad in November, I stood in awe at what people can do to each other. Pakistan's Interior Minister arrived with a tight huddle of officials surrounding him. They walked him through and in, and on top of the carnage. He stood outside the Embassy building – its entire northern side sheared off by the blast – and gave an impromptu press conference. As I fought to work through the pack of reporters, I stopped short. Looking down at a chunk of flesh – pink and bloody – lying in the mud and grass next to a man's Afghan wool cap. The shattered and shredded bone and muscle were no longer a human being. Our violence reduces humans to random, unidentifiable pieces of meat.

• • •

May 5, 1996 (Islamabad): It's 11 p.m. on a Sunday. Islamabad is quiet, except for the bullfrogs and crickets that chatter in the ravine behind my house. A gecko clucks now and again in the distance. An old motor scooter's engine whines into this bucolic setting and fades away down the street.

The fragrance of jasmine growing wild by the stream blends with the smell of fresh mint in my garden. The moon is almost full; its pale light trickles through the tree leaves, casting weird shadows. The vines overgrowing the brick wall at the back of my yard rustle as a stray cat struts out. He freezes, balancing atop the wall when he sees me – an intruder in his world of darkness. It's quiet, peaceful tonight. But I can't help wondering what the night conceals in Pakistan.

Bombs and guns are a part of life here. Only the calm of the night lulls you into feeling at ease. A bomb explosion on a bus in Lahore killed dozens of people in January; before that, seven were killed when a bomb hidden under a sofa tore through the waiting room at a cancer hospital. A cancer hospital! What in God's name goes through people's heads?

In the ten months I have lived here, well over 200 people have been killed in bomb explosions alone.

It's always the same: women, children, and men going home, packing their belongings with care onto a bus. Mothers, friends, somebody's father at the market picking up flour, or eggs, enjoying a cigarette over milky, sweet *chai*. Students, labourers, travellers waiting in line for their papers, or waiting to meet someone.

It's always the same: there are no warnings. Nobody has a premonition; you don't see it coming because it happens on any day, anywhere. There's a flash of brilliant light. All other sound dies, swallowed by the clap of thunder that echoes for a lifetime – somebody's lifetime. A wall of air – the shock wave – flattens everything in its path. Oxygen is sucked from lungs, glass is plucked from windows, and trees are stripped of leaves, birds and branches.

In an instant it's over. A crater is left behind. Burned, disfigured limbs litter the ground. There's no sound. The world stops for a heartbeat. Moments later and the journalists arrive, notebooks and cameras in tow. It's a story for a day. Then the officials follow to the scene. They shake their heads and wag their fingers for all to see their horror, preferably on camera. Then they leave, retreating to offices and tepid tea, and piles of untouched paperwork. The journalists too head home to computers and word processors. They tap out their well-thought dispatches and later brag of their heroics. But the fathers and mothers and friends and loved ones are left behind to gather the limbs; gather together what was a life an instant ago. It makes no sense. Should it? Maybe that's who we are, what we've become: Muslims, Jews, Christians, Hindus and Buddhists alike. We look to God for answers; we implore God for strength, but why should God care when we certainly don't.

$$\cdots$$

May 17, 1998 (Abidjan, Ivory Coast): Three months here, and Africa is as enigmatic as ever. There are some basics that are easy to grasp, but some of the more bizarre concepts – the cruelty, the inequity and injustice are just a little too tough to get my mind around.

Exploited-and-dumped-upon-Africa seems like an unfair place to me. Understandably there is anger directed at foreigners, by which I mean to say "whites", but there too is a deep, inexplicable capacity for horror that I cannot fathom.

In Sierra Leone a 13-year-old boy learns how to hack off people's hands and fingers with a machete knife. And in Nigeria, police think nothing of using strands of wire and rope to slash at crowds.

I suppose I can say I understand. No, not understand. I can see how humans can do that to one another ... no, I take that back. I can't understand, or see, or empathise. I can't figure out what the hell drives people to such fury that they will raise a rusty blade into the air and repeatedly slam it down into another person's flesh. What scares me the most here is the insanity of mob justice. The frenzy, the seething blind rage – is that the sum result of centuries of slave trading, corporate exploitation, colonialism and Cold War brainwashing, or indoctrination? Have we created Africa as it is today? And are we now content to let it sink, or swim? If so, then Africa certainly is our crime through the centuries.

Ian Stewart is a writer based in Northern California, where he lives with his wife and 7-year-old daughter. He was nearly killed on assignment in Sierra Leone in 1999. His first book *Ambushed: A War Reporter's Life on the Line* chronicles that assignment and his career overseas.

Note from the editors: Ian Stewart sat next to Myles Tierney in the car in Sierra Leone which was attacked on January 10th, 1999 resulting in Myles' death.

Chechen comedy hour

Greg Marinovich

Midsummer in the Caucuses. Clearly this was where all fairytale writers went on sabbatical. White, yellow and blue flowers soften meadows, and gentle hills and streams gurgle while soft clouds float across a sky of deep, brilliant blue. So blue. A blue that needs a thesauric contrivance to ensure I accurately convey the sense of heaven to you. As a believer in participation, I will let you look it up.

I am happy. Tramping along in liberated southern Chechnya, following a chess-playing fighter who would take on the entire Russian army to keep me safe. The fact that he and his fellow rebels regularly take on the Russians for sport does little to diminish his heroic status. My guide halts suddenly, turning his heavily-bearded face to me, a merry smile shows how generous dentists in the Caucuses are with precious yellow metal.

"Mine," he says, pointing down at the dirt road we are hiking along. Phonetically it came out something like "Mean–eh".

My mind grinds through the glossary of barnyard Russian it contains. Should I pull out the phrasebook? Mean–eh? Mines? Landmines? Oh no. Oh yes. The gold teeth glint maniacally in the gentle sunshine. I freeze, struggling against the massive adrenalin surge that wants me to run. He was chuckling at me, now he is roaring with laughter. I always get skinned at poker, so perhaps my terror and shocked disbelief are not as hidden as I imagine.

As the illusion of heaven changes to the reality of hell, I cannot see the humour in the situation unless he is joking. Of course he's just kidding, but nonetheless I decide to hold fast a little longer.

The hardened mud makes it impossible to discern unnatural disturbance, but on the other hand it all makes sense – we are strolling through one of the nastiest war zones ever. "You're joking, right?" He is laughing so much he has difficulty saying *"nyet"*. Instead, he mimes explosions as he jumps up and down on the dirt road. He is a heavy man and his booted feet come down hard on the minefield.

The weight of my pack and the sudden vulnerability of my feet are excruciatingly apparent. He ceases imitating a lunatic and beckons me forward – come, come. This is now even scarier. What does he want? Why is he doing this to me? I realise that I really do not know this man at all. I placed my trust in a desperado who carries a Kalashnikov and an RPG with several rockets instead of a lunch pack to work each day. I shake my head. I am not Chechen, my sense of fatalism not as finely developed, nor do I believe that tiptoeing through a minefield entitles me to the martyr's share of 72 virgins in the hereafter.

I have a tremor running up and down my right leg. Banjo leg, I believe it is called. My recently dear friend takes to stomping about, to allay my fears. I recall the sounds of him making love to his wife the previous night carrying clearly from their makeshift bed on the kitchen floor through the wall to me who sleeplessly occupied their bed. I remember too his love, nay, passion for killing Russian soldiers. Perhaps he too is not in a rush to ravish the 72. I stretch out a foot and ease my weight forward.

It is kind of like the moment of no return in bungee jumping, but infinitely more stupid. I take a second step, all the while vividly visualising the pain and horror that lie in store. I try to spot mines, but that of course is as futile as any of the other desperate escapes I have tried to imagine. I wonder how long it will take to perfect levitation.

Then a thought occurs to me: "What kind of mines are these?" I demand in suddenly improved Russian. It is as if he will die of laughter: "Tank mines!" as he jumps up and down once more for effect.

Greg Marinovich, born in South Africa in 1962, is co-author of the best-selling non-fiction book *The Bang Bang Club*. He covered wars for 12 years and won the Pulitzer Prize for Spot News in 1990.

Millennium moments

Max Quinn

I often wonder why I was privileged to be chosen to join a team voyaging to a tiny dot in the South Pacific to witness the very first sunrise of the New Millennium. But I was. My task was to direct a television outside broadcast of that event to millions around the world.

The Republic of Kiribati (pronounced Kiri-Bass) had the best credentials to claim to be the first to see the light. This island nation is an enigma. Covering an ocean area the size of the USA but a land area no bigger than Long Island, it is the only country to straddle the International Dateline. This quirk of time legitimately places its atolls to the east of the dateline in the same day as those to the west – in fact half an hour ahead of arch-rival New Zealand. So I found myself on the aft deck of the Kiribati Government freighter *Nei Matangere*, eyeing the horizon for a tiny uninhabited speck that would become home for the next three weeks leading to the 1st of January 2000.

But my millennium experience had already begun, albeit by chance two months earlier while on assignment in the bitter chill of Antarctica. It was the 24th of October 1999. Nothing particularly unique about that until the Scott Base manager pointed out that at midnight the sun was setting for the last time this year. Because of the tilt of the earth's axis the golden orb would be permanently above the horizon for the next four months, thus making it the last sunrise of the old millennium in Antarctica. At midnight on the 31st of December the sun would be shining brightly above Scott Base. So that evening a group of us set off to climb nearby Observation Hill, site of a memorial cross, erected in 1912 by Captain Scott's surviving men, to record the magic moment. The temperature was minus 25 degrees. The summit gave us a marvellous 360-degree view across Antarctica. But our eyes and cameras were all focused on the southern horizon for where the sun was about to momentarily disappear below the horizon before re-emerging on its low trajectory around the Antarctic sky.

As it reappeared its golden glow glanced off the wind-blasted timbers of the cross. I could just make out the inscription hammered into the wood 87 years ago in honour of the five who perished on that fateful South Pole trek. Cameras whirred and clicked. It was a breathtaking moment and the first of a triumvirate of millennium moments I was to witness in the coming months.

On Monday the 20th of December I was plucked from the frozen wastes of Antarctica and into the equatorial heat of the Pacific Ocean. Our ship was lying just off Caroline Atoll – now renamed Millennium Island for the occasion. On board were over 80 Kiribati concert performers and supporters who had enchanted us with their sublime harmonies during the past four days of sailing. Also on board were the millions of dollars worth of sophisticated television paraphernalia needed to mount a telecast of this complexity. Salt-water and electronics usually don't mix, yet throughout the day, tiny overloaded lifeboats piloted by skilled locals managed to navigate the reef without so much as a drenching. Reef sharks darted among us as we waded ashore like ancient explorers stepping onto some newly discovered land. As our gear slowly piled up on the blistering beach those of us in the TV crew bashed our way into the cool of the tropical forest to find a spot to set up camp.

Our next task was to seek a location where we could mount the telecast. It had to be on a level portion of beach preferably against a backdrop of coconut palms with a clear outlook to the eastern horizon. Amazingly within 100 metres of our camp was the perfect spot. Over the next two weeks we would rig cables, lights, and rehearse with cameras and videotape machines for the precious few minutes that so much had been invested in.

As the 31st of December approached the performance segments were slowly coming together. We were responsible for two ten-minute inserts at midnight and sunrise that would lead a worldwide broadcast mounted by global news giant APTN. As the director I had to call the shots from a temporary control room set up in an old army tent and plan how we could make our part of this global event stand out. My major concern (apart from doubting if the generators would keep running at the crucial moment) was to identify the exact spot where the sun would appear. Possibly the most crucial shot of my life, I had decided to place a remote camera pointed at the horizon to capture in close-up the sun's first appearance; easier said than done. We knew to the second when it would appear but exactly where was another matter. Having the camera pointing a degree or two either way would ruin the shot and I wasn't waiting another thousand years for my next chance!

So in the preceding days I dutifully made my way down to the beach in the early morning gloom to take a bearing on the point the sun appeared each day. After several days of this ritual I was confident I could calculate exactly where it would rise on January 1st.

The full dress rehearsal on the morning of the 31st of December was a triumph. The sun hit the spot, as did all the performers and camera team. Now to repeat it the next morning ...

Communications with master control in New Zealand was by satellite phone while the pictures and sound would go via two temporary satellite dishes erected specially for the occasion. On making contact with New Zealand my nerves were rattled. The first words I heard crackling over the airwaves from our Scottish producer were ... "come on Auckland, get your shit together ..!" There was obviously a panic going on and we being the first live insert into the global telecast did not make my nerves any calmer. But as midnight approached we seemed pretty relaxed and, before I knew it, I was counting down and cueing the haunting call of an elder seated by a fire on the beach. He chanted a farewell to the old millennium and requested us all to take a fresh step forward into the next. Then on cue the choir came in with a glorious pronouncement, that the new era brings us good health, peace and prosperity. Right on midnight the Kiribati President handed a local boy a flaming torch representing peace and hope for the next thousand years. As he sailed away in an outrigger, proudly holding high the burning beacon, a vigorous dance called *Tekeraoi* started exulting good luck and congratulations to all. Before we knew it the ten-minute segment was up and we were off the air. Now for the dawn.

Sunrise at the equator is a sudden thing. So when we assembled for our second and most important insert it was still pitch black. Things also seemed a lot calmer at master control. The broadcast had already been around the world once and now they awaited part two – the first view of the new-born sun. Once again the chanter called us to attention "as we await the birth". Then the chorus began – so exquisite in its harmony that it still haunts me to this day. Above this a falsetto voice cries "This little island alone in a huge ocean ... so far from everywhere ... ready to meet the new dawn ..." At the point of sunrise a warrior sounded a conch and I mixed through to our locked off camera so carefully positioned on the horizon. But today, on perhaps the most important sunrise of our lives a long shroud of grey cloud would block it out at the crucial moment. We waited with hearts pumping. Realising it wasn't going to show I quickly called for a cue to the next segment – a celebratory dance as young girls flirted with the new-born sun. But our disappointment at its non-appearance was only fleeting as, suddenly, glorious crepuscular rays burst forth from behind the billowing clouds to provide a startling climax to the broadcast.

As we made our way back to camp for a well-earned breakfast one of the journalists accompanying us emerged from his tent asking if he had missed anything. This was definitely not an occasion to sleep in!

On our shipboard journey back home we celebrated by casting a bottle containing sand from the beach and a heartfelt message from the team. It was a bit of fun and we thought "that will be the last we'll see of that…"

One week after my arrival back in New Zealand, I was packing again. My destination was the small Alaskan Eskimo village of Kaktovic where my assignment was to film aspects of life in the Arctic winter. Located well above the Arctic Circle they had yet to experience the first sunrise of the new millennium. However I knew the sun would soon be making itself known and would give me a chance to observe yet another millennium moment. On the 26th of January I headed off to the outskirts of town in temperatures more frigid than I had experienced in Antarctica. I set up my camera and waited. Apart from keeping an eye on the southern horizon I needed to be wary of rogue polar bears that had been seen around the township in search of an easy feed. The sun's trajectory near the poles is, unlike the equator, close to the horizon so I had a glorious crimson sky for company. Finally, through a gap in the Brooks Range, a blast of light like a torch being shone directly into my eyes pierced the sky signaling the first light of the new millennium in the high Arctic. Once again my camera rolled as I recorded my third millennium sunrise. But here, I was on my own. Only a few local dogs snapping at my heels witnessed it with me. For the locals it was just another part of the annual cycle their ancestors have been witnessing for thousands of years.

Exactly one year later in the warmth of my office as I went through the morning ritual of checking my e-mails, I was caught by surprise. It was from the leader of an Aboriginal tribe near the tip of Cape York in Australia: "Dear Mr Quinn, I would just like to inform you that we have found a bottle on a nearby beach that you threw into the sea on the 1st of January." Our millennium bottle had drifted over 4 000 kilometres west avoiding a myriad of islands not to mention negotiating the Great Barrier Reef before finding landfall. I could not think of a better way to end my millennium experience.

Max Quinn is a New Zealand producer/cameraman with over 30 years experience in television production. In the past decade he has specialised in Polar films and has filmed and observed emperor penguins breeding in Antarctica in winter. His assignment for APTN to Millennium Island is one of his recent tropical assignments.

Buffels and Bullets

Stephen Davimes

Sometimes I miss the reek of teargas and the thwack of a sjambok or rubber bullet. A good adrenaline rush of yesteryear could really clear the head and do wonders for objective reporting. These days I think a lot of reporters are muddled, mendacious and have it too cushy.

As a reporter and then photographer covering news in the old regime, times were too interesting but also deliciously ironic. Anyone remember the Key Points Act? Well, because of it I wanted to invent the SA photographer's underpants. Everyone's familiar with the macho photographic vest for keeping spare film, batteries, lenses, and Zippo lighter, even if you didn't smoke, for burning paper in front of your face to ward off teargas. (This I learned at Soweto's Regina Mundi Church, and you never used water on your eyes because it spread the pain.) The government experimented with types of gas, different "bouquets".

Well, because of the aforementioned Act, a scientist friend and I were arrested at a chlorine plant where I was taking photographs. We'd gone there because workers complained their cars were rusting in the parking lot because of the toxic levels of chlorine which my friend sampled and proved. As the security advanced on us outside the plant I surreptitiously replaced my film in the camera and dropped the exposed roll down my trousers. I was forced to hand over the fresh roll from my camera. We were firmly told that chlorine was a strategic material vital to combat the "total onslaught". Despite saving the film the story was never permitted to be published. Custom underpants for the press with secure compartments might have been revolutionary. I used this technique successfully more than once - the notorious "towser" method, practiced at prison near the Constitutional Court, not withstanding. This was a 'scientific search technique' explained to me by photographer Alf Kumalo, where the police or warders would make a naked prisoner star jump and yell "towser!" to dislodge a concealed item.

I once recall photographing a young and innocent-looking, can you believe, Winnie M.M. at Wits University long, long ago where these underpants would have been essential. On the same day and place I was shot with a rubber bullet, well a "37mm solid nylon baton round" that might have knocked some sense into me. I temporarily lost a little hair in front. I could have tried to sue the police minister for a hair piece. Anyway, someone picked up the cracked rubber round, which I still have. I read that the Johannesburg Art Gallery bought a brick used in a riot for a couple of thousand and displayed it as apartheid art. I might have been able to flog it my rubber bullet too!

The minister who had caused all the fuss at Wits in the first place, interestingly, was FW, known then as hands-off–Wits de Klerk, remember, then proposing punitive academic measures for students who protested.

I remember covering an AWB rally in Krugersdorp where I was tripped in the hall but luckily I fell on a brown-shirted old lady who broke my fall. Terreblanche ranted about the Joodse, Swartes and everybody else but especially about the Engelse and their Oorlog. But that didn't stop 'die leier' arriving fashionably late by crimson British Jaguar.

Again when the right wingers staged a rally in Pretoria's Church Square and clambered over the statue of Oom Paul Kruger with anti-Karl Marx placards reading "that damn Jew", little did they know that the statue they were on was donated to the city by another Jewish Marks, Sammy.

In the old days, newspapers had official police spies and unofficial ones unlike those in Nusas which only had one kind, and you could usually tell which they were, unlike Nusas it would seem. They usually surfaced later in the SAP with rank after the democratic elections.

I still have my permit from the West Rand Bantu Administration for entering Soweto for the purposes of news coverage, "between the hours of..."

I have fond memories of the *Rand Daily Mail*, SAAN and many of its larger than life characters. I recall Doc Bikitsha, Sophie Thema, Robbie Tshabalala, the news editors, colourful photographers and dart players and many others who taught me so much. I always carried my own camera even as a cadet and whenever I bumped into the late Mike McCann in its corridors he would throw its lens cap into the dustbin until I got the point.

A piquant memory I have of reporting under apartheid was when it rained in Springbok for the first time in many years. As a young cadet on the RDM (the "blerrie" Communist rag owned by capitalists), the news editor instructed me to get reaction from the townsfolk. So I'd thought I'd do a clever telephonic colour piece. I called the town's police station and effusively asked the desk sergeant what it was like to finally have rain.

He said politely, "Sorry, I'm not allowed to talk to the Press."

Stephen Davimes is a cynical retired journalist and photographer living in Johannesburg with his wife Claudia, their two sons Joshua and Dominic and his pocket Alsatian, Bagela.

Fifteen days in hiding because of an email address

Donna M'Baya Tshimanga

January 2001: the second DRC war is in its third year and the Congolese don't hide their disgust towards the government of Laurent Desiré Kabila anymore.

They are tired of war. Didn't the man who overthrew Mobutu Sese Seko say at the start of the rebellion in August 1998 that "the war will be long, popular and will end where it started", meaning Kigali? But what the former rebel leader probably didn't predict is the social and human cost of the war. Growing poverty. Total destruction of schools and medical infrastructure. More than three million dead.

Some kind of negative solidarity had set in between Kabila and his citizens who were intoxicated and doped up on anti-Rwandan propaganda. The message was loud and clear. The collapse of the nation was the fault of Rwanda and the rebel puppets of the Rally for Congolese Democracy (RCD). Facing this dead-end street, the Catholic Church decided to break the silence. The Archbishop of Kinshasa, Cardinal Frederic Etsou Bamunggwabi, called for a demonstration under the banner "A Cry for Congo". Thousands of Kinois gathered at the Notre Dame Cathedral in the capital and demanded an end to all hostilities. Local and international media covered the event. But the images weren't aired on the national Radio-Television Nationale Congolaise thanks to Dominique Sakombi Inongo, a former hardline Mobutu supporter and now Kabila's Information Minister.

Journalists from the state broadcaster complained to Journaliste En Danger (JED), a Kinshasa based non-governmental organisation for press freedom, which then issued a statement comparing this censorship to that which was practised under Mobutu. The international media used the statement to tackle Sakombi. But the next day he broadcast a censored version of the gathering and sent a statement to the French radio station RFI. In it he denies any intervention and labels JED and its members as "crazy". JED is now in Sakombi's firing line.

JED sends Sakombi's statement to Radio France Internationale (RFI) and to other local and international media, including to Walter Mbayirindi, the then presenter of the Swahili news for South Africa's Canal Africa radio station. Sakombi discovers that his statement was sent to Walter's email: mbayrindi@usa.net.

What follows is a farce based on an e-mail address.

Sakombi declares that Walter Mbayrindi lives in America and works for Deogracias Bugera, one of the leading figures within the Rwandan-backed DRC rebels, based in Goma. The message to the paranoid population in the capital is clear. Walter is a traitor. And I, working for the JED, and the organisation's secretary general Mwamba wa ba Mulamba, are said to be passing on intelligence to the rebels. Automatically this means that we are now on the "wanted" list of the COM, Kabila's special military court to which there is no appeal. We have become hunted animals overnight.

Monday, January 15th, 2001: A newspaper vendor on the corner of the street warns me that the daily *Le Palmares* claims on page three that "the two enemies M'Baya and Mwamba have been arrested". The newspaper declares we have been arrested on the 14th and that during our interrogation we have admitted to be traitors in the service of Rwanda and the RCD. I pinch myself. Here I am standing free on the corner of the Avenue du 30 Juin and the former Avenue du 24 Novembre. Am I dreaming? I remember sleeping at home last night and not in a police cell.

I read the article again. And again. Then I realise there must have been a plan to arrest us but something must have gone wrong. So Mwamba and myself were now clearly marked, wanted and thus on the run. We had to disappear.

I call Mwamba who was still asleep. I just tell him to leave his house right away and to meet me downtown.

My worries are confirmed when a few minutes later I get a call from two journalists who tell me to disappear urgently because we are now officially hunted because of "collaboration with the enemy during wartime".

At 10 a.m. on Monday, January 15th, 2001, we went into hiding because of serious but fake accusations orchestrated by the Information Minister.

So we go underground and our only contact with the outside world are our cellphones. We call trustworthy friends in Kinshasa to explain our situation. We stress that Walter never lived in the USA and never had any doings with the RCD. In fact he works for the state radio and TV station where he still reads the news in Swahili.

Walter's surname, Mbayirindi, looks somewhat like a Rwandan surname. And his e-mail address ended on usa.net. Washington was perceived by Kabila and co. as Kigali supporters and thus anti-DRC.

All our friends tell us to lay low for the time being. But Minister Sakombi hasn't had his vengeance yet. His agents contact the owner of the building in which JED has its offices. They demand that JED is closed down and expelled from the building. The owner is warned that his refusal would lead to problems with military justice because "JED works together with the pro-Rwandan rebellion" and that there is "clear evidence" in this matter. The owner, Fundu N'Kota, is a good friend and a "brother", as we say in Africa. He was a bureaucrat under Mobutu's reign. He even made it to Provincial Governor under the *Marechal*. He stayed on till May 17th, 1997, when Kabila's forces took the capital. He was arrested for a few days, and crossed the river after being freed. But in 1998 he returned home. Fundu didn't want to get involved in this "collaboration" case and certainly didn't want trouble with the Kabila regime. The doors of the JED offices were bashed open and all its contents were looted. Our secretary could only save two computers and some files.

Twenty-four hours after we went "underground", at around 11 a.m. on January 16th, Laurent Desiré Kabila is shot in his palace.

At around 4 p.m., not knowing what had happened, Mwamba calls fellow journalist Severin Bamanyi, who is part of the "presidential press corps", to ask him to help clear our names.

Severin tells Mwamba: "The country is adrift. Lost. In turmoil. Where are you? Put the TV on!" We do and see Colonel Eddy Kapend, aide-de-camp to the President. With a monotonous, dark voice and enraged eyes he orders the closure of all borders and calls upon the military to remain calm and in their barracks. My first reaction to Mwamba is "this brass has just overthrown Kabila". We switch on the radio to RFI. It's here that we hear about the assassination.

For the Congolese establishment the hand in this murder is clear. Rwanda. And this tragedy comes just hours after we have been branded traitors and Rwandan collaborators. Our situation just gets worse and more complicated by the minute. I call Polydor Muboyayi, the editor of *Le Phare*, who was trying to get us out of Sakombi's clutches. Polydor tells us to stay put. "The army is in the streets. But I don't know who is in command. If they catch you now you are in serious trouble because they might link you to the murder."

For the first time since going into hiding I fear for my life. I fear for my family. I call Modeste Mutinga, the director of the daily *Le Potentiel*, for advice. He tells me he is in hiding himself and that the only advice he can give us is not to get caught because that would mean the worst. We knew what he meant.

We decide to contact our JED partners in the US, Canada and Europe. Disguised, I go to the other JED offices. From there I could send e-mails.

I ask Mwamba to stay put because it would be stupid if both of us get caught. Our partners responded quickly and advised us to get out of the country as soon as possible. But the borders where closed. And Mwamba had no valid visa. I had a Senegalese one.

Luckily the airport re-opened soon and, still disguised and thanks to friends at the airport, I managed to get on the Cameroun Airlines' flight to Dakar.

Two weeks later Mwamba calls me and tells me everything is quiet again and I could return to Kinshasa. I follow his advice and meet my family again.

Kabila Junior had followed Kabila Senior. Sakombi was too busy trying to save his political career to worry about us. And the truth came out – Mbayirindi never was on the RCD's payroll, nor did he live in the USA.

… and during our underground-life Walter just kept reporting from the national broadcaster.

Donna M'Baya Tshimanga is a freelance journalist, living and working in Kinshasa. He is president of the NGO Journalistes En Danger, which promotes and defends press freedom.

Baptism of fire

Hilary Andersson

I had never set foot in Nigeria before; I didn't know one person there, and that night I was flying in to take up a three-year posting there for the BBC. Against all advice.

Nigeria was in the grips of the dictator General Sani Abacha. He had recently hanged an internationally famous human rights activist, and had taken to arresting foreign journalists.

The British Airways flight delved through the darkness, and landed. As it pulled into its parking bay, a gigantic menacing Nigerian face, painted on the tail of another aircraft, slowly moved in to completely fill up my oval window frame. Its cheekbones were hard, its angry eyes were piercing, and they looked straight at me.

In my hotel room that night, I woke up startled by the ring of the phone.

"Is that Miss Harper?" the voice mysteriously asked. No-one knows my middle name is Harper.

I asked the voice what it wanted. It asked me if I had lost anything.

The first page of my passport flashed into my mind like a photograph. Emblazoned across the top of the photo page is "Hilary Harper". My surname, Andersson, is on the line below. The voice wanted money. I wanted my passport. So the next day I bought it back.

The drive to my new office was down a long road, clogged with cars stacked nose to tail, with less than an inch between them.

Suddenly frantic honking started and a siren blared. My driver screamed "shut your window, shut it quick". A military commander, a man with the power of a god in the madness of Abacha's Nigeria, wanted to get through.

His men were hanging off his car wielding huge black whips which they violently lashed out at all of us innocents. And so, desperate to be obedient, we lurched madly, in the unbearable sweaty heat, one whole inch towards the car in front of us. A thousand cars lurched too, and the commander squeezed through.

The next day I attempted to master "the lurch" myself, and inadvertently knocked a soldier off his moped. I fled in terror as he leapt back on his bike in a rage. I crashed through the appalling traffic, and tore around a corner. He followed. I ducked into a private driveway. The gate guards there, sensing my panic, threw a cloth over my licence plate, and the moped sped by.

I moved into my flat in Lagos later in that first week of my posting, hoping for a sanctuary from the chaos. On my first night cockroaches crawled across my face whilst I was sleeping. I leapt up, stood on my mattress, and shouted at them for at least an hour whilst emptying an entire bottle of bug spray into my room. The cockroaches retreated to the bottom of my pillow-case where I found them the next morning.

But there were bigger concerns. The BBC had called me from London about rumours of a coup plot in Nigeria, rumours that Abacha was being held hostage in the presidential mansion.

I made a few discreet calls to check these rumours, but nothing could be confirmed so I went out for an errand in downtown Lagos.

As I was preparing to go home, two men in plainclothes approached me and flashed identity cards at me. They carried the dreaded letters "SSS". The State Security Service. I was under arrest.

They wouldn't tell me why. Nor did they have a car in which to take me away, so they asked me if I wouldn't mind driving. What could I say?

"Oh sure, please, get in," I said opening the door for them.

Absurd as this was, my sweat was turning cold, and my stomach was hollow. I felt nauseous with fear.

At intelligence headquarters they stripped me of my phone and watch and ushered me down a corridor. On its dirty wall was a poster with the caption "Shhh Shhh, Secret Secret", and a picture of a man holding his finger to his lips.

There was nothing to confirm that I wasn't now playing a part in a sinister cartoon.

They put me in a dark little room with two damp and torn brown armchairs. There was a tiny window high up, and the walls were scratched with the graffiti of other inmates. None of the guards would tell what their plans for me were.

I was given one book, the Bible. I started reading Revelations to keep my mind off things, but it wasn't very calming. When I asked for another book they gave me one about a woman who had been arrested during the Spanish Inquisition, complete with vivid details about her torture.

A lipsticked ex-prostitute, turned evangelical Christian, was sent in to guard me personally. Such people are recruited by the SSS for lowly minding duties. She spent the night trying to save my soul.

Finally in the dead of night I was called in for interrogation. Two men sat behind a wooden desk. One of them held a long ruler, which he waved about threateningly as he tried to force me to write a statement that they were dictating. I refused.

The statement they were trying to get me to write would have indicted me in an attempted coup plot against the Head of State of Nigeria. The sentence for that is execution.

Fortunately I am able to talk, endlessly. And so I gabbled and gabbled and gabbled, and argued and argued and argued, until they were so sick of me they sent me back to my cell.

The next day, exhausted, I waited for hours and hours knowing it was the brink of a long holiday weekend in Nigeria, and that if no-one let me out soon, I would be there for days or even longer. The waiting was the worst, because fear was gnawing at the insides of my stomach.

Eventually I was called out again. I was taken to a big plush room and told to sit on a very low couch. At the other end of the room on a huge chair, and behind an enormous polished desk sat a large Nigerian man with a chiselled black face, an enormous blue traditional robe on, and a tall Nigerian hat. He looked just like the face I had seen from the aeroplane window.

Without smiling he slowly moved his head up to look at me, and said, "Welcome to Nigeria. This is your baptism of fire."

Hilary Andersson was later released – thanks to the intervention of the American and Lebanese Embassies. She reported for the BBC from Lagos for three more years.

The protest

Elizabeth King Humphrey

Her mop of chestnut brown hair bobs and swirls in the damp wind. Her grey Italian hiking boots kick the walnuts which have ripened and fallen from the trees. She tries not to keep in step with the others. The small cluster skip along the frosted autumnal grass, intermixed with crispy, early fallen dull leaves and walnuts. Every so often, when she finds herself catching up, she stops and scours the ground for more delectable, fresh walnuts. She picks them up, placing them in her coat pocket to open later.

Jonathon takes the lead, as usual. He always needs to be first. And his loud, boisterous voice always makes sure he is. His words furiously emerge before his breath has time to interact with the frigid air. Everyone else sees breath in front of them. Jonathon is already ten steps past when his breath finally turns to smoky air. His gait is forceful, brisk, rapid fire – mimicry of his life.

The three walk behind. Not following, just moving at their gentle pace. All of them are determined to ignore the quizzical looks of the locals. They progress towards the shore of the grand, mythical river searching for the demonstration site. The river strolls along – oblivious to the action on its shores. Jonathon darts about – leading without knowing that no-one is following. His camera and camera bag clank along his hip. They bounce along to his frenetic pace.

She looks behind them to see a dark figure slow his pace in unison with hers. She had seen him near their hotel. Jonathon would scoff at her if she mentioned it. She remains silent – until she can say it without fear of humiliation – if it ever came to that.

Their path brings them towards a decrepit iron bridge. Built for utility, not for its mastery of design or form with nature – the object emerges as electric power lines do, in the middle of a pastoral, romantic scene. But it is devoid of protesters, of people – the essence of the journalists being there.

She peers back to look at the stranger. She tries to disguise the panic she feels, so she airily moves towards Pavel. He would be the one to stand near if the stranger made his move. Pavel could speak the language and would certainly protect her.

Out of Jonathon's earshot she mentions to Pavel that they are being followed. He looks at her and puts his arm around her shoulder, "I know. But don't worry; he's just observing us. It's a former police state and they've just forgotten to tell the police that democracy has prevailed. Don't worry, we're the press, they won't bother us as long as we are just doing our jobs."

His calmness has a temporary effect and she steps away, finding her own rhythm again. She fiddles with the damp, fresh walnuts in her pocket. She thinks about food and where they will find a place to eat on an overcast day like today, in this unfriendly neighbourhood. Since mentioning food while they are lost – or at least not where they should be – is not a good idea, she starts trying to open a walnut against another. She can't manage to break them open within her coat pocket, so she takes two and positions her hands as though in prayer – with a walnut in the base of each hand. They break open easily and the walnut meat collapses in her hands.

Jonathon hears the noise of the walnuts and turns around. She looks up at him – caught in the act of varying the journalistic mission without his permission. He glares and continues his search for news.

The stranger marks his pace.

Elizabeth King Humphrey received her BA from Columbia University and MFA at UNC Wilmington. She has worked for CBS News and The Associated Press.

I'm confused

Milton Nkosi

It was the beginning of the year 2000 when I began producing a film on South Africa's coloured community for BBC's Newsnight programme. The focus of the film was the challenges facing the mixed-race community in the new South Africa.

Following extensive research we discovered a man in the small town of Murraysburg, neatly tucked away in the Karoo in the Western Cape. His name is Mr Isaac Dokter, who was classified a coloured in the old South Africa. This racial classification allowed him access to the slightly better public amenities compared with what black people had. According to the laws in South Africa prior to 1994, coloured people were slightly better off than black people purely because of the colour of their skin; they were a touch whiter. The apartheid system thrived on divide and rule; it pitted brother against brother. In the case of Mr Dokter, he enjoyed the half-comfort zone, a luxury black people could only dream of.

When we arrived at a Murraysburg township, locally known as Julwe location. We found a family that was undecided on what surname they wanted to use in the new South Africa. Isaac was in the process of changing his surname from Dokter to Mosotho. "Why?" I asked, and he answered, "because I want to go back to my roots".

But why now? It turns out that Mr Dokter was a Mosotho before he converted to Dokter. He did this so that he could at least attend a better school. An opportunity he wouldn't have had, had he remained a Mosotho. In the 80s things were so bad that he changed his surname from a traditional black South African name to a surname that was acceptable to the apartheid regime. Being a Mosotho, he'd have had to endure the indignity and humiliation suffered by black people who were, by law, classified as second-class citizens. So Isaac Mosotho did what he thought was the right thing. He changed his name to fall in line with the requirements of the Separate Amenities Act. He got all of that – he went to the right schools, played in the right parks, spoke the oppressor's language, Afrikaans. Life wasn't that good, but it certainly was better than what the majority of South Africans enjoyed.

He then married Marelda, a coloured woman from the Western Cape. They were blessed with two beautiful children, a handsome boy, Ashley, and gorgeous little Lisa. Then, came the historic, all-race elections of 1994. On a beautiful late autumn day, May 10th, Nelson Mandela was inaugurated as the first black president of South Africa. Black South Africans had their dignity restored. Then, came the airforce's flypast – for the first time in the history of South Africa black people felt they belonged to South Africa and that it belonged to them too. No-one felt the need to change their name to feel accepted by his or her master. We were the masters of our destiny.

One of the millions who stood in the long queues snaking into the distance was Isaac Dokter, and he too had his dignity restored. He then embarked on a long and drawn-out name-changing process. He wanted to be African again! He wanted his father's name back. He wanted to be Mosotho again! As Archbishop Desmond Mpilo Tutu chanted: "We are free, all of us black and white together, we're free ..." And the crowd followed behind him.

It was with shock and dismay that the children heard from daddy who announced to his young family that, they were changing their surname. As from that day onwards they were to call themselves Mosotho and not Dokter. Together with my BBC colleagues, Jane Standley and Glenn Middleton, we then posed the question to Marelda – you married a coloured man, you're coloured, your children are coloured, what is your reaction to the name change plan and what does that make you? She replied, "I'm a coloured, no I'm an African, no I'm confused." We asked the question, are your children also coloureds then? Same answer – "confused".

We had a good laugh at the situation because at the beginning it felt like a laughing matter. But later that night when we were flying to another coloured stop in Cape Town, I was overcome by sadness thinking that people had to resort to these tactics just to survive the harshness of the apartheid system. Young Ashley who was eleven years old at the time said that he didn't mind being a Mosotho, but he was concerned that his African relatives will tease him because he couldn't speak their language.

Mosotho emphasised that he was doing it for his kids. I was quickly reminded of a story we once covered on coloured utility rates protests in Westbury, when one coloured lady said to us that coloureds are always squeezed between the blacks and the whites. Then she delivered the killer sound-bite: "During apartheid we were not white enough and now in the new South Africa we're not black enough!" There were many others too, like: "I buy a colour TV and all I see is black and white"!

Due to apartheid legacy, even ten years after democratisation, most politicians right from the top, still refer to various groups in the country as, whites, Africans, Indians and coloureds. Although most speakers hasten to clarify that the term, "blacks" includes Africans, Indians and coloureds. Some people in the coloured community still feel that post-apartheid reconstruction programmes such as affirmative action, have a heavy bias favouring black Africans at their expense. They feel alienated by empowerment programmes that are geared up to fast-track the advancement of black Africans. According to a study conducted by Idasa (Institute for a Democratic South Africa), a think-tank group, there's no scientific evidence to demonstrate that coloureds are being discriminated against either by the government or by the people in the new South Africa. At present there are just over a million people who constitute what could be described as the coloured community. The majority come from the Western Cape.

Mr Mosotho, still lives in Murraysburg, and his wife and children speak very little of any of the ten official African languages. English is the eleventh official language.

I will tell you more another time about the coon festival, where coloured people paint their faces! It is the minstrel street dance, generally accepted to be a coloureds-only tradition. As you can imagine, it was difficult for us to use the term "coon" on BBC television – a point we made clear to our interviewees, although they were proud to be called coons.

Die storie gaan aan – the story continues!

Milton Nkosi is the Africa Bureau Chief for BBC News. He was born in Soweto and was educated in South Africa, and did part of his journalism training in London. He's covered many conflicts around the world. He's married and has two children, Kgosietsile and Khanyisile. He lives in Johannesburg.

The speech I never gave

Sheila McClure

We were meant to be going to Nepal, the mysterious Kingdom of Nepal. It was what I'd been looking forward to for the past two months and not going had put me in a funk.

I thought I'd set up enough stories. I had secured us a meeting with the Dalai Lama in Dharamsala to kick off the trip - then we'd head up to Kathmandu. We had plans to do a story on garbage becoming an increasing problem with the increasing flow of tourists. Another story - hard to set up, but interesting nonetheless – was going to look at a problem with native Nepalese being evicted from neighbouring Bhutan - a hint at ethnic cleansing the world was choosing to ignore. Or maybe it just wasn't aware. There were festivals to cover and a rarely seen slave market and beautiful mountains and interesting faces to film - but I could confirm just about nothing.

Poor phone lines or insurmountable language barriers kept a "sure thing" at bay. The only guaranteed story we had was the Dalai Lama interview but, owing to heavy exposure from a recent US-European tour, the editors thought it wasn't worth the money.

Instead we were on the train platform at about 11 or so at night – waiting for a train to Rajasthan. The desert. At the beginning of summer. It was already over 40 degrees Celsius. Every day.

Rishi Lekhi is one of the best cameramen I've ever worked with. He was on staff at APTV after his elder brother - who had previously held the post - left for a new job at the BBC. Their father, too, had been a cameraman. I'd agreed that his wife, Vimmi, and their new son, Rishabh, could come along. We'd all been hoping to go to Nepal and his wife had never ridden on a plane or been out of the country - so it would've been a series of firsts for her - and I felt privileged that I could be part of this historic adventure. Rajasthan in the summer certainly wasn't top of their list - but they couldn't really afford vacations and one of the towns we were visiting was also home to some of their relatives.

For some reason - and I'm not strictly sure which reason - I had thought travelling to the hottest spot in India with a cameraman, his wife, their new child, a photographer and a pile of gear would be a hoot. It was definitely a hoot alright.

There are stories pouring out of India. Fascinating features there isn't time to show on the news anymore. Terrorism updates, government over-spending and celebrity scandals seem to dominate now. But this was before 9-11 and the war in Iraq and 24-hour access to the US military. We had our trip approved – although it was made clear that I needed to watch the pennies as the news coffers were never too full for these sorts of adventures.

We'd just missed an enormous camel fair. And we were out of season for elephant polo. Not that everything was fated to turn out horribly on the trip. Our first stop – after a harrowing jeep ride a couple of hundred kilometres from the train station (although I found most vehicular travel in India harrowing) – was a rat temple. It was there I discovered that tall, strong, mustachioed Rishi Lekhi was afraid of rats – and I would have to shoot the story.

I thanked the heavens – although I should've probably just thanked the rat gods for they were more present – that I had worn socks that day. The shoes had to come off at the front gates and I can assure you going in barefoot would've put me in a much crankier mood. Ahead of me at the temple were a newly married couple paying their respects. They couldn't have been more than 15 years old. There were various nooks and crannies throughout the temple – some filled with beautiful statues surrounded by offerings of coconuts and sweets and other morsels of food – as well as piles of flowers. Above all, though, there were rats. Every which where. Rats a go-go. Rats up the proverbial wazoo.

As I made my way through the temple with the camera – gingerly setting it down from time to time on a rodent-free surface – I kept reminding myself that this was really good TV and how many other people in the world get paid to travel to exotic locales to film, uh, rats?

The socks went straight into the garbage and my body went straight into the shower. Our accommodation was really lovely and it cheered me up. It was something silly like $20 US a night and I was convinced my room was a full wing. Until I saw Rishi and Vimmi's room. They had a wing. On the way to dinner we saw camels pulling carts precariously stacked with dozens of colour televisions. I loved the contrast. I wasn't grumpy anymore.

The next day we went to prison. Most of the men, we learned, were local murderers and thieves. It appeared the bulk of the murders were men who either suspected, knew or suspected they knew that their wives had been unfaithful – so they had killed them. Beyond that – they were harmless. Or so it seemed. We were let in around midday. I expected lots of crude hooting and catcalling from rows and rows of cells. Instead all we were met with were a bunch of loosely guarded men who were napping.

We actually had to wake some of the men up in order to film the story which was detailing their punishment: Rug-making.

That's right. No rock quarries or chain gangs for these rural life-takers. They were sentenced to years of dying, preparing and weaving rugs – sold at cost through the front of the prison. Some of the rugs were truly spectacular and, to the number, every man I spoke to had either killed his wife or raped a local woman.

When we had finally wrapped all the stories, and packed the four billion bags we had collectively brought along into the car that the driver had finally decided to appear in, we arrived at the train station in the early evening ready for our train. Our train that we were only wait-listed on. Our train that I'd forgotten couldn't confirm our seats until those few precious moments before departure. Our train that was so full there wasn't a chance on earth we'd be finding our way into a cool, first-class overnight cabin.

We stood on the platform and waited. Rishi kept checking with the conductor at my impatient insistence while Vimmi tended to a squirmy Rishabh. I was a black cloud of unpleasant thoughts about India and all it had to offer. And then came the final straw.

Rishi approached with his head hung low. I knew he wasn't going to have good news. I also knew it wasn't his fault but I didn't care. That speech had been waiting far too long for a good outlet.

Rishi and Vimmi looked aghast. Up until then I had been a good-humoured guest in their land. Delighting in the new foods, sights and sounds. But now I had turned into the Evil Producer from Overseas. Rather than being truly cruel I'd started by screaming about budgets and timetables and no wonder things were never on budget here with such a hodgepodge system of ticket-booking when, all of the sudden, one of my gesturing limbs got caught in the beaded glasses holder I was wearing and beads flew everywhere.

Little black and red and brown beads went absolutely everywhere. Rishi and Vimmi just waited in horror for my reaction.

A moment passed in silence and then I began to laugh. Laughed like a looney hyaena. As I calmed down, I silently thanked my arm for intervening before I got to the meat of a speech that I should never have begun.

I got a grip on myself and announced we were going to go back to the hotel, find a travel agent and buy some airplane tickets (given that there wouldn't be free train berths for several days, if not for a couple of weeks) and some Elephant Beer. I wasn't quite sure in which order.

In the end it didn't matter. I think we got beer at the travel agent's. I didn't ask. It's easier not to and now I was in a good mood. I'd made a pact with myself that I'd take any heat rather than blame India if the budgets were questioned. In the end it was going to cost a grand total of somewhere around $250 for us to stay on, fly home and eat at the really posh restaurant in the Raja's main palace. Then we went back to our sumptuous rooms in the cousin's palace and made merry in the Lekhi's room, dancing and singing to our own songs. I sang some of mine. They sang some of theirs and we were relaxed, happy and laughing.

It was the best $250 (that wasn't mine) that I ever spent. Vimmi got her first plane ride - Rishup too for that matter. We saw dozens of women making their way across the barren landscape in their saris, dotting the landscape with rich colours that I was too far away from to make a snotty judgement about whether the fabric was silk or synthetic. For once, I just let it be pretty.

And most importantly I remembered that I was the guest, and that not only were the Lekhi's my hosts, but so was their country. And it was time to stop being an ungrateful, air-conditioned-hotel-centric visitor. It was time to stop making up speeches, and time to enjoy India. At its pace.

Sheila McClure got her travel bug from being raised in a navy family. She has worked for AP Television for nearly 10 years, and recently hung up her hat to explore, perhaps not greener, but different pastures.

Three weeks on the remotest island

Masako Osada

For seven days we saw nothing but the horizon and a few albatrosses. Then, one foggy morning in October 2000, the triangular shape of "the remotest inhabited island in the world" appeared in front of us.

Tristan da Cunha. A British overseas territory in the South Atlantic Ocean, halfway between Cape Town and Buenos Aires. The entire population, less than 300, lived in one village, the Edinburgh of the Seven Seas. Their ancestors came from Scotland, England, Ireland, Holland, the United States, St Helena, Italy and South Africa, in the 19th century. The circular island with an average diameter of ten kilometres had no ports or airports. A South African fishing boat kindly gave us a lift from Cape Town.

The lucrative fisheries concessions with South Africa, Japan and the United States enabled the government of Tristan da Cunha to provide free health care and education. There was no unemployment and virtually no crime. The police officer's main job was to teach children about road safety.

The volcanic island was breathtakingly beautiful. The snow-capped peak rises to 2,060 metres from the plateau. Cows and sheep stroll around the green pasture. Over the cliff lies the ocean of every different shade of blue. The sky is vast. Here, even the laziest photographer could take stunning pictures.

For us, a TV crew making a documentary on moral issues surrounding genetic research, it was a different story.

The islanders were understandably distrustful of journalists. A lot of reports about Tristan had been purely sensational. The genetic closeness of the islanders (there were only seven surnames) and the remoteness of the island fuelled unkind imaginations, looking for physical and mental abnormalities and eccentric customs and traditions, which we did not encounter. An angry islander told us that an Italian journalist once wrote that their wedding cake was made out of cardboard. We suspected that, even if a brave resident wanted to speak with us, living in such a tight community would make it difficult to break down the barriers.

That the islanders had little concept of filming didn't make our work easier. Their main communication with the outside world was through a radio telephone link via Cape Town. There was a satellite phone. Internet became available at the Administrator's office in 1999. Still, the postal service relied on fishing boats and letters arrived only several times a year. There were no newspapers, radio (except for a local Tristan Broadcasting Service) or television as a means of instant access to the outside world.

To watch a "telly", one of their favourite pastimes, meant video tape viewing.

Most of us become nervous in front of a TV camera, but we know more or less what is expected of us. A reporter may interview you on the street and you may see yourself on a small screen on the seven o'clock news. That never happened on Tristan.

People were almost superstitiously suspicious of a TV camera. It was, for example, impossible to film a group of people. They just turned away and dispersed. We had to do something to earn the islanders' trust before the ship decided to leave, which could be at any time, depending on the fishing and the weather.

We spent the next few days walking around the village and greeting people. "Hello." "How are you?" "Nice day, isn't it?" Nothing personal, nothing offensive, just broad smiles. Gradually, people started to respond to us. Conversations started to flow. When we went to film the crayfish factory several days later, we encountered overwhelming hospitality. People were still shy but much more open to us. Very few turned away from the camera.

With the help of Donald, the resident doctor, we selected, filmed and interviewed several asthma sufferers. Despite the lack of air pollution, about half of the population on the island was asthmatic. It was genetic and, with precise family trees, it was not difficult to guess who brought the gene to the island. Scientists came to the island, took blood samples back, analysed them, identified an asthma gene and patented it. Tens of millions of dollars were said to have changed hands. The scientists verbally promised free medication to the islanders if the cure for asthma was developed. Without being properly informed, the islanders signed the document to waive their claims on any future discoveries and developments. They simply trusted the scientists who seemed nice and believed what they were told.

Many islanders trusted us in the same way. We were not just a TV crew but became their guests. A frail Agnes insisted on knitting socks for us and her ageing husband Gilbert offered to milk a cow for the camera. The 80-year-old Cyril picked his prime lettuce for us (fresh vegetables were few and precious). Brian wanted to make a model long boat for each of my male

114

colleagues. Jerry and Terresa invited us to their son's birthday party. The whole village gathered for our farewell party and Jimmy, the Chief Islander, thanked us for our "sensitivity", which does not often happen in our business. There was a special kind of warmth, like going back to your hometown after fifty years.

Without the 24-hour-a-day exposure to radio, television, Internet connection and telephones, time passed slowly on Tristan. Initially, we communicated freely with the outside world, using the satellite phone we had brought from Tokyo. We were part of a broader world, the world we were used to. Then, one day, all the satellite signals were gone. Japanese, American, French, German, British … we tried every single satellite that we could think of. Still no signals. I thought, if a nuclear war wiped out the rest of the world now, we would not know. That was a very strange feeling – a sense of complete isolation. It was scary, and at the same time, liberating. We learned to control our own lives without outside pressure. Time meant very little. Life became leisurely.

As technologically advanced communication systems swallow wider areas on the map, the world becomes smaller. In 2001, they installed a huge satellite dish on Tristan. The islanders can now enjoy reporters' "breaking news". They are more "connected" to the rest of the world. And, another place where one can feel both lost and fulfilled may be disappearing.

Masako Osada is a Japanese freelance journalist and media co-ordinator based in Johannesburg. Her recent publications include *Sanctions and Honorary Whites: Diplomatic Policies and Economic Relations in Relations between Japan and South Africa* **(Greenwood Press).**

The heaviness of a dream

Hamilton Wende

I met somebody years ago, on a Greyhound bus when I was travelling in America. He asked me a question I have never forgotten. "Who is it?" he asked me. "Whose eyes are the ones who watch us in our dreams?"

I didn't have an answer, but you know how it is when you have a dream that starts off all right, but soon you are plunged into a nightmare. One where you are caught in a situation of heart-stopping terror, surrounded on every side by something unutterably frightening. You try to run but you cannot move. Your arms and legs are immovable, weighed down by the heaviness of your dream. Who is it in the dream who watches you suffer such terrible fear?

That's what it felt like the day I went to Soweto to cover Chris Hani's funeral. He was an immensely popular black leader in South Africa who was gunned down by a white extremist in April 1993. The anger black people felt at his murder was overwhelming. It threatened to derail the transition to democracy. Nelson Mandela appeared live on national television to speak to black people and prevent South Africa descending into all-out racial war.

But even Nelson Mandela could not guarantee that the rage of his people would not explode into civil war. For days the country teetered on a knife-edge. For those of us working as journalists, going out into the streets to cover the story was terrifying. Seventy people were killed in riots across the country. We didn't know what would happen next.

I was working as a soundman. On the morning of the funeral, Mark, the cameraman I was working with, and I went in early to the office. I don't know how I slept the night before, but all that morning I felt within me that heavy, immobilising fear of a nightmare. The SABC was going live and on the television screens huge orange flames and dark smoke were rolling out of the sky above Soweto. Gangs of angry youths rampaged around the stadium where Hani's body lay in state. They were smashing the nearby railway station, and had already set fire to the houses of white people who lived nearby.

Mark and I were silent in the car on the way to the township. There was no mistaking the stark truth of that morning. We were white and heading into the epicentre of black rage. A white traffic cop stopped us on the outskirts of Soweto. "You'll take responsibility for what happens to you?" We nodded, and he let us through. I could hardly speak. My lungs felt weak and empty with fear.

Outside the stadium a vast crowd was gathering. The police and the ANC marshalls were co-operating, but neither of them could control the mob violence at the fringes of the crowd. A row of pretty turn-of-the-century houses stood nearby. They were close to Soweto, and trendy, racially liberal whites lived in them. The mob surrounded them, smashing windows and doors. One or two of the houses had been set alight.

Mark is one of the bravest people I know. He pointed to the burning houses. "I'm going there. To get some pictures. But you don't have to come with me. It's completely your choice."

I don't know why I went. I didn't say anything, but I was so frightened I could hardly breathe. I could feel fear burning in my legs and arms, almost paralysing me. And yet, I took the microphone and followed Mark into that crowd.

Some of the youths spotted us whites and shouted insults. At one point a police armoured vehicle drove up and fired into the crowd. The youths ran at first, then they turned back. One of the policemen saw us. "Get out of there!" he yelled. "They'll kill you."

The police fired again and drove away at high speed, terrified for their own lives.

Somehow we reached the burning houses. A bleeding dog shivered on the ground, dying a terrible death. The youths were torturing it with burning brands. Smoke and flames filled the air. We didn't know it then, but at least one person was trapped inside one of the burning houses. One can only imagine how he died.

We filmed for a few minutes before the crowd noticed us. They pointed and shouted at us.

"We'd better go," Mark said. "Don't turn your back, and don't run."

Terror filled my mind, almost like a drug. In a daze I began to back away from the burning houses. Very quickly we became the target of the mob. The youths gathered in around us, the shouting at us grew louder. Faster and faster, they advanced on us. Two or three of them emerged at the front of the mob. They had become the leaders and we their next target. It all seemed to be a dream. My mind entered a rushing tunnel. We had been chosen as victims. The attack would come soon.

Suddenly, one young man appeared in front of us. The whole crowd watched him.

The teenager pointed at us. "Just go," he shouted.

We looked at each other. His eyes stared directly into mine. He wanted me to understand. He was trying to save our lives.

"Okay," I said. "We're going."

He put all the energy in his young body into the expression on his face. "Go *now!*"

He was making himself, and not us, the focus of the mob. It was a very risky thing for him to do. The crowd might easily have turned on him as a "sell-out".

The boy raged at me. "*Just go, go.*"

It worked. The energy of the mob changed direction. They forgot about us. We stumbled out of the edges of the crowd – unhurt, but only just.

I don't know what might have happened to us that morning. It felt like a terrible, frightening dream. I will never forget that teenage boy who appeared in the middle of it all, and the courage and humanity that lay in the depths of his eyes.

Hamilton Wende is a freelance journalist, television producer and author based in Johannesburg. His most recent book is *Deadlines from the Edge — Images of War Congo to Afghanistan* (Penguin, South Africa).

The man who died in the sky

Marcelle Katz

Roko greeted me with tangible warmth and a passion for life, his family, his building. His face was strong, open. His hair – sweaty brown, he was dressed in rough denim dungarees. This, I felt, was an ordinary man who lives an extraordinary life.

Born in Montenegro, on 31 August 1941, Roko Camaj had one of the most unique jobs in the world – a window cleaner at New York's World Trade Centre, the second tallest building in the world.

He hand-washed 200 windows a week suspended from a harness on the 110th floor.

This is his story.

"My world consists of windows and reflections. You see everyone else from the other side of the glass. I don't get too philosophical about it, except I choose to be on the outside looking in. I am the one who is free. Inside, it's like a jail.

I wouldn't ever want to trade places with the big shots sitting inside in their leather chairs. As I pass their air-conditioned cages, I can see they'd just love to rip off their ties.

Me, I don't have any stress. I'm always having fun and my face is always tanned from being outdoors. When I'm in the automatic washer, I make like a clown through the window and the girls love it. Sometimes I open the door of the cage and pretend to walk into space and go arrgggh. The people inside go nuts.

I'll never forget February 26, 1993, the day Muslim extremists set off the bomb. There was so much smoke I didn't know where to go down. I thought everyone was going die. Like cockroaches.

Women with high heels left their shoes everywhere. It was like a carpet of stilettos. If I'd been hanging outside, I'd have got stuck and they'd have had to lower me by hand.

I start out everyday at 4.30 a.m. and have the same breakfast each morning – a nice, greasy American breakfast bagel, bacon and eggs and tasteless coffee.

The Trade Centre is relatively quiet first thing in the morning. It starts buzzing from 7.30 a.m. when the 'suits' arrive.

Window cleaners are really weird guys. I think it's because when you work hanging down the side of the building it's a completely different world. You look straight ahead and everything's normal. Then you look down and whoaaa, there ain't nothing for over a thousand feet.

The city looks like a toy town with tiny cars and toothpick people.

I'm even higher than the clouds and aeroplanes. When they fly by I have an inexplicable urge to jump out and ride on the back of them.

Everything has to be very secure in the window washer cage. You can't even have loose change. God forbid if you drop one penny from here, you can kill someone down below.

The thing is, I love life – I love my family and I love this job. The people downstairs call us crazy. They even take pictures of us as if we were urban freaks.

But my office is outside, in the sky. I am free."

11 September 2001

The last call from Roko to his wife was when he was on the roof on the 110th floor of the south tower. He saw an airplane dive into the spine of the building. His voice was steady. His son recalls: "My mom was very panicked, but he told her, 'Don't upset the kids, we're all in God's hands. Everything's okay.'"

He died one hour later.

What does one do with a pile of grief? Of raw pain, confusion and anger? "The only meaning of life," said Roko as he gripped me in a goodbye hug that day, "is the meaning you give it."

In memorandum: Maria - Denmark submitted: 11/01/2002 - By the words, written by people who were close to you, I can tell that you were indeed a very special person! I'm sorry that you had to leave the world like this – may your memory live on forever in our thoughts and hearts.

Marcelle Katz is a Capetonian. She worked as a feature writer for various South African media – *Argus*, *Fair Lady* – before attending the Cannes Film Festival and ending up staying in France for 10 years. Currently she is a freelance writer for the London *Sunday Times Magazine* and has an agent in London who syndicates her features worldwide - including Paris, London, New York, Sydney, Malaysia and the Czech Republic. Based back in Cape Town this year but still travelling to Europe and beyond for new stories, places and people who live both small & big lives.

Wise and gentle

Owen Smith

I'll never forget that brave, strong boy – wise and gentle beyond his years.

It's the early nineties in the war-ravaged Balkans. We arrive in the Serbian capital Belgrade – the war seems a long way away that first night as we eat and drink too much in a restaurant in the old town.

We are the ITN crew sent to relieve our colleagues who had been covering the siege of Sarajevo for four weeks. We are in good spirits – arrogant, immortal. I'm the producer, Terry Lloyd the reporter.

The rest of the crew are more experienced than I, but we are a good unit. We are professional and we are looking forward to doing some stories and maybe making a name for ourselves.

The following day we are on the long journey south to the bleeding heart of the Balkans that is Sarajevo.

Surrounded by Serbian nationals the sophisticated population of the Bosnian capital are suffering the ravages of a medieval-style siege.

Our driver is a young Serbian architect making ten times his normal salary by ferrying journalists and their equipment to Sarajevo. Dangerous work but it eventually pays for a new life for his family.

We arrive at the hotel in Ilija next to the dangerous Sarajevo airport controlled by the Yugoslav army and nationalist Serb militia. The departing ITN men give us a quick briefing – they are anxious to leave.

"Get up early, get into Sarajevo, do your story and get back here before 11 a.m. That's when the Serb snipers wake up after a night on the plum brandy – you don't want to be around then.

"Most days if you hear the sound of a car's horn you know somebody's been hit. It's too dangerous to get them so the horn only stops when the battery goes flat."

We begin to feel uneasy, less arrogant.

We rest up and get out early the next day. We bluster our way through the Serb roadblock, race down sniper alley and talk our way through the Bosnian checkpoint at the other end of the airport road.

We have heard that the UN has permission to move two busloads of children out of the besieged city and we decide that's our story for today.

On the way we notice people crouching and hiding at a busy city centre crossroads – a sure sign of an early rising sniper.

I am disorientated by the banality of the violence. An elderly lady, just like my own mother, jogs across the dangerous street with her shopping bags as she makes her way home for tea.

That danger passes and we find the children on a school playing field, the buses' engines are revving impatiently. It's a chaotic scene of bewildered children, crying parents, stressed-out UN officials and nervous Bosnian soldiers.

Before the buses are half full we hear the noise. Like thunder it swoops at us from the sky. Sleekly dangerous, grey, angry and very frightening. The Banshee engines scream, doppler-like, as the jet fighter races past, skimming the rooftops.

The strangely beautiful killing machine turns for another pass. I am frozen to the spot. Fear grips my whole being. Around me children are running for cover, screaming in terror. Some fathers are shaking in anger, weeping with impotency.

The cameraman steadies himself and films it all as Terry helps spot the shots – true men.

I am still pathetically immobile. I look to my right and then I see him.

Tall for his age, slim and straight-backed. A still calmness among the blur of pandemonium, he is dressed in a black raincoat, scarf and cap – like an English schoolboy, circa 1960.

His arms envelop a small boy sobbing silently into his protective caress. He gently soothes him as if he had merely fallen and grazed his knee, rather than facing being blown to bits by a weapon of cruel destruction created by the brilliant minds of men who should have known better.

He lifts his head and looks at me. It is not a look of fear or bewilderment or anger. He nods down to his brother, smiles and knowingly shrugs his shoulders in my direction. Even though I cannot hear him or speak his tongue I know what he means. He is saying, "Kid brothers eh! Got to look after them, haven't you?"

He smiles again and looks skyward as the death plane climbs away without attacking – buzzing the children for kicks has slaked its lust, for now.

The boy leads his brother by the hand and they get onto the second bus. Then they are gone.

We, the crew and I, are back in the comparative safety of Ilija by the sniping hour of 11 a.m.

We have a number of close calls in the weeks to come, eventually escaping over the mountains into Croatia.

Since then I have been to many places and seen many things. Terry Lloyd has been lost to us and I have grown older and now have a son of my own.

But every day that passes I wonder what happened to that brave, strong boy – wise and gentle beyond his years.

Owen Smith is a British TV journalist formerly with ITN and APTN. He now lives quietly in London with his partner and two young children.

"This is what I remember of Miguel"

Jeremy Bowen

This is what I remember of Miguel.

In Sarajevo, he drove around on a motorbike. Most of the rest of us had armoured Landrovers. He was a tall, wiry man who always looked tired. It looked as if he was pushing himself too hard. I think he was shooting stills as well as video. He always seemed to have a selection of cameras on his shoulder.

Later, while the war was on in Kosovo, he shot some of the most authentic combat footage I have ever seen. He was with a group of Kosovan fighters who were being hunted by Serb forces. The fear and desperation on their faces showed they were having to fight not just the Serbs, but their own conviction that they were about to die. His determination to follow a fundamental rule of reporting, to narrow the distance between yourself and the story, was paying dividends. But he realised as much as anyone the danger that came with his dedication to the truth.

In 1999, at the height of the NATO bombing campaign in Kukes in Northern Albania, I disappointed Miguel in a big way. The Kosovo Liberation Army had offered Miguel, Elida Ramadani, Vaughn Smith (from Frontline News) and myself, the chance to cross the border into Kosovo, not just for a day or two, but for the rest of the war. The way out was going to be with NATO, assuming they were going to come in.

We met at a café early one morning. Kukes was packed with hundreds of thousands of refugees, all waiting for a chance to get back across into Kosovo. No-one at the time really knew what was happening on the other side of the mountains – we had a chance to find out. But I had come to the café to tell Miguel and Elida that I had decided not to go. I can still remember how Miguel's face fell when I told him. For me it was not a good use of time. We were producing strong stories every night in Kukes. I reckoned that that if I disappeared into Kosovo it might take weeks to get something out – and by then it might be history, not news. I was also scared. Perhaps we all were. But for me, the sums did not add up and I did not feel in the mood that day to risk my life.

I had huge admiration for what Miguel was doing. He was in no sense high on adrenaline or scornful of danger. He thought hard about what he was doing and its implications. His strong Catholic faith helped him deal with the big questions that every intelligent, experienced person who does war reporting eventually asks and tries to answer.

I heard that Miguel and Kurt Schork had been killed the day after I had been in Beirut at the funeral of another friend, Abed Takkoush, who had been killed by the Israelis. Three friends dead in two days on different continents. I still wonder how news stories can ever be worth such losses.

Jeremy Bowen has been a BBC foreign correspondent since 1987, including five years based in Jerusalem. He covered stories in more than 70 countries, including ten wars, and won various reporting prizes from Royal Television Society in UK, New York TV Festival and the Monte Carlo TV festival. Jeremy is now BBC News Special Correspondent, based in London.

My big brother was watching me

Shafiek Tassiem

"The cops chased me and Jimi with batons and I jumped over the wall with all the heavy equipment. And I think Jimi was impressed so I might get the job," he said, breathless with excitement. This was the start for Aziz. He got the job as soundman with Visnews covering news stories in southern Africa. He was on top of the world.

From then on, his life became big stories and the chase for news. The competition just got hotter with WTN, their main opposition at their heels. Aziz always got a kick out of beating the opposition to a story. I could never understand what it meant or how it all worked. Why would they cover a story and then race off to the SABC only to put a video tape into a machine and shout into the phone "the bird is up". And then scream down the line that the opposition was trying to disconnect the cables.

I began to piece it all together when I started working with Aziz. He had graduated to camera work and needed me to carry the sound recorder and point the microphone in the right direction. More often than not, in those violent apartheid years, he needed me to watch his back.

There was going to be a student protest at the University of the Western Cape. He was filming and I, attached to him by a so-called "umbilical cord" plugged into the heavy sound recorder I would lug around after him, tried out as his soundman. I was so afraid of making any mistakes that I broke out in a cold sweat, but I forced myself to keep concentrating. We knew the police would be out in force and that some action was likely. Aziz started filming as the students, chanting anti-apartheid slogans, toyi-toyied to the campus gates where the police were waiting. Some picked up rocks and lobbed them across the road at the uniformed enemy. More students began advancing towards the police. And then there was teargas. Some canisters landed near us, their noxious gas swirling out and into my lungs.

I couldn't see properly and could hardly breathe. Aziz tried to tell me to sit down behind a concrete barrier to avoid the rocks and the canisters which by now were flying in all directions. I tried not to panic and Aziz remained very cool. A big bang! I thought, "damn, not more teargas, I'm about to throw up". But no, seconds later I felt this burning sensation on my legs and all over my back. Instinctively, I reached onto my back and felt my back. Blood on my hand.

Then I heard Aziz shouting, "We've been shot, we've been shot – get down!" We were pinned behind the barrier while Aziz kept filming. Seeing the blood streaming down his face, I panicked even more. When the mayhem subsided I started feeling the real pain.

I think Aziz was more concerned about me, although he looked really bad. He finished filming and took me to a doctor while he went to the office to edit and feed the material – even though he needed medical attention more than I. It still baffles me today.

We received our fifteen minutes of fame. Our bosses in London sent us "herograms" and we even made it into the papers. A Sunday paper wrote a feature on Aziz that weekend.

Aziz never missed a beat, nothing could surprise him. It was he who always delivered the surprises and I kept dreaming to one day be like him. His passion for sport, whether it was cycling, cricket, soccer, table tennis or volleyball always led to me believe that he would become a professional sports person. But when he came home that day with headphones firmly jammed to his head and a handheld microphone linked to a heavy machine, I knew this was it.

It all ended for him on a dusty road on 4th August 1991 when he was driving to cover the rescue of passengers off the sunken cruise ship the Oceanos. He lost control of the vehicle. His colleague, Jimi survived. It must have been traumatic for those who lived through the ordeal that day. I can only live with the memory of getting the news of his death later that Sunday. But I still dream to be like my big brother.

Shafiek Tassiem is a Reuters cameraman based in Cape Town where he lives with his wife and son.

Love of danger: front lines and marriage

Christina Babarovic

The city of Pristina looked as tired as Bartley's wearied expression; its buildings pock-marked with bullet holes, broken windows, the streets littered with burned-out cars and soldiers on patrol.

Bart took a long, lazy drag on a cigarette as he sat on the windowsill of the once grand Grand Hotel. It was sunny and hot; and the stench of backed-up toilets lingered in every corridor of the building. He certainly wasn't expecting a producer to burst into his room and my enthusiasm was more than obvious as I introduced myself. "Hi! Tina Babarovic from Washington!" I said with a smile and shook his hand. It was hard to hide the excitement of my first overseas assignment and the thrill of driving into town with British troops and tanks. Bart didn't seem exactly pleased to meet me so I bounded off to somewhere else.

So, it wasn't love at first sight, but more an attitude of disdain or dismissal. I thought this tall Kiwi with a big cocky grin was cynical, jaded and had been in one too many war zones.

He saw me as a US-based producer who was too perky, too green and not worthy of much notice. Plus, he didn't like my khaki shorts and baseball cap! I was just too ... well, producers like me were "a dime a dozen", passing regularly through this cameraman's familiar territory over the last ten years.

Who would have thought that I had discovered the love of my life, scowling at me from the open window?

Our first encounter ended without any fanfare. There were a few weeks of reporting, cajoling and arguing, which produced good, solid pieces shot and edited from Kosovo.

Bartley had to be bribed to work with me ... with a promise of a plane ticket out of Kosovo after months on assignment. I had no idea about this arrangement, until years later. And I had thought it was my smile that had won him over ... Ha!

I returned to Washington DC filled with stories of my recent adventures, without so much as another thought about Bartley Price ... and for his part, he barely noticed that I was gone.

The story should end there. And probably would have, if I hadn't been re-assigned, six months later, to ABC News' London Bureau. A casual hello and wave inside the newsroom was the only acknowledgement of our previous time in Kosovo.

In London, you change. The pace of life flows differently, my shorts were gone and my hair grew longer. After several assignments together, mutual respect turned into ... well, friendship.

We stalked the grounded Concord in Paris to find out why it crashed and flushed President Clinton's bad boy Marc Rich out of hiding in Switzerland. I was learning the trade secrets of overseas journalism and Bart was a bit more tolerant of my energetic approach to stories.

I still smiled a lot, though.

From there, a whirlwind romance began. Yes, while out on assignment. And three months later, we were engaged.

Two towers exploded into flames and the world changed forever. Bartley headed off to camp out in northern Afghanistan and I flew to Pakistan to wait for the United States' response to terrorism. Our budding romance still sparked over bad satellite phone connections, proving distance can make the heart grow fonder.

It's one thing to be engaged – it's another challenge to actually follow that promise through with a wedding and begin a lifetime together. I have learned that in the news business, it is impossible to plan anything beyond one week in advance! We decided to get married in London, during a four-week break between assignments in Afghanistan, just before Christmas 2001. It meant friends and family had to scramble, but we did have a wonderful day!

Two days after Christmas, Bart was off to southern Afghanistan, in Kandahar, for ABC News. Three weeks, later I followed him there. A honeymoon in a war zone ... nights filled with stars and tracer fire, days packed with deadlines ... it seemed to be the appropriate place to begin our lives together.

Tina Babarovic is an ABC News producer based in London. She's been working with ABC News since 1985 where most of her career was spent in Washington DC. Her speciality for several years was covering aviation and plane crash investigations.

Tina has recently been covering post-war Iraq for ABC News.

Bartley Price is a freelance cameraman who has covered almost every war since 1990. He spent much of his time in Bosnia during the conflict in the 1990s and later much of his time in Baghdad along with most other foreign news freelancers.

African snapshots

Alexander Joe

"Don't speak to me like that"
Mogadishu, Somalia
When the UN mission to Somalia was coming to an end, its troops withdrew from the city to the airport. One Sunday morning they left the airport for the beach and anticipated that the Somalis would go on a looting rampage. The media were given a position to cover the final withdrawal of the UN troops. As the tanks rolled onto the sand dunes gunfire started.

An American marine started shouting at the media to "get out of the area!" But none of us moved. The shouting continued as rounds whistled over our heads. Then the marine came closer and shouted, "Get the fuck out of there!"

One of the photographers, a woman, replied indignantly: "Don't speak to me like that, I'm French."

The AP photographer, Ricardo Mazalan, and I, could not hold it in and just dropped down onto our knees, laughing our heads off.

Sometimes we are human
10 August 1991
Covering Madagascar's six-month strike, I saw the people march on the President's Palace, hoping to bring his government to an end. They marched for about 18 kilometres and then were stopped by government forces, two kilometres from the Palace.

After a short stand-off, the soldiers opened fire with teargas and then started firing live rounds from a helicopter – so did troops on the ground. Many people were killed and many were injured. The army started to advance on the few people that were still around when I saw this great picture – of a body and advancing soldiers.

I took several photos and then moved away when I heard a voice saying "Eh you!" I turned around to find out where this voice came from. Then I realised that the body was not a dead person but a wounded boy. I called his friends to tell them their friend was wounded and they should come and take him away. As they tried, a soldier cocked his weapon and pointed it at them. At this point I lost it and went and picked up the boy to take him to his friends, but the same soldier then pointed his gun at me. I told him he either shoots me or lets me go.

The next day in the hospital, photographing the wounded from the day before, a boy suddenly jumped out of his bed and hugged me saying: "Thank you, thank you!" I did not recognise him until a friend reminded me who he was – the wounded boy from the day before. That day I felt that I was human, unlike other times when you photograph people in terrible conditions and never know what happens to them after you leave.

All black people look alike
Burundi/Rwanda

During the Rwandan genocide, the Red Cross invited the media to accompany them in a convoy carrying food into Rwanda from Burundi. Two French women journalists and myself, a black photographer, accepted their offer.

When we got to the Red Cross in Bujumbura they refused me permission to accompany them. I was told by a white Red Cross worker that it was too dangerous for me as a black person to enter Rwanda.

"If the Tutsis don't kill you, then the Hutus will," he said. In his eyes all black people look alike, despite the fact that I come from Zimbabwe. A Rwandan or a Burundian black person could see from a mile away that I don't come from the same region.

So the two women and I decided to go into Rwanda on our own. At the first checkpoint of Hutu militia we came across, they immediately started shouting "Belgium! Belgium!" at my two white colleagues.

It was quite ironic for me that now to black people "all white people looked alike"; to the Hutu militia during the genocide all white people were the Belgian enemy, and if it weren't for me, my white friends would have had a hard time. The Hutus, could see I was from a different part of the continent without me even having to say a word.

Alexander Joe is a Zimbabwean-born photographer. He wanted to become a fashion photographer, but as the war to end white-minority rule in his home country escalated he turned towards documenting the political struggle in Rhodesia. He worked for UPI and several British newspapers and is currently based in South Africa for AFP.

On the edge

Eric Miller

Covering Africa often comes down to a simple issue of logistics. You have to arrive safely, work safely, and leave again. To do this you rely on local people who look after you at no small risk to themselves.

Take Edison for example. On several visits to Zimbabwe, Edison has been driver to me and Swedish correspondent Gorrel Espelund, and on many occasions to other visiting journalists. Edison rarely earns more than US $50-100 a day for his efforts. But Edison has on occasion confronted, in the line of duty, threatening and irate war veterans, often at risk to his own safety and merely so he could help us in the execution of our responsibilities. Edison is philosophical about some of the dangers he has experienced on our collective behalf. "It's what happens when one works with journalists" he said stoically, and in Zimbabwe jobs and hard currency are hard come by. On one occasion Edison was beaten up and had his car confiscated. Being associated with foreign journalists often makes one a lightning rod for the anger of the prevailing powers.

In South Sudan it was the jovial and gregarious Karaba who was not easily fazed by adversity. On a trip to the front line, he took us across a small river avoiding a bridge he said was "mined". When one wheel of our land cruiser slipped over the edge of a weir, Karaba took command and delegated to us the task of collecting rocks to build up some traction for the loose-hanging wheel. He covered the windscreen with a pile of leafy branches, "So the Antonovs don't see the reflections and bomb us."

Rushing back to cross the Ugandan border before it closed, Karaba hurtled along the stretch of land called "road" (not dissimilar to a lunar landscape), hell-bent towards the bridge "But Karaba, I thought you said the bridge was mined?"

"Not any more it isn't," he grinned broadly.

In Port Harcourt, Nigeria, I was photographing a queue of people at a local filling station who had spent the night waiting to get their cars filled. I was surrounded by a squad of incredibly angry and aggressive policemen within about 1/60th of a second of taking out my camera.

Although I had not noticed them taking "contributions" from drivers, they had quickly noticed me. They hauled our driver from the car, and delivered a quick whack to his head with a rifle butt. I was shocked. But as he desperately held onto the policeman's ankles, begging and pleading, I did not immediately understand his fear. My Danish colleague Jesper Strudsholm and I became the focus of a torrent of verbal abuse from the cops.

After several hours, going from police station to police station, the cops finally released us. There had been a discussion of payment, our driver said, but eventually they did not extort any money, apparently in deference to the fact that we had all the necessary paperwork. It later emerged that the driver had spent many months jailed and tortured for political reasons, hence his fear of arrest.

Strudsholm and I once landed late in Kigali. It was the day of the first scheduled public executions of some of the ringleaders of Rwanda's genocide. We both quietly acknowledged that our lateness might have been fortuitous. Neither of us relished the idea of watching a public execution and taking pictures would be almost impossible – and hugely risky.

Our driver took us directly to the main execution site, a stadium. By the time we arrived the bodies had been removed. The police confronted us and the small camera hidden under my shirt felt heavy and bulky. Ordered to leave, and mindful of the sullen animosity of both the milling crowd and the police, we complied. For some reason our driver took it upon himself to challenge the police. Arrested immediately, he spent several days in jail.

Pilots who fly in Africa are another breed altogether. I am convinced they all share a genetic heritage that predisposes them to danger. One of the most rampant displays of machismo I have witnessed, was inflicted on me by a fine young woman pilot in the Okavango Delta. She couldn't resist "testing" me with some below-tree level flying, waiting till the frighteningly last moment before a gut-wrenching vertical climb to clear the trees. Not even her sweetest, most innocent, eyelid-fluttering enquiry of "Are you OK?" could persuade me to unclench my sphincter until we had landed safely in Maun. To rub salt into my wounded sense of self that evening, she wiped the floor with me in the local pool hall.

But it was the mad Texan in Sudan who really got my grey hairs going. In his rattle-trap twin-engine, antique-looking aircraft he promised to get Strudsholm, myself and a TV crew to the remote villages. We ought to have been forewarned by his late-night tales of pulling his own aching teeth with naught but a pair of pliers and a bottle of whiskey. We ought to have been more alert after he told us how one of his previous wives had tried to kill him by misdirecting him during a night landing, or how he had once worked for the CIA and almost managed to help them assassinate Yassir Arafat. But after being stuck idle on the border for four days Strudsholm and I were pretty desperate to get into Sudan.

The plane was overloaded. Most of the seats had been stripped out to accommodate supplies for the villages. After a bladder-punishing four-hour flight (of course the plane was too small to have a loo) we finally made our approach to the village landing strip, and had a bumpy touchdown. Most of the passengers ran for the nearest clump of bushes. Their newfound looks of relief disappeared instantly when Tex informed us that "Sorry, this was the wrong village." Everyone had fled after a recent government attack and we would have to leave immediately as there was still a threat there.

The only problem was the airstrip was too short for a fully-loaded plane, a fact that Tex took as a personal challenge. It took him three utterly frightening and soul-destroying attempts to lift off before he finally managed to squeeze the last remaining guts from his abused engines. I left clear imprints of my fingers in the metal armrests of my seat. Tex landed us safely, promising faithfully to return at a pre-arranged time. Suffice to say he did not. Happily we never ever saw him again, and fortunately another plane agreed to take us back to Kenya. We discovered later that Tex had lost an engine (it literally fell off!) and had had to make an emergency landing in the region, hence his no show.

We had been warned by the Red Cross in Abidjan that the airstrip in Monrovia was "dicey". Just the previous morning a plane had failed to negotiate the short strip and ended up in flames at the end of the tarmac. OK, I thought, what are the chances of two planes crash-landing on consecutive days at the same airstrip? I assured myself that the pilot was not suicidal, that not since Japan's defeat in the war had there been a squadron of suicidal pilots, and that we would be delivered safely to our destination. I assured myself that the pilot probably also had a family and a hot dinner waiting – surely he would not put his own life at risk? This has long been my flying mantra, one that I whisper to myself on almost any flight I take, including our national airline. Despite the still-smouldering wreck of yesterday's flight lying at the end of the runway, we landed safely and had no more to deal with than a full-frontal attack by touts and protectionists on the tarmac.

It was only a few weeks later, when an Air Botswana pilot in a suicidal fit of pique apparently prompted by a lover's tiff, stole an Air Botswana plane and crash-landed it into several other planes on the tarmac, killing himself and destroying the country's entire fleet. It was only then I recognised the fundamental flaw in my flying mantra. Clearly there are some pilots with a death wish.

Eric Miller is a South African photo journalist who has worked in over 25 African countries. Together with Jesper Strudsholm and Gorrel Espelund he published *Reality Bites: An Africa Decade* **(Double Storey Books) in 2003.**

Everything by God

Joan Baxter

It's said that every dark cloud has a silver lining. In many places I've lived in Africa, I had the impression people could find gold in a slag heap or a manure pile. Many of the best stories that have happened my way over the years have nothing to do with real headline news or catastrophes or politics – they have to do with real people living real lives and making do – despite real news, catastrophes and politicians. People who know how to take the "mis" out of misfortune.

The people of Tamale, a northern town in Ghana where I lived for four years in the 1990s, even found a way to turn mishap into happiness, and potholes into small gold mines. Each year the rains turned much of the town's main road, Ghana's north-south lifeline, into a muddy quagmire. And potholes, of gargantuan dimensions, had long since swallowed up the last remnants of pavement.

One of the deepest of these washouts was about 100 metres from my front door. There, on a Friday morning, an overloaded lorry overturned, spilling its contents of timber, produce, livestock and passengers into the ditch. Fortunately and miraculously, no one was injured. It took two days before a tow-truck, after itself getting stuck, managed to get the lorry back onto its wheels, and on its rumbling way to its destination in the uppermost region of Ghana. I watched with detached interest, as one after the other, more trucks got stuck in the same place. I noticed, but did not register, the large number of people who gathered to watch these lumbering vehicles flounder in the mud. I had no idea that this section of road was turning people into millionaires – even if only in Ghanaian Cedis.

The reason it took me so long to hear the ringing of the jackpot outside my door was that I had never paid much attention to the lotteries. Yes, I had seen the clapboard "lotto" kiosks painted jittery shades of blue, pink and red, perched over the open gutters in town. I knew that the lottery was a thriving business, partly because little else was in northern Ghana. At these booths people staked their claims on local lotteries with names like "First Class", "Patience", "Sunrise" or "Victory Stars". You bought a ticket for a few cents and you wrote down two numbers between one and ninety. Then you waited, until on Saturday afternoon, a computer in Accra – hundreds of kilometres to the south – "dropped its numbers". If your numbers "came down" and got chalked up on the fronts of these kiosks, you went and collected your winnings. Very straightforward, I thought. People staked their precious income on vague hopes and unforgiving statistical probabilities, gambling away children's school fees and food budgets. A familiar story.

I should have known that there was a hidden twist, that nothing was as straightforward as it might appear. Not in Tamale. Choosing the numbers on your tickets there was not guesswork or a question of luck – it was a local art, science and African para-psychology all rolled into one. There were people in Tamale who called themselves "Lottery Professors" or "Doctors"; fast-talking individuals who pointed to long sheets of previous winning combinations, spouting numbers, formulae and predictions as though they had outsmarted the computer – and perhaps they had. But when they were consulted, for a hefty fee, by would-be lottery players seeking magic winning numbers, they claimed that the numbers they offered had been given to them in dreams and visions. Or, they said they chose lucky numbers from the licence plates of accident vehicles.

The numbers on the licence plate of the lorry which overturned that Friday in front of my house were 78-50. The numbers on the licence plate of the tow-truck that came to upright it, were 48-54. All four of these were winning numbers that Saturday. Sheer luck, or soothsayers' magic? Or is there a difference?

Turned out that just about every lottery player in Tamale used the numbers from the licence plates on the overturned lorry and the rescue vehicle. They'd won collectively more than 100 million Cedis (equivalent to US $400 000) – a windfall, a truck full of money, in a town where people earned (if they were lucky) about 15 000 Cedis (about US$60) a month.

Within hours of the first accident women had already got fires going and set up chop bars, cooking yams for the crowds camped out at the scene of that mishap, waiting for another accident – looking for more lucky numbers on the licence plates.

But alas, a week to the day after the first big accident, contractors appeared at the site with heavy graders and began to smooth out the mud, filling the gulleys with tipper trucks full of gravel. The people in the adjacent village – many on shiny new bicycles they had bought with their winnings – came out to hurl insults at them, chastising them for fixing the road. There would be no more lucky numbers for them, they said.

When that bit of road was more or less smoothed out, the repair crews packed up and disappeared to wherever it was they hibernated in northern

Ghana. The rest of the roads remained just as they were, treacherous ruts and holes, accidents waiting to happen.

It was shortly after my neighbours filled me in on this "lottery lorry story", that I remembered I had seen some words written across the front of that overturned truck which had brought luck to Tamale. The letters had been blue and gold but I couldn't quite remember the words. I asked Iddrissu, a young neighbour and the proud owner of one of those new bicycles, if he recalled, perchance, what words had been written there. He said, with a big grin, "Yes, I remember. The words on the lorry were EVERYTHING BY GOD."

Joan Baxter is a Canadian journalist and writer who has lived in and reported from six African countries over the past two decades. She has two children who share her deep affection for the continent.

Shooting pictures

Denis Farrell

The helicopter rose into the sky and we were quiet. No-one was talking but we were all thinking about the momentousness of the day. The first day of South Africa's first democratic elections.

Our day had started well before sunrise, to have us in place as President FW de Klerk dropped his vote into the ballot box in Pretoria. The paper containing his historic "x" was barely deposited when a frantic call from the office told of an explosion at Johannesburg's international airport.

"Leave immediately and head for the airport to pick up film" was the command from our usually London-based photo editor. He had relocated to Johannesburg to run the election coverage on site. En route the plan kept changing and alternative arrangements were made to get the pictures back to base. With all the chopping and changing I thought the planned helicopter trip would not materialise. And it had required some planning. Getting a seat on a chopper from which I could take photographs had not been easy on that politically sensitive and highly-charged day.

Praying nothing else would delay me, I made it to Rand Airport with just minutes to spare. The next two hours would be spent observing from clear blue skies the queues of people patiently waiting to cast their votes. Voting queues were what we needed to beat our opposition. They had beaten us hands down with their picture of a voting queue in the recent elections in neighbouring Namibia. The picture showed a queue which wound around a hill to the voting station at the top.

The rotor spun against the calm sky as a local radio station reported on events unfolding on the ground. We did not know what to expect. Flying over golden mine dumps, watching mine workers standing in a disciplined squared-off queue. Had I done the right thing by taking to the sky?

Ahead on the horizon was Soweto. I was filled with excitement. The queues were bigger than anyone had anticipated. In an open field was a snaking queue of hundreds of people, lining up one behind the other in a curious M-shape. Leaning out as cool air rushed through the cabin, I began to capture history. The pilot circled three or four times, but he couldn't drop any lower for fear of being fired upon. A 200 mm lens brought the scene closer.

The radio reported a four kilometre-long queue of whites and blacks lining up together in an up-market white suburb. Would that be the definitive shot? Would I be better on the ground? Then I thought of the struggles in the townships that had cost so many lives. I thought of my colleagues Abdul Sharif and Ken Oosterbroek. They had died shooting pictures in townships where people were shooting bullets, not too long before the elections they had not lived to see.

After two hours of hovering we landed and the rush was on again. I reached the office in record time, dropped off the film and headed off to the northern suburbs for those extended queues. The jovial atmosphere among black and white voters prevailed. No-one seemed bothered by the fact that they had been waiting for many hours. With the light fading I headed back to the bureau with more images.

In the days that followed the world learned that as expected the African National Congress had come to power. Nelson Mandela, whose victory was eerily foretold in my queue of Soweto voters, was inaugurated as the county's first black president.

Most of the international press corps went on to cover the Rwandan genocide, some a little disappointed that our elections had not started a civil war and that life in South Africa would find its own normality.

A year later a call announced that the Soweto queue picture had been nominated for a Pulitzer Prize. I didn't get it, but for me the greater honour was having Mandela's signature on the photograph that defined for me the end of an era and the dawning of a new one. Every day in the office I see it, framed and signed and taking pride of place. Every day it reminds me of those whose lives were sacrificed for peace.

Denis Farrell is a South African photographer and since 1987 the Southern African Photo Editor for The Associated Press based in Johannesburg. He has also dabbled in fashion and advertising photography and is a good cook.

Survival and dignity

Teresa Turiera

Rafael was a former diplomat who abandoned his miserable salary to work as a taxi driver. He had a Lada with which he criss-crossed Cuba, from Vinales to Santiago. But every time it broke down, he had to wait until a tourist friend of a friend of his brought the part in from Europe. I myself brought him a set of four window cranks so he could roll down the windows.

Because it seemed that these were a rare commodity in Cuba, every time we left the car and parked anywhere we religiously collected all four of them and took them with us for safekeeping.

I met Rafael on my first visit in July 1996, just after Clinton had announced sanctions against European companies that invested in Cuba. And the debate, as to whether the island was surviving thanks to programmes set up by the socialist revolution or because of growing investments of Europe and Canada, was hotter than ever.

Getting gasoline was also not very easy, but our friend Rafael had his resources, the same resources that every Cuban has had to look for in order to survive with dignity. Rafael stopped the car in front of a mortuary in Holguín.

"I am going in to say hello to my father, who works here as a guard of the bicycle parking," he told us.

There was a funeral going on inside the house. Half an hour later the hearse made its way to the cemetery, with the cortege made up of relatives and friends following behind. When the hearse came back and the members of the funeral cortege had all taken their bicycles and gone home, Rafael´s father signalled to us to bring the Lada into the garage.

The employees of the funeral home closed the door and gave Rafael a piece of rubber, which he used to skilfully siphon the gasoline from the hearse to the Lada, all for the exchange of a few dollars, which would allow the families that worked there to buy a kilo of meat or powdered milk for their children that month.

While the operation was underway, an employee of the funeral home gave us a piece of paper with the address of his parents in Spain, so that we could send them his greetings, and a present. It was a book about the revolution, written by Fidel Castro!

When I arrived at Havana Airport we foreigners – who were mostly tourists from Spain and Italy – were greeted with a first taste of Fidel Castro's media campaign. It was a huge billboard that said, just in case anyone was in any doubt at that point: "Mr. Imperialist – In Cuba every child goes to school and none of them die of hunger."

But in the four weeks I was there I filled my suitcase and my memory with many other messages of the revolution, but above all, its real characters, the Cuban people who face a hard and daily grind with dignity.

Spending the night at the home of a happy family in Havana, every one of them staunch defenders of their leader, and resigned to the political and economic situation of the island, one of the teenage sons ran into the salon where we were talking. "Mami! Mami! The traitor's envelope has arrived."

The "traitors" were a part of the family who had one day risked their lives as *balseros* and now religiously sent an envelope full of dollars to their relatives in Havana while living an almost tolerable exile in Miami. The men left for the United States, where they began other families, whilst the mothers and grandmothers stayed behind taking care of the children, who legally could not leave the island until they came of age. This was another of the stumbling blocks put in place by the Castro government to dissuade those that no longer believed in the virtues of the revolution and were willing to face the dangers of leaving the island – the sadness of knowing that they could never come back.

Strolling down the *malecón*, three teenagers approached me wanting to talk. They wanted to know what was happening "out there", about the Europe that they dreamed about travelling to one day. They asked me what I did for a living and were disappointed to hear I was a journalist. They wanted to be doctors, or engineers, or farmers or pilots … any profession that was beneficial to the community, that dignified them before the revolution.

In Santiago I met a teenager who rented out foreign magazines and newspapers. A cousin of hers worked in the brigades that cleaned the airports and easily got her hands on the "precious booty" in the planes that arrived from Europe, Canada and Latin America. The most coveted were the European tabloid magazines and the Spanish newspapers critical of the Castro regime. They would be passed around at an ever-diminishing price as the glossy paper began to show its wear and tear.

I asked what her name was – "Usnavy!"– she said with a thick accent from the south of the island. Well, what an original name I thought. It is not a Spanish name. Where does it come from? Proud of its origin, the young girl answered: "My father was a marine in the US Navy, but he left a long time ago, and never returned. That is why I was named "US-NAVY".

From a street not very far away came the tinny sound of a radio. As I turned the corner, I saw a group of neighbours huddled around a radio listening to the voice of their leader. Fidel was giving a speech in honour of the anniversary of the attack on Moncada. As always, after about four hours of talking, the event finished to shouts of "Socialism or Death. Motherland or Death. We will triumph!"

Three years later I returned to Cuba, to cover the IX Ibero-American Summit. The Miami "traitors" were still sending dollars; "Usnavy" continued to dream about one day going to the United States and never coming back; Rafael no longer worked as a taxi driver because the Committee in Defence of the Revolution had turned him in. The Lada had no window cranks – they had all been stolen.

Teresa Turiera is a journalist living in Barcelona. She is a Chief of Programs for Catalunya Radio. Previously, she worked as diplomatic correspondent in Madrid, as a freelance reporter in New York and as European Affairs correspondent in Brussels.

Breakdown

Dina Kraft

The black tarmac at the Mombasa airport is broiling and the Israeli evacuation team of soldiers, doctors and nurses is exhausted. Everybody wants to go home.

It's been a sleepless night–turned–to–day, tending to the wounded and the shocked following the suicide bombing attack on the beachside Israeli-owned "Paradise" hotel the day before.

The Israeli medical experts and soldiers fly in by the hundreds on planes from Israel into the sweltering Kenyan night. Kenyan soil, Israeli soil – it does not matter. Israelis have been attacked. They are here to rescue.

Medical teams swoop in with stretchers, plastic drip bags and morphine supplies and ferry the wounded to waiting planes. Soldiers and security guards lug silver boxes of unknown content, their Uzis and M-16's thwacking the backs of sweat-soaked uniforms. They even bring their own food: crates of bananas, canned pickles and corn, mini-plastic bags of chocolate milk.

And now the hard work is over. The injured treated, the most seriously wounded Israelis and Kenyans evacuated to Israel's modern hospitals, the traumatised tourists counselled, and the area secured.

Home, home. Everyone aches for it, shuddering at the reach of terror even here, on this humid East African beach coast of holidaymakers and escape. Nowhere is safe.

Passing the time, some play cards. Others huddle for the sparse bits of shade under airplane hangers. A small group prays around the Torah scrolls retrieved from the bombed-out hotel. An army psychologist squints in the baking sun and muses on the non-stop cycle of violence and how it is changing Israel's people.

Abruptly we all turn to hear voices raised in argument. One voice booms louder, more desperate, his words turning into a pitched cry. It is the voice of one of Israel's leading trauma surgeons. He's asking why he is not already homeward-bound. Why are they still waiting to board the plane?

He shouts and shouts. His long, intelligent face turns purple, veins throb in his neck. He nervously runs a hand through his silvery curls. He cannot be calmed.

"I have no life, I have no life," he screams. His voice cracks, mixing with choked sobs.

"My wife is calling me, she is crying into the phone. I *waaaaant*, I *waaaaant* to go home!"

The army clerk he has accosted pleads for him to calm down.

"Breathe. Breathe. Relax already!" he implores. He too is now beginning to snap.

But there is no consolation. Not for the surgeon and not for those of us watching him. This man who takes charge of Jerusalem emergency rooms often filled with bombing victims now crumples into a puddle of exhaustion and despair.

It's all too much: the horrible reality of these last years of Middle East violence now puncturing our hearts far away, under the African sky.

The doctor standing next to me is one of Israel's leading blood specialists. He says the surgeon's breakdown is not about this attack, but is born of two years of piecing together bits of torn and seared children.

He tells me he has served in three wars as a front-line doctor, but nothing has been as bad as this most recent Palestinian uprising.

"Do you know what we do in the operating rooms? We cry," he says, rubbing his scrubby white beard. "It's the pressure. It's awful. The last two years were the worst of my life... You see children burned, babies in shreds. And each time we cry and cry."

In the Kenya attack he met the father whose two sons were killed in the hotel lobby when the suicide bombers set off their explosions, ripping open the hotel. One brother could only be identified by his retainer. All that remained of the other was a hand with a watch still strapped to the wrist.

"We are supposed to be the healers. It's considered a mark of shame to say we are close to breaking down," says the blood specialist gesturing towards the surgeon who continues to wail under the blistering sun.

Dina Kraft is a journalist based in Tel Aviv. For over six years she worked for The Associated Press, first in Jerusalem and most recently in Johannesburg. She has reported from throughout Africa as well as Pakistan, Turkey, and Jordan. She has a Masters degree in History from Stanford University.

A journey to Hell

Moyiga Nduru

Suddenly, the chopper whirled, and began descending, almost touching the canopy of the trees below. It was shaking violently and, if I may add, uncontrollably. My heart jumped.

I felt sick, and uncomfortable, wanting to throw up. But I held back, controlling my bowels. There was no point messing up the helicopter since it was going to crash anyway. Yes, it was going to crash at any moment. I would soon be dead. So would everybody on board. A few beads of sweats formed on my forehead. My palms, too, were developing specks of sweat, a clear sign of nervousness.

Oh my God, why are you forsaking me? I heard myself saying, silently. I had not prayed in years. The violent vibration of the chopper took about a minute. But, to me it seemed like an eternity.

We were traveling in unfriendly territory. Our guide, composed, and craning his neck, looked down and remarked: "Some of them hide here." He was referring to the rag-tag Hutu rebels in the *kibera* ("dense forest" in Swahili, a lingua franca in east and central Africa) just beneath us.

My colleague, an African journalist, did not show any emotion. I wonder? I seemed to be the only person on board gripped by fear and nervousness.

"Supposing the rebels shoot and bring down the helicopter?" I asked. The pilot laughed. "They don't have the means to bring down any plane."

We were five in the chopper: two journalists, two pilots and the guide, who was a very important person in the tiny strife-torn central African nation of Burundi.

The year was 1996. Major Pierre Buyoya, a former military ruler, had just been recalled from retirement by Tutsi officers – who seized power from Sylvestre Ntibantunganya, a Hutu – to do what, they believed, he knew best: rule. Regional leaders, nervous of coup d'états, reacted by imposing sanctions on the land-locked Burundi. My trip to Burundi was to cover the impact of the sanctions.

Flying from the Kenyan capital Nairobi, I spent a night in Kigali, Rwanda, since all flights to and from Burundi had been banned, thanks to the embargo. In Kigali, a beautiful city still recovering from the 1994 genocide in which up to a million Tutsis and moderate Hutus were slaughtered by a blood-thirsty Hutu militia, called *interahamwe*, or "those who fight together" in Kinyarwanda, I learned that the Burundi chargé d'affaires was travelling to the border to pick up an African ambassador. The ambassador was returning from a fact-finding mission, or, to put it bluntly, "busting" the embargo choking Burundi.

Neat and clearly parcelled farms dot the road from Kigali to the Burundi border. The terrain, especially the countryside, reminds one of Holland or Switzerland.

I had no idea that the good African ambassador would be dropped at the border with a helicopter, and ride back with the chargé d'affaires to Kigali by road. That was our luck, riding in a chopper and avoiding the killing roads of Burundi – but not for long.

Back in the forest, the chopper found its feet, gained its height, and a few minutes later we landed at Bujumbura international airport. The airport, whose control tower building resembles a Middle Ages mosque, was virtually empty except for a few ageing planes, parked in the hangars or on the unused runway.

At the hotel, a heated argument between a French journalist and an army spokesperson turned nasty. "If you're not careful," the army officer warned, "you'll return home horizontally, not vertically". What he meant of course, was that the journalist would return home in a coffin.

We were scared. Would the officer carry out his threat? Was the threat meant to frighten foreign journalists staying at the hotel, or was it only a warning? We didn't know. I didn't sleep that night.

In those days, only reckless journalists and brave aid workers ventured into Burundi where ethnic violence had claimed more than 250 000 lives, mostly non-combatants, since 1993. Some of the aid workers complained openly about the former Belgian colony going down the drain. The only people making money were top army officers or smugglers. They supplied fuel, salt, soap, rice and cigarettes, commodities that were scarce in the country. And they made cool bucks.

Returning to Nairobi via Kigali after a two-week adventure into Bujumbura was another nightmare. Only one soldier, armed with an AK-47 assault weapon, was assigned to accompany us to the border, the highway being infested with rebels.

Sitting at the back of a 4X4 vehicle, the soldier struck me as someone who would abandon ship should rebels open fire. As we approached rural Bujumbura, we spotted two soldiers by the roadside, flagging down our

147

vehicle. I pleaded with our guide to let them ride with us – to boost the firepower of the lone soldier. The driver, God bless him, stepped on the brakes, and the two soldiers jumped in. What a relief!

The first 30 kilometres from Bujumbura was hell on earth. Every kilometre we met a pair of soldiers patrolling the highway. Some waved to us – some exchanged greetings with the driver, himself a soldier. I didn't see a single civilian on our 30-kilometre journey. The distance between one patrol and the next was like walking ten kilometres, dodging bullets and landmines as you go.

The feelings were tense until we spotted another pair of patrol soldiers. They waved, and we smiled. Not a genuine smile, of course, but a fake one. Every moment I expected a rebel bullet to be aimed at our vehicle. After the first 30 kilometres, another ugly face of the war appeared: displaced persons, mostly old people, children and women occupying the abandoned houses by the roadside. Where have the young people gone? Only God knows. You didn't ask such questions in Burundi at the time.

Halfway to the Rwandan border, life returned to "normal". A bit of sanity prevailed here and there; a few cows, goats, sheep and chickens mingled with peasant farmers. Occasionally, farmers could be spotted tending their fields in a country soaking with blood.

At the border, I only experienced a minor hitch. The immigration officer demanded an explanation: how I slipped into Burundi without a visa. Burundi was under a military rule – and my first guide didn't bother to get me a visa. Luckily, I had established good relations with some members of the junta. That saved me.

Officially, there is no record of me visiting Burundi in 1996. It was as if it was a dream.

Moyiga Nduru is a journalist with Inter Press Service (IPS), an international news agency, based in Johannesburg, South Africa.

Is that all?

Donna Bryson

On the first full day of voting in South Africa's first all-race elections, I met a black woman who got to her polling station in Johannesburg's gritty Hillbrow neighbourhood at 9 a.m. She stood in line for three hours before she got inside, only to be told her expired passport was insufficient ID.

A stranger immediately volunteered to drive her to the Home Affairs office downtown, where she got a temporary voter card on the spot. She returned to Hillbrow and in a few seconds had marked her ballot.

"Is that all?" she asked the polling station attendants. She'd enjoyed mingling with blacks and whites in line, the festival spirit that led a stranger to help her out with a ride when she most needed it, and, above all, the thrill of voting for the first time in her life. She just wanted it all to last a little longer. But she'd asked the question of the day.

South Africans were embarking on their democratic experiment, and voting was far from all there was to it. Ahead lay violence, political setbacks – disillusionment for many. Democracy is hard work. On that April day in 1994, it seemed no-one was shirking it. Voting was being described in super superlatives. One woman told me it was "orgasmic".

A polling station officer presided over a tent on the edge of squatter camp with so much pride he could have been sitting in a marble-halled palace. I met another woman who'd given birth to a girl five days before the voting. She named her Day, "like new day. Maybe we'll get a new future," she said.

Hope is a powerful force, perhaps powerful enough to sustain South Africans through the work of building a nation. Back in 1994, I didn't fully understand. But as later reporting took me to places like Rwanda and Zaire, Kashmir and Kosovo, I began to see the pattern.

A Hutu mother darting onto a dirt road to thrust a letter pleading for help for her half-Tutsi children into the hands of French peacekeepers, and then taking the troops to other Hutu women who had married Tutsis and were just as fearful for their children.

The master painters and sculptors who kept holding classes long after the dictator stopped paying their salaries, and the students who kept coming to the moldering fine arts campus that once had been a Kinshasa showpiece. The Hindu accountant and the Muslim shopkeeper sharing tea in Kashmir. A dozen firefighters, most of them British volunteers joined by a handful of ethnic Serbs and Albanians willing to work together, throwing themselves at nightly arson blazes in the Kosovo capital.

Despair and resignation are more rational responses to the world's casual brutalities. Hope takes courage.

Finding joy in just standing in line, naming a baby for the future – because they were acts of hope, they were everyday acts of courage.

Donna Bryson has worked for The Associated Press since 1986 – first in Johannesburg, then in Delhi as news editor for South Asia, and then in Cairo as news editor for the Middle East.

Music, monkeys and mayhem

Cynde Strand

The day Robert proposed that pleasure cruise, he billed it as a TV journey into the "Heart of Darkness", a chance to document the most notorious river in the world, the Congo; CNN's most notorious producer offering me "the trip of a lifetime".

I had been on many "trips of a lifetime" with Robert and they usually involved wearing a flak jacket. But it was winter in Bosnia and one thousand miles of music, monkeys and mayhem sounded pretty good.

What did I really know about the Congo? I knew the Kurtz character from Joseph Conrad's famous book *Heart of Darkness* went mad living on the banks of the river. I should have taken that as a portent of things to come.

After Zairean independence in 1960 anything associated with its Belgian past was chucked. In 1971 President Mobutu Sese Seko re-named the Congo River the "Zaire". It became known as the river that swallows all rivers, and Mobutu became known as the president that swallowed everything.

The river was and still is a lifeline for the people. Tugboats push barges from the capital, Kinshasa, to Kisangani and back. For many, these waterlogged shopping malls are the only way to buy and sell goods.

A pigmy with an elongated head wearing a raincoat and no shoes opened the door for me at the Kisangani Airport, our departure point.

We boarded the "Colonel Ebeya" with bottled water, coffee, canned tuna, 40-proof ten-year-old "malaria medicine", and ten cases of television equipment. Our first class *cabine deluxe* was a dark room with an airless air-conditioner.

Atop one of the four barges lashed alongside the "Colonel Ebeya", we waited for the big departure scene – and we waited and waited.

No matter how many hours you are delayed, departures in Africa are always a last-minute scramble. For us there was yet another departure fee for yet another official – you see life then in Zaire was like a rotten tooth and no how matter how much you paid, the pain would never go away and you would always find yourself paying more.

The only other thing you could always count on was the not-so-secret secret police, always lurking, watching, and demanding to see permits. We had permission to film whatever we wanted as long as we maintained *le strict respect de la dignity humaine*. Which translated meant that anything good was going to cost us hours of negotiation. Our permit also said we must not film any *situation bizarre* which was pretty much everything we saw and why we were there.

The "Colonel Ebeya" was like a city, with a class structure and different neighbourhoods. The elite sat high in the Hollywood Hills of first class, and looked down on those sleeping on mats outside in no class. There were shops, food stalls, bars, barnyards, churches and a jail. Babies were born. People died. And the mayor of our little town was Captain Louis Bela, a man whose belly was as big as his voice.

The most popular entertainment was cheering for the villagers as they paddled out to the "Colonel Ebeya" and the frantic acrobatics involved in balancing their goods and lassoing one of the barges. They arrived with pineapples, dried fish, catfish, antelopes, monkeys, pigs, goats, hens, crocodiles or furniture, and they left with everything from shoe tacks to condoms to salt to safety pins.

The first night out Captain Bela came by wearing a winter coat, shivering in the stifling heat – malaria. I escaped to the first-class bar. No exotic bar snacks like parrot sushi or monkey paw paté, just smoked monkey, its face frozen in a silent scream, the way mine was beginning to look after just one day on the river.

Zaïrean music sounds like wings flapping and was played incessantly; the people on this boat though would never fly away. This was the cruise to nowhere in a country going nowhere.

Day three and a dead monkey peed on me. I began counting the minutes and watching for signs of Ebola. I couldn't stop asking Captain Bela, "When are we going to get to Kinshasa?" But he would always look at me with his alley-cat eyes, raise his finger, and say, "On schedule Madame, unless of course there is *l'imprevu*, [the unexpected]".

The first *l'imprevu* came on the third night. One of the barges sprang a leak and began to sink. Panicked passengers heaved their bundles and babies over the rails. The only lifeboat I saw was full of livestock and I doubted many people could swim. Most were angry – another humiliation and no hope of compensation.

By sun-up our first-class passageways were choked with third-class refugees. As we pulled away from the half-submerged barge, scavengers paddled out of the jungle, hungry to strip away anything they could. In Africa things may rust and rot but nothing goes to waste.

"Hi, this is Cynde. I'm calling from the Congo." At sunset we hauled the satellite phone to the roof. A relaxed cool replaced the irritating heat and the lush beauty of the rain forest slowly graduated into total blackness as we crossed the equator.

The second *l'imprevu* came from the heavens – they opened up. Since there were no windshield wipers on the "Colonel Ebeya" we had to stop and wait or risk getting stuck on a sandbar. From the captain's deck we waited and watched as most passengers huddled under sheets of plastic, the continent's great panacea.

By day eight the passageways were so slimy and heaped with animals, both living and dead, we could barely make our way through the barges. It was as if Stephen King had rewritten the story of Noah's Ark. We took refuge inside our *cabine deluxe* knowing that just outside our door unspeakable things lay waiting with their throats slit.

We fought over the *The Guide to the Leading Hotels of the World*, and took turns playing Kurtz, massacring innocent roaches with bug spray.

It was going to be close, we were down to the last baby wipes. Not only were we forced to ration them; we were going to have to tear them in half. Captain Bela came by for his last payoff. After ten days of commandeering the best of the river's bounty he seemed content with the last of our coffee and canned tuna.

Though Kinshasa is merely a static version of the "Colonel Ebeya", just seeing the dilapidated buildings and pulling into the rundown port was cause to rejoice. There was just one problem – our African version of Water World was bigger than the parking space.

We waited just a few feet from salvation, clean sheets and a shower. For me the journey was almost over, but most would turn around for another ride on this ramshackle merry-go-round.

The few journalists who booked a seat on that cruise can quote all the Conrad they want, all I can do is applaud the courage of people who are forced to survive in the belly of the beast.

Cynde Strand is a producer, cameraperson, editor and sometimes reporter. She spent most of her career as one of CNN's human cannon balls. Now she is a mother and travels less, but the journey is just as exciting.

Beams over Baghdad

Stephen Claypole

The lights, when they appeared in the dusty gloom of a Baghdad evening, caused deep unease among the transmitter engineers and security men working in the debris of the bombed and looted TV headquarters beside the River Tigris.

Torch beams were probing a few hundred yards away along the ninth floor of the equally bombed and looted Mansour Milia Hotel.

"That's new," said Mike Furlong, an ex-US military man heading the efforts to re-construct broadcasting in Iraq. "Looks like the Saddam Fedayin are back. We could be in for a heavy night."

A few minutes later Furlong ordered his team of about ten engineers and ex-Special Forces men to take their sleeping bags to the shelter of a sturdy apparatus room. "We will have to stay all night otherwise we will lose everything we have done all day," he said.

Sure enough, after an hour, some loose gunfire zinged around the al-Salhiya transmitter tower where the Furlong team had been working for the past 12 hours. At the nearby Nasser Square, the young American soldiers sitting on an Abrams tank ignored the shooting. Just the sounds of a Baghdad night. Nothing special.

The ex-Special Forces guys at the TV station, although heavily armed, hunkered down but did not return fire. It came to an end with a round from an RPG-7, the grenade just missing a shiny new Japanese generator trailer but sending shrapnel tinkling against the red-and-white steel struts of the transmitter.

This was the reality of broadcasting in Iraq in the aftermath of the supposed cessation of hostilities. Nobody quite knew who was treating the Coalition as invaders and not liberators, but suspicion fell on former Baath Party apparatchiks.

At the end of the compound there was a local character, Abdullah Al Sheik, who had occupied the DG's offices with a bunch of heavies and proclaimed himself the new DG. Nobody locally could recall his past achievements in broadcasting.

Across town, at the vast and modern conference centre built by Saddam Hussein opposite the Al-Rashid Hotel, another struggle was underway to get post-war TV up and running.

The Great Leader had built himself a State apartment and fortified bunker on springs in case he got tired or bombed on one of his frequent visits to the centre. The robust air-conditioning of Saddam's suite made it the ideal place to set up editing – actually in a grand, ornate bedroom – and a two-camera studio in the drawing room. From here the evening news was to be broadcast.

In the car park outside an antiquated scanner, driven all the way from somewhere in Europe, provided the electronic heart and vital transmission link in what became known as the Iraqi Media Network.

The logistical struggle to launch Iraqi Media Network was nothing compared to the struggle to control it. This was where I came in and out – swiftly.

In late March I got a call from Major-General Tim Cross, the British deputy at the Office of Reconstruction and Humanitarian Assistance in Iraq, then based at a sprawling resort hotel beside the Gulf in Kuwait. Would I be prepared to drop everything and come out to help ORHA with what he called "the media piece"? It turned out that Kate Adie had dobbed me in.

A few days later I was taken on by a super-efficient American defence contractor called SAIC – otherwise known as a Beltway Bandit – and asked to help ex-General Jay Garner, Director of ORHA and Tim Cross with the public roll-out of the new civilian administration.

At about the same time President Bush asked the American Ambassador in Morocco, Margaret Tutwiler, an ex-State Department Spokesman to do the same thing. Alastair Campbell despatched a young Downing Street Press Officer called Emily Hands to the identical cause. Not to be outdone, the FCO thought it ought to be done in Arabic as well, so Charles Heatly, a young political officer arrived from somewhere in the Gulf.

A few days later we broke free of the Kuwait compound and flew with Jay Garner on a Hercules C-130 transporter to Baghdad, landing in the dawn and going straight away to a looted hospital in the north of the city where we were met by a sullen crowd of doctors, nurses and a few remaining patients. It was there and then we were confronted by the magnitude of reconstruction in Iraq.

The next few weeks, for me, were riveting, hard and ultimately dispiriting. ORHA settled into a vast palace called the "Four Saddams" – its roof was dominated by four huge, helmeted busts of The Great Leader.

The building was three times bigger than Buckingham Palace and with more sinks, gold taps and lavatories per square yard than any building I have ever visited.

The plumbing was irrelevant to begin with because we had no running water, mains electricity and hot food other than chemically heated army rations – MREs. The palace floors were covered with dust from the desert and the rooms infested by mosquitoes, sand fleas and large black rats.

This was the setting in which ORHA began its work, further complicated by a directive that we couldn't go anywhere without FORCE PROTECTION, meaning a convoy staffed by soldiers and Special Forces.

It was no wonder that early on in the mission Washington began to fret that Jay Garner was not "relating" to the Iraqi people. The pressure increased by the day to get the Iraqi Media Network TV service on the air.

No thought was given to why the military had precision-bombed most of the TV and radio stations and transmission systems in Iraq. On the ground the only means of communication was by Thuraya satellite phones that worked so poorly they were known as "Thuraya Heaps".

"We need a network evening news to talk to the Iraqis," said Washington. What the Administration wants, the Administration gets.

Originally, the Iraqi Media Network was to be given a degree of independence under a former Director of Voice of America, Bob Reilly. But as the hysteria about "Jay not relating" grew, Margaret Tutwiler and ORHA public affairs took control.

It was the stuff of the dreams of the White House and Number 10 – direct control over the contents of the evening news. "We have got to have vox pops" became the mantra, so that the Iraqi people can see themselves talking in an atmosphere of liberty.

When the vox pops came back to the temporary studios with anti-American opinions they were shelved for a day or two to be inter-cut with official ORHA reponses.

Into this dodgy mix came Hero Talabani, the exotic and cosmopolitan wife of the leader of the Patriotic Union of Kurdistan – a great favourite at Santa Barbara coffee mornings. Mrs Talabani convinced Miss Tutwiler over dinner and champagne that she was the arbiter of public taste.

So the next mantra became: "What will Mrs Talabani think of this?" After one morning meeting with IMNtv team, it was decided to take a taped package to Mrs T's house for her to comment on the editorial content. The Iraqi exiles who formed the majority of IMNtv's staff threatened to strike.

As I padded through the vast halls of the Four Saddams Palace, I reflected that control of the media had not changed much since The Great Leader's day. I was relieved when a C-130 Transporter came to take me home on a day when the temperature reached 107 degrees fahrenheit.

Stephen Claypole is Chairman of the London-based broadcast advisory company DMA-Media Ltd. He was the temporary international media advisor to the Office of Reconstruction and Humanitarian Assistance in Iraq and previously advised the OSCE in reconstructing broadcasting in Kosovo.

The correspondent's tale

David Eades

My first foreign trip did not go quite as planned.

My enforced stay in Khartoum had cost me dearly ... my pallid complexion, as befits an Englishman emerging from a long, cold, overworked winter, had found the fabulous Sudanese sun unforgiving. For three days I had enjoyed cups of tea, sipped between mouthfuls of crumbly sweetened bread, on the vast open terrace of the Grand Hotel. For all its cracked walls and faded mosaic paving, it still exuded the splendid, old colonial "how they must have lived" ambience, a musky waft of life before the Battle of Omdurman and the fall of Khartoum. Waiters in crisp, white *jelabeahs* served out of the old family silver, while one mad dog Englishman was thinking for just a moment he was on his summer holiday ... sunstroke and sunburn were on the menu ... and I had just ordered them both, my head soon to peel like a dried onion.

It took me three days to escape Khartoum, three days waiting for a permit that the "authorities" – that is, the man sitting at the table I had to report to every day – could happily have approved the moment I appeared ... or just as happily rejected for all three weeks I was in Sudan.

To get away in three days was considered reasonable; it could, I was advised, have been a lot worse. And at least I could still fulfill my mission: to meet the good folk of Shendi – a market town of relative plenty in a land of virtually nothing.

It took a five-hour crawl across the desert to reach Shendi. There were tracks to follow – but they had been obliterated by the sandstorm; we relied instead on the in-built radar of our well-travelled driver. I was sand-soaked – dust in my eyes, ears, hair, in my clothes, shoes, socks ... I was crusty and as dry as the Sudanese Sahara desert we had been traversing.

There was worse to come. My crisp, brand new jacket – designer wear for the tough outdoor life – was already battle-scarred: one side eroded clean away by a puddle of battery acid.

I accepted it with stoicism – a badge of honour from my first real foreign trip as a reporter. Why Sudan? In the most honest terms, it was to visit my sister, Alison, who was working on a voluntary mission (VSO) in Shendi. Her challenge: to halt the sand creep of the Sahel by teaching the

Sudanese, a people so shorn of necessities, let alone luxuries, that they had stripped every tree, every bush they could find for fuel and timber. And so the sand crept closer to the modest villages and towns, the Sahara maintaining its relentless, arid progress, edging south, creating dunes over all obstacles in its path, even the very houses built from the timber which had kept the sand at bay.

The intrigue for me, though, lay not so much in the idea of the project, as in its execution. This was education by puppetry, a mobile puppet theatre, staffed by Sudanese puppeteers and supporting a team of local foresters encouraging people to plant their own trees.

Not everybody knew what puppets were, so they would pour out after sunset in their hundreds to watch these shows with fascination. It was something I had to see.

And in just a couple of days the puppeteers were to set out – with me in tow – on their latest adventure across this vast, empty country, spreading the word of sustainable development.

The short time I had before the trip was spent gathering snapshots of an extraordinary world, none more vivid – and ultimately more significant – than the scene on the banks of the Nile. There, beside the old ferry stop, with the clapped-out ferry criss-crossing non-stop, I met the brick-makers. They were shaping deep brown bricks from the slush and sludge of a great waterway – the sun for a kiln.

We talked, though neither they nor I shared a common word between us, scarcely even a gesture. We laughed too; I took pictures as they posed in stately Victorian style, unsmiling, before revealing their giggling white, cracked teeth once again. They invited me for *fatuur*, their breakfast: thick, hot *lugma* - a sort of dirty semolina, with *okra*, or ladies fingers, all of us scraping from the communal old can, itself thick with years of previous servings. I smiled, I gagged ... but I ate.

And so to the preparations for departure. The day before leaving, we rehearsed the loading of the lorry. All the puppeteers gathered – Mustapha, with the smile of an angel, Chinese, given to convenient bouts of malaria when the physical work beckoned, Magdi, the streetwise, Karoma the lute player and Shadia, stunningly beautiful.

It was hard and heavy work, all under a forty degree sun, and I was beginning to feel just a little queasy. By the evening, I was feeling worse. Too much sun again? Possibly ... but lurking in the back of my mind, the slimy dollops of *lugma*, sliding from my cupped fingers into my mouth, before running as if through sluice gates into my stomach.

By morning, the lorry laden and ready to go, my fears were confirmed. I was going ... nowhere. Nowhere beyond the confines of my bed and the toilet next door. The trip was postponed for the sick Englishman. After five days, it was postponed indefinitely. By then my routine was well rehearsed. I could get no further than the adjoining room, which I visited on a regular basis. I was fed a diet of saline and banana shakes, a cassette of the Travelling Wilburys and a steady stream of BBC World Service Radio.

Alison was beginning to worry. After a year in Sudan she was immune to the local dietary differences, and she had thought little of my plight. But these things are meant to come to an end and mine wasn't. A trip to the surgery was required.

"How are your stools?" enquired the doctor. "Liquid," I replied. "Show me them," he retorted. "How?" I rejoined. The nurse proffered a small object, which the doctor then passed ceremoniously to me. It was a cigarette packet. Players Number Six. A small one. Was I condemned to die? Was this my final luxury? I opened the packet nervously. Inside ... nothing; nothing bar the tumbleweed strands of tobacco which gathered in the silver foil wrapper. It was an empty cigarette packet, nothing more. I looked up bemused but the doctor was already engaged in other, no doubt more pressing cases.

In my state of bewilderment, I could only surmise this was the receptacle for my stool ... my liquid stool!

The nurse ushered me outside to the back of the surgery. Beyond stood only a toilet hut. I weaved my way towards it, faint with weakness, but racked with confusion and anxiety at what I was about to do.

Suffice to say, I managed to provide what I surmised the doctor had ordered. With great precision, I made a watertight vessel out of the silver foil, and returned it to the Players packet.

I walked ever so slowly back towards the surgery. I appeared round the door and approached the nurse. She looked at me blankly. Suddenly, I was struck with an awful fear: was I meant to put money into the packet to pay for my treatment? I froze, the cigarette box tight in my hand. She moved towards it and, ever so weakly, I allowed her to take it. She left the room. I waited for a cry of horror or roar of indignation. But there was nothing, no histrionics, only the briefest of inspections, and an almost instantaneous diagnosis.

The prescription followed and, needless to say, I survived.

I never made the puppet tour. I only just recovered in time to return to Khartoum and at dead of night, fly out heading for home. I had failed spectacularly on my first assignment: acute sunburn, chronic diarrhoea – no story.

For a decade David Eades travelled as a BBC correspondent from South Africa to China, from Moscow to Washington. He had postings to Brussels and Ireland, before covering Sports News. David now presents for BBC television and radio.

Never assume anything

Robyn Cohen

"You people", he barked. "Well, uhhm …", I spluttered. "You people. What's wrong with you people, hey?" And again: "No, honestly I can't believe you people!" Sunday morning and a deserted part of Cape Town, June 1999. Here I was, a lone Jewish woman facing the wrath of a Muslim man at a community radio station. Backed into a corner, this hulking man lunged towards me and I thought, *oy vey*. Mobile phone battery dead. Escape routes? None. I am an arts and lifestyle writer, but this kind of drama I wasn't expecting.

At the time, the Jewish and Muslim communities were at loggerheads – as they often are in this beautiful city of Cape Town. Funny though, I cannot recall what that particular turmoil was about. It's a bit like remembering the fight you had with your husband, sibling or best friend. The pain and the anger are easily conjured up. You can picture exactly what you were wearing, that you were eating a lemon-and-poppy-seed muffin and drinking cappuccino with Sting singing "Fragile" in the background. Try and remember the details of what you were fighting about? Nope. Zilch. The fine details get mulched, deleted. Makes you wonder. It couldn't have been very important, could it?

And so with this particular conflict between us Jews and Muslims, I really cannot begin to recall. Nor do I have any interest in digging into the archives to see what was going on at the time. The purpose of my visit to the radio station was in order to be interviewed for five articles I was writing for the *Cape Times*. Called "One City, Many Cultures" (yes, laugh at the irony), the series examined themes viewed from the perspective of many cultures in Cape Town. Focusing on rites of passage from birth to death, freelance writers were asked to focus on at least five religions or belief systems. There are many differences but there are also so many similarities as our convictions of faith frequently intersect and collide at common nodes.

My brief was "Growing Old". Acutely tuned into the ongoing tensions between Jews and Muslims, I went out of my way to focus on rituals from a Muslim perspective. Measure the column space of my features and the words devoted to the Muslim rituals and it's clear – I have given it more space than other faiths I had selected.

Friends (Jewish and others) admonished me to expect trouble. They were wrong. I got none – not even half a second's trouble or even a quarter glance of hostility. Researching my stories during a heat wave, I was served refreshments and food wherever I went and was treated with the utmost warmth and hospitality by the Muslim community, and indeed by all religious and cultural leaders I encountered.

From writing "One City, Many Cultures", I discovered an incredible level of interfaith co-operation between South African organisations working with the elderly. Across all the religions, senior groups regularly socialise with one another, have fun, fundraise. Even the feistiest, most recalcitrant oldies I came across were able to let go of their idealism and join the crowd for an hour or two. Perhaps when you reach a certain age, when half your friends are dead, you realise that life is too precious to waste spitting at each other across cultural barricades.

So there I was at the radio station with this huge man leering at me and shouting, "You people!" over and over again. After what felt like an eternity and about ten reiterations of "you people", the man finished his sentence: "You people … are not giving our leader any coverage."

Yasser Arafat was in town and it transpired that he felt that the Press was snubbing Arafat with its reporting. As a freelancer, I was seen as a member of the press-at-large and hence the jibes. There was no racial agenda in his refrain of "you people", or at least that is what I felt instinctively. Once he had finished his piece, I realised he had not shown any animosity. I learnt in that encounter that as a writer you should never assume anything; ever, no matter how threatened you feel.

Later on when he took me up to the interview room, I discussed some of the images I was dealing with in my articles and I muttered, "well, you know I am Jewish," as an aside. "Really?", he answered without a hint of sarcasm and I believed him. "That's nice and thank you so much for coming in today. Can we offer you something to drink?" He added, as if to say, "Isn't it a lovely day?".

Robyn Cohen is a writer and artist who lives and works in Cape Town. She is a regular contributor to the *Cape Times*, *Sunday Independent* and other publications.

When I am outside

Jo-Anne Richards

The boys scuffled among themselves. One stomped his buddy's feet while another, hysterical with giggles, rubbed a shoulder limp from lammies.

There were eighteen of them, teenage boys for the most part. And all of them faced two charges of murder.

I can't remember quite what I expected. They were charged with stabbing and burning two men they had randomly stopped at a home-made roadblock. But these were the 80s. They had been mob-crazy, running on rhetoric and singing of "guns in Angola".

These were the times. They also faced charges of terrorism, in the old, stupid sense of the word. This could involve anything from knowing too many political choruses, to a fist in the air at the wrong time. I suppose I expected them to be committed struggle-istas at least, staunch in austere ideals.

"Hey Miss, Miss. Ah please Miss, could you bring us some sweets? We like chocolates best."

With much giggling and nudging, a couple of them had called me over on my first day in court. "Hey Miss, I am Accused Number 2 and this is my friend, Number 17."

"Yes, Miss," Number 17 added, "And some James Hadley Chase. You know James Hadley Chase?"

The cops were indulgent, in court anyway. In the end, they didn't even check my bags of sweets and James Hadley Chases from the second-hand bookshop. It's lucky he was so prolific.

They were shy with me. I was the only woman they'd seen in months, besides the court stenographer, who had to be 106. On one of my early days, they called me over.

"We wrote letters for you," said Morgan, handing me a grubby, much-folded scrap of paper. We'd now made the bold move of progressing to names. I unfolded it gravely; aware they were watching intently.

"Great is my joy for this opportunity of writing this letter for you," he wrote. "In reference to health I am highly in progress and my wishes are to hear the same from you.

"I asking you to think about me and pray for me to have a success of my trial. Every waking step or second I thought about you because my wishes is for our friendship to continue when I am outside."

Outside. This young boy thought he would walk freely from this place of pompous white men. He still believed that we could meet on the outside.

I couldn't look up. I heard their giggles, but I couldn't look up and face them - these children who had been forced by circumstance to play MK and boere rather than cops and robbers.

Morgan and I, and sometimes his co-accused Raymond, wrote letters through the trial that I covered for much of its two-year run. Early on, one of these hardened politicos so feared by the state wrote of his longing for the outside. "I cannot tell what I can do when I am free," he wrote, "Since my education is at an end. Perhaps I can be your garden boy."

But for the most part, they were letters of friendship. It was an odd friendship, but we exchanged small details of ourselves and the things that made us glad or unhappy.

"I am only short of words to express my feelings at this time, but at any rate you know perfectly well about my situation. I only hope and wish that the almighty will secure our souls until the aimed goal is achieved. Kindly permit me to pen-off here. Pass my kindly greetings to all at your house and the Comrades."

After three years inside, my letters transferred from Pollsmoor Max to Private Bag Robben Island. Now they were men.

The judge had said the crimes had flowed from a sense of grievance, "but we have only the greatest condemnation for the manner in which these grievances were expressed". He had called Raymond "an evil man", who had stabbed a man as he sat in a puddle, his burnt flesh draped in streamers to the ground. I had seen the photographs in the file.

He was sentenced to twenty years while Morgan, who had played "a leading role in the events" was sentenced to fifteen years.

"I enjoyed the Christmas season very well," wrote Morgan the following year. "I'm in a good state of mind and I hope that you be my guide and mother at all times ... I'm learning here, continuing with my academic education. Please don't worry. I'm always with you."

Later that year he wrote "from the distant Island", to "apprise you of my state of affair at this captivity. I must inform that at least life is bearable or rather interesting here ...

"The conditions here are conducive for one to become not just an ordinary learned but an exponent of the hidden social processes which take place in the society. I should think it's worth mentioning the fact that knowledge becomes the material force, only if it corresponds with reality, and highlights social processes."

I guess he no longer wished to be my "garden boy".

When I left Cape Town, he wrote: "Johannesburg! I have never been there Jo-Anne. But I gather that it is a place of fast life … Many of my people from Nyanga and Gugulethu are to be found in that city. They work there every day of their lives and sleep in hostels and come back home to tell stories about it. Some do not come back.

"Someday when I can be able to walk and speak without fear I would like to visit this legendary place."

And perhaps he has. Ten years on, Robben Island became a place that tourists visited.

If he did, I never heard of it. When the *Rand Daily Mail* and *Sunday Express* closed down in 1985, I wandered overseas on retrenchment pay, deciphering Turkish newspapers on states of emergency back home. When I returned, I wrote to Morgan on the "Distant Island", but he never replied. Perhaps he never received them.

He could be anywhere or anything by now, I suppose. Even in government. Perhaps he has his own "garden boy". Who knows?

Jo-Anne Richards is the author of three novels, her latest being *Sad at the Edges*. She is a journalist of more years standing than vanity allows her to mention and now inflicts this strange obsession on tender young minds at Wits University.

Tingi-Tingi

David Hands

A child is lying down, covered in a black blanket. I see her from a distance. I did not notice her at first in the midst of the destruction that surrounds me. I am standing in what used to be a refugee settlement. The refugees fearing for their lives, fled when the rebel army came. The temporary homes that housed the refugees now lie empty; their presence only a reminder that life once existed here. Clothes, shoes and cooking utensils are scattered amongst the dead and the dying.

From this distance she looked tiny, and cold. Her motionless figure blended in with the scattered personal belongings that were left behind. She looked dead. She was lying on a hill, and behind her lay the abandoned camp. I picked up my camera and walked closer, the thought that it would make a "great" shot crossing my mind. Approaching her, I noticed the dark blanket was moving, and when I got really close the blanket rose into the air and buzzed around me. Flies, millions of them, kept her covered until my presence momentarily made them uneasy and forced them to fly off. Then they started settling down again; I was no threat.

The girl's back was turned towards me, and as I walked around her my eyes never left her skinny body; I wanted to see her face. As I came to a standstill I just stared, not knowing if I should film or not. She once must have been beautiful, now she was an image to haunt me probably for the rest of my life. Her eyes were shut, her face was withdrawn back into the bone, her cheeks had disappeared, and her head looked out of proportion with the rest of her body. Her skin barely covered her bones, it was holding on as a last attempt to protect her.

I set up my camera and as I was getting ready to film this breathless child, her eyes slowly began to open. Can she be alive? How can anybody survive such severe malnutrition? She desperately tried to focus her swollen eyes, probably only seeing a bare shadow standing above her. For a moment she seemed frightened, maybe she thought I was one of the soldiers that caused her suffering and had returned to finish the job. But then, when her eyes adjusted she saw a white man standing looking down on her, and with all the strength that she could master she forced all her remaining energy into raising her hand towards me. Her palm slightly open, her lips moving, but I cannot hear what she is saying, but I know, and I begin to feel helpless. I stand there frozen, just staring.

I called out, like a frightened child, I called for anyone to help. Charlie, a UNICEF officer, came running and just for a minute stared at the living dead, the same as I did a few moments earlier. Once his initial shock was over we started organising a stretcher to carry her away. That is when I started filming. I knew I missed the best shot earlier, and for once it did not seem to matter. I followed her all the way to the field hospital, and once she was in the hands of the experts, I turned and walked away.

I found a bit of shade and sat down. I had had enough for the day, it was humid and very hot, and I just sat and waited for the plane to take me out, anywhere, as long as I was able to get far away from that place. Charlie soon joined me, and without even knowing if I could handle the truth I asked what chance the little girl had. He looked down on the bare earth, as if looking for the answer there and he spoke and told me what I did not want to know. She probably will not survive. She was too weak and tired. Her body had had enough. If she did survive, she will never be normal again, and it would take years before her system would be able to survive alone.

That night in the safety of our hotel in Goma, I sat and had dinner. I did not eat much – it doesn't matter anyway, and on the TV I saw my images of the day. I had a world exclusive, as I was the only cameraman at this refugee camp. This usually brought satisfaction to me, knowing that millions all over the world would see my pictures. And yet, I felt I had cheated. Could I have done more for her? Why was I so desperate to take the plane out without offering my place to the girl, with the possibility of her getting better medical treatment? Why did I not offer to look after her, to pay for the best doctors? Why did I use her suffering, her death to broadcast my pictures?

I thought that the girl's image would fade slowly with the passage of time. It did not, I am writing this years after I left Tingi-Tingi, and her image is still bright in my memory. Maybe that is the way it should be.

I never even asked her name.

David Hands is a freelance cameraman and editor based in Cyprus. Over the last 10 years he covered news stories and documentaries in the Balkans, East and Central Africa and the Middle East.

A last act of love

Abraham Fisseha

We drove up to a food distribution centre in the town of Wollo, north of Addis. We had not yet got out of the car when we saw a young woman with a child on her back. They were heading to the centre to get food, some relief from the drought-related famine.

We started filming and followed her to the centre. Seeing our camera and the promise it carried of publicity and increased aid, the officials gave her priority. She didn't have to wait for her rations of a 12,5 kg bag of cereal, some biscuits and a litre of oil.

She smiled. At least she had something with which to sustain herself and her child for the next few days.

Still smiling, she turned to take her child off her back to feed him. As she got him down, the smile was shattered. Her child was lifeless. He had passed the point of no return. Gone forever.

I will never forget that moment when I witnessed how hope can be dashed in a minute. I was a witness because of a job that no-one understands. But to do it I have to be compassionate, humane and courageous and trust the Almighty, the merciful.

The image of that woman and her child remained with me. They prepared me for another drought, another famine.

It was a year later in Dollo, a town in the southernmost tip of Ethiopia. All around I saw the horror of children and the elderly losing their struggle to live. I filmed as much as I could before I needed a break from the pain of what I saw.

I moved away from the camp to compose myself and then I saw him, an elderly man slowly digging at the hard earth. He was struggling to make an impact on the unyielding ground. And even though he could hardly breathe, he continued with his task.

"What are you doing?" I asked him.

He looked up and indicated something on the ground nearby. It was wrapped in a worn-out cloth. He said it was the body of his dead child.

He was struggling to dig a grave for his son.

He had to continue, he said, because everyone else in the camp was as weak as he, and no-one there was able to assist him.

"I do not want to see him eaten by wild animals." It was his last act of love.

I decided then and there that there was nothing else for it; I called on two of my friends and colleagues to help.

We three healthy strong men made a meal of the task and before long, the grave was ready. As we turned to fetch the child's body, we saw his father lying on the ground. He was not breathing.

His last breath had been used on his digging. Now the father was also gone.

Our journalistic activities had to be suspended.

We had to become grave diggers for the day.

Abraham Fisseha has been a journalist in Ethiopia since 1979, working first for local media and then for international broadcasters, wire services, and the TV agency APTN. Since 2003 he has worked for AFP.

Die another day

Orla Guerin

Did I look a killer in the eye? If so, it wouldn't be the first time. There have been others over the years – KLA fighters in trenches in Kosovo, Serbian paramilitaries in bombed-out buildings in Sarajevo, Russian troops on the Chechen Border. But this encounter was in suburbia – in the neon-lit landscape of my local shopping mall in Jerusalem. Had the skinny young man in the row behind me come to blow himself up, or was he there – like me – to see the movie?

Living in Israel, you think twice about a lot of things. This is a place for surreal self-examination. Am I risking my life to go for a coffee in a popular café? Is it better to get a take-away lunch rather than sit outside in the sunshine among the crowds? Should I shop at 10.00 p.m. when no-one else is around?

So we debated the wisdom of a trip to the movies. Suicide bombers like enclosed spaces – a blast inside four walls has greater deadly force. A bomber who boards a bus can take far more lives than one who blows himself up in the open air at the bus stop.

We assessed the temperature of the conflict, like you might check the weather report before going out anywhere else. How high was the level of tension? How long since the last suicide bombing? When was the last Israeli assassination of a Palestinian militant leader? How tight were Israeli security restrictions on the West Bank? How many incursions had the Israelis carried out lately?

The answers weren't comforting, but this Sunday night we needed an escape. Our little band of three weary reporters headed for the multiplex to bask in the unreality of the latest offering from James Bond – "Die Another Day".

We arrived to lax security at the entrance to the mall. No metal detector, no-one checking our pockets or our bags, just a paunchy middle-aged guard in a greasy uniform whose mind was probably on paying his bills. Upstairs at the cinema a few bored teenagers kept watch at the entrance.

They barely looked us over, before the queue behind us swept us through the door. We didn't turn back. Living in a war zone requires you to believe that you will witness the horrors but never be sucked in.

The opening credits roll – we burrow deep into our seats, ready to listen to whatever Bond has to say. About fives minutes pass. Then he comes in – light flooding in behind him, silhouetting his narrow frame. A skinny young guy – jeans, rumpled T-shirt, light jacket, something dangling in his hand. I turned back to the screen, but the newcomer never even looks at it.

He stands stock-still, gazing at the audience, ignoring the movie he has paid to see. "Looking for a friend," I thought. But no-one acknowledged him from the crowd. Then he walked forward slowly, uncertainly, and sat into the empty row right behind me.

I felt unease, like a cold wind wrapping its arms around me, and turned back to stare. On either side of me, my friends were turning too. All three of us were accustomed to running on instinct. Each of us sensed danger, without a word being said.

Behind us he perched on the edge of his chair, body slightly twisted, eyes darting around. He was tense, uncomfortable, ignoring the action on screen. "Maybe a drug addict," I thought. But then, immediately, a less comforting thought - an addict wouldn't waste money on a cinema ticket.

My eyes were on his hands. What was he carrying? Had he put anything down? His T-shirt was loose. Was there anything underneath? Were there any wires around his body?

By the flickering light of the screen I could see no sign of a bulky explosive belt. His fingers were still clutching the small bag he had brought it. Too small to hold a bomb, I decided, unless militants had found a new way to make one.

He stayed silent – and so did we. But our scrutiny seemed to unnerve him. He got up fast and left. I headed out the door after him. By the time I reached the security guards at the front entrance, he was gone. They followed me back into the cinema, shining their torches under his seat, but there was nothing to find.

Their search was enough to send two young girls in the row behind running out the door. For reasons that my two friends and I later found hard to grasp, we stayed put, waiting for Bond to achieve his predictable victory. Maybe we needed the reassurance.

We had no proof of anything. Nothing but our suspicions or perhaps our paranoia. But afterwards I called the police and the army, asking them to alert the owners of the mall, to make sure they tightened security in case the young lookout came back. That's what we believe he was – a scout sent to check the cinema, to survey security inside and out, and report back to someone who might be ready to carry a bomb.

So far, there has been no attack on that cinema, or that mall. But there have been massacres elsewhere – down the street from my office, at the café around the corner, on buses not far from my home. I have raced to the scene of these atrocities, and counted the dead being carried away – seen tiny broken bodies, fathers crying for missing sons, seen patches of scalp, with hair still attached, lying on the ground at my feet. And I have wondered: what is the bomber's final emotion, in the final moment before killing and being killed? Does the attacker who sets out to kill at random, on the largest scale possible, know even a moment of pity for his victims. Does he hesitate? Do his hands shake? What does he feel? Is it triumph or fear? Hatred or euphoria?

It's no longer just the angry young men, unemployed, poor, and without prospects, who are setting off the bombs. They've been joined by married fathers and mothers, college graduates, a granddad, an Israeli Arab – even a teenage girl.

• • •

I interviewed an Israeli bus driver, 24 years behind the wheel, who stared a suicide bomber in the face. Baruch Neuman is a tall and sturdy-looking father of three. He and a passenger rushed to help a man who slipped while trying to board Baruch's bus. When they pulled back his shirt, to check his injuries, they saw the suicide belt.

"We pinned him down, and yelled to everyone to get away," he said. "But the bomber kept struggling and we were terrified the bomb would go off. After a few minutes we ran. He stood up, walked a little while, and blew himself up." The bomber managed to kill one woman, not the scores he hoped to take with him. I asked Baruch how he felt, face to face with the stranger who wanted to kill him, and everyone else on the bus. He gave a surprising reply. "I didn't see him as an enemy," he said. "I felt pity because I knew he was about to die. I held his hand, and I thought 'this poor man, why is he doing this?'"

If you travel the West Bank and Gaza, as I do, Palestinians will give you plenty of answers to that question – the humiliation of life under occupation, the lack of dignity, the lack of freedom, the lack of hope. To the Palestinians, suicide bombers are "martyrs" not killers, and this is what many children now tell you they want to be.

• • •

On a cold afternoon, with the light fading, I found nine-year-old Mohammed and his friends playing in the ruins of his family home in Gaza. Israeli troops demolished the two-storey building because one of his relatives was a militant. The large extended family would be sleeping outside that night, and perhaps for months to come.

Before he has even reached his teens, Mohammed dreams of death. "I want to be a martyr when I grow up," he told me with a shy smile, "because I love my land, and I want to liberate Jerusalem," – a city he worships without ever having seen. As a child in Gaza he lives in one of the world's largest prisons, locked in behind an Israeli fence.

Mohammed held up his school exercise book for me to see. Instead of pictures of soccer stars, the pages were plastered with photographs of his heros – the latest additions to the ranks of suicide bombers.

Orla Guerin is an award-winning Middle East Correspondent for the BBC, based in Jerusalem. Prior to the Middle East she reported from the Balkans. Before joining the BBC in 1995, she was Eastern Europe Correspondent for the Irish state broadcasting service, RTE, reporting on the collapse of the Soviet Union and the break-up of Yugoslavia.

Bosnia's finest

Nino Bantic

Marriage:

As far as many people in the town were concerned She had chosen the "wrong side", and His position wasn't considered to be any better, either.

They were simply a couple who happened to be at the wrong place at the wrong time, and yet they were not together. To tell the truth, when they got married no-one told them that all the business about the groom's side and the bride's side would become deadly serious. He was a Muslim married to a Croat, and She was, obviously, a Croat married to a Muslim – and that clearly wasn't a winning marital combination in central Bosnia in the spring of 1993.

After the wedding She moved to His house in the oldest part of the town. His neighborhood was predominantly a Muslim area while the rest of it was mostly inhabited by Croats.

One morning in April He went downtown to see his friends. She stayed at home to prepare lunch. But He was unaware of a new fact: that day was the first day of the war between the Bosnian Muslims and the Croats, and He was shocked to find He couldn't return home, as the Croatian militia had sealed off the whole area.

He remained stuck in what was to become the Croatian side, and She found herself stuck on the Muslim side of town.

It took Him 10 months to test her cuisine again.

Ceasefire:

"Tomorrow, on the first day of the ceasefire, we are organising an extraordinary family reunion," said the Captain, but the rest of us didn't share his enthusiasm. Nor did he, frankly speaking.

The Captain was the spokesman for the British UN peacekeepers in central Bosnia, and we were journalists who had been covering this conflict for more then a year. We all knew well that those ceasefires never lasted longer then a day, at best.

"This time it looks serious, it was signed in Vienna, by the Croatian and Bosnian foreign ministers under US supervision," my London editor told me via satellite phone. "Maybe", I said, "but I can't see a reason why these guys here would ... why would they stop fighting just because someone somewhere in Europe wanted it so?"

As a matter of fact the whole conflict in central Bosnia started because someone somewhere wanted it so. But when the borders, so easily drawn somewhere else, were transferred to the reality on the ground – the situation got somewhat more complicated.

"You see that blue car over there?" a local Croatian officer asked me once, "you see that car? OK, that's the current border of Herceg Bosna (Bosnian Croat Republic) here in our village. By the next week we will push it across the road, all the way to the school."

"And then what?" I asked.

"Then one day we will connect this area to Croatia," he replied.

"But behind the school are some Muslim positions, then further on are Croatian villages surrounded by Muslims, then there are a few hundred miles of Bosnian Serbian territories, and yes, there is finally Croatia, yet still occupied by Serbs. How are you going to do that?"

"Let us deal with that bloody school first", he said.

Reunion:

The "ceasefire trip" was organised by the Captain and his UN guys. They took along an official interpreter, a Bosnian girl called Lejla, to help other journalists with translation.

Usually UN interpreters are not allowed to help journalists, but the Captain understood the importance of today's assignment.

A small convoy of journalists and UN officers was on the road. In our car my crew was talking about footage we filmed the evening before in a Croatian war hospital. While we were there a man was brought in with severe head injuries. A Muslim sniper shot the guy while he was patrolling along the frontline near his house.

"If the ceasefire really holds, we have the excellent pictures of the last soldier killed in the conflict", said the colleague.

"But he's still alive", I said. "No, no, he died later," he said. "We've got some excellent stuff."

Preoccupied with the conversation we hadn't realised that all Croatian and Muslim checkpoints had disappeared from the road.

It looked like the ceasefire was for real this time.

At noon on that February day in 1994 our convoy came to the town where He and She lived their divided lives. Slowly and carefully we drove across no-man's land and entered His neighborhood, the smallest Muslim entity in the valley, a symbol of the Muslim resistance and survival – almost like a small Stalingrad. The whole place wasn't bigger than two streets; all in all there were about 50 houses, but there was a school, a field hospital in what used to be a garage, and a graveyard in someone's garden. A washing line with blankets was stretched across the riverbank – protection from Croatian snipers.

"Something went wrong," said the Captain "it looks as though locals don't like the idea of filming the reunion of the couple."

He and Lejla had just got back from the Muslim commander.

The same story on the Croatian side.

"That issue is very sensitive", said the Captain. "Both sides are basically angry at both of them."

"Have you seen the guy?" I asked Lejla, in the language we use to called "our language" to avoid political problems in naming convention, as I was Croatian and she was Bosnian.

"Look, both of them are scared they will get shot. He was drafted by the Croatian militia and was fighting for the Croatian side. He was probably shooting at the town many times. There wasn't too much choice for him. So, He is not really welcome in this town anymore. She, on the other hand, became a nurse in the Muslim field hospital, so – for Croats – She helped the enemy ..."

He left the Croatian side and walked to no-man's land, escorted by a group of British soldiers. She left the town escorted by another group of British soldiers. The two groups walked down towards the burned petrol station, and I wasn't able to see them kissing, as they were completely surrounded by the peacekeepers.

While they were kissing, one colleague saw an older man. "Are you happy? Are you happy because of the ceasefire?" he asked him in English.

"Back off, you vultures," he said in "our language".

"What does he say?" the colleague asked Lejla.

"That they are very, very happy with the ceasefire," she replied.

From the very first moment I saw Lejla, I knew she was an excellent interpreter.

One of Bosnia's finest.

(note: for safety reasons, Lejla is not the real name of the translator)

Nino Bantic was born in Croatia in 1965. His successful career as a radio comedian was disrupted by the war in his country and in 1991 he became a war journalist. Since then he witnessed the less funny side of life in Croatia, Bosnia, Macedonia, Sierra Leone and Albania. Nino currently works for Associated Press Television News in its London HQ as a senior producer. He's married with two children.

Chasing opportunities

Sello Motseta

They sit perched under trees like vultures stalking their prey, and rise spontaneously to compete for scarce jobs as soon as a vehicle slows down near them.

These hordes of mainly glum and rather modestly clothed Zimbabwean "illegal immigrants" can be seen chasing vehicles in the scorching heat – like bees following honey – in pursuit of piece-meal jobs, to get some of the much needed currency to take back home.

Luckmore Shoniwe is one of them. This 23-year-old final year A-Level student who still dreams of going to university, travelled over 800 kilometres from Harare to what he had hoped was a better life. He has found that Africa's much-vaunted democracy can be a rough neighbourhood from which to try and eke out a meaningful existence.

"Living here as a foreigner is a problem," he says. "It is true that some Zimbabweans are thieves but we are all classified as thieves by locals. Even where there is place we are denied accommodation because they say Zimbabweans are thieves," he adds in disbelief and resignation.

Shoniwe tells of life in White City, the small dusty, debilitated slum bordering Gaborone's Central Business District, so far from home.

"Where I used to live there were 20 people in the room, each paying 70 pula a month for rent. Sometimes I can get a job cleaning yards, digging a trench or as a builder's assistant for 20 pula a day."

At other times he is not so lucky and has to spend days "fasting" because he cannot afford to buy something to eat. Even as he talks to me his alert eyes are continuously darting left and right, in case our rather animated conversation deprives him of his daily bread.

My heart goes out to them, especially in view of the apparent indifference to their plight by regional leaders and the growing xenophobia from fellow Botswana.

Botswana's President Festus Mogae can however hear or see no evil in his next-door neighbour's actions. African apologists call it African solidarity. It is a carry-over of the patriarchal notion that what one man does in his own house is no one else's business. But this mindset is out of step with current realities and the "botho" principle in African culture that informs dealings across kin by encouraging good neighbourliness.

Despite these pleasant cultural offerings, the Botswana government will build a 2,4 m high game-proof fence separating the two neighbouring countries – to stop the growing number of Zimbabwean illegal immigrants entering Botswana. This is despite the Southern African Development Community leaders' stated ambition of creating a free-trade area in the region over the next eight years.

This is capitalism gone very awry with many of the Zimbabweans often being abandoned by Tswana employers once they have completed menial tasks assigned to them because they have no recourse to legitimate legal advice. It is a brutal and stark choice that most of them have to face.

My advice to my beleaguered fellow Africans is to stick it out in President Robert Mugabe's Zimbabwe, despite the deteriorating economic situation in that increasingly turbulent nation. If you have to take your chances in unfamiliar territory, neither family nor friends are waiting with open arms.

Sello Motseta is a freelance journalist based in Botswana who has written for The Associated Press, IRIN news, the South African newspapers _Business Day_ and _The Star_, _Botswana Guardian_, and _Mmegi –The Reporter_ (Botswana). He holds an MA in International Studies from Rhodes University, Grahamstown.

Waste

Kathy Chenault

The sign warns in multilingual
yellow and black:
Don't drink the water.
Don't swim in the water.
Don't cook in the water.
Afrikaans, Setswana,
Zulu, English.

We live like this. Why?

One tone. No demands.
The words run off
this Soweto man's life –
24 years, fermented.
    Sewage swirls in clumps,
    gurgling over trash
    washed into clumps,
breaking blue, to black,
the brackish stream.

    And the water runs on.
    Downstream, the smell
    spirits the air, stinging
    eyes and nostrils.
    Grimaces, sighs, dull eyes
never go away.

    You never get used
    to the stench.

The squatter's sullen, soft face
apologizes for the putrid sky.

We tell the children
to stay out of the water.
But they are children.
And children play in water.
This Shit River is
the only running water here.

Two children crouch
on a rock, on the bank,
poking sticks into
the river, piercing
oily, rippled rainbows.
They know not
to swim in it,
not to drink from it.
But sometimes they do.
That's what kids do.

A grandfather nurses
his daughter and grandson
back from cholera. He changes
soiled clothes. Spoons
water through craggy lips,
presses lumps of meal
into desert mouths.

This Shit River kills
us, a little each day.
What can we do?

This is our home.

Never, forever

Kathy Chenault

The visions descend
with vengeance.
The words of victims
empty into decay.

The scenes, more
than readers want to see
in their newspapers
with morning coffee.
(That's what the editor said.)

There is no way
to say: Here is Rwanda,
just love this land
rugged in earth steam.
The peaks, now shrouded,
the hollowing of souls,
defy that prayer.

Writing genocide,
we drove those roads
across fields cutting
deep creases into horizons
baptised in rituals
of fire and flood.

Stilled, and yet
after years and years
those images turn and turn –
my melancholy, my madness.

No one heard
the boy's pleas

as he ran bleeding
into the valley
of banana groves,
haunted and gnarled.

Somehow, bony arms,
legs escaped, escaped
the frenzy of death clutching
at the country church.

Fathers and brothers sent them,
believing in God's refuge.
Thousands died, their bodies
shredded into the wooden floor.

Bones and skulls decompose
in a mass of bloodied clothes
and scattered pots and books –
all the flock could carry.
A pencil lies
on the floor.

My words fail, fall,
rot in notebooks, shelved.
I stare into that,
but can't describe it.
Couldn't imagine it, even,
except there it was.

These were people.
This was flesh, molting
from red to brown
to vapour, foul, enduring.

The Virgin Mary, cast
against a mural of too-blue
sky and surreal hues,
rests as witness
to the sacrifice of innocents.

That 9-year-old boy recalls
men binding his mother,
brothers, sisters, with
cord and rope. The men
thrust knives and spears
into the hands of children
and yelled: "Kill! Kill!"

A neighbour, the father
    of a schoolmate, now
    gargoyled in hate
    raises a machete higher
    and higher. The blade
    hacks the boy's skull,
    his blood oozes cold
onto bare shoulders.
He runs and runs and runs.

    Those painted skies
    pale at the altar
    where spirits in silhouette
    look down on me.

    I can't forget that.
    Never.
    Now forever.

K.M. Chenault is a writer based in Johannesburg. Her work has appeared in several publications, including *The Dallas Morning News*, *Newsday*, *U.S. News & World Report*, *Newsweek* and *BusinessWeek*. Previously, she worked for The Associated Press as an International Desk supervisor, as a reporter at the UN, and as a foreign correspondent based in Beijing.

Rose, Sierra Leone

Adam Roberts

Some reporting trips throw up a memorable person who is strong, witty or defiant enough to linger in the back of your mind for years. At random, unguarded moments you find yourself asking "What ever happened to bald Mr Kazzimi in Hama who dared say a little about Syrian politics?" or "Is Mr Jish still counting the books of his crumbling library in Massawa?"

In November 1998 I was in Freetown, racking up encounters with people who left me wide-eyed. Clifford and Winston – local writers – told how they had survived in Sierra Leone's capital when murderous rebels snatched power a year before. Nance, employed by the United Nations, interrupted a story of how her family escaped rape and killings to show me a great cotton tree thick with fruit bats. Graffiti on street-side rubble told of passing violent years – *"de throw society"*, "thug life", "black justice", *"rod to pis"*. Incongruously a new sign on the airport road gave a "Welcome to Sierra Leone, the Athens of West Africa."

To reach the second city, Bo, I passed through 25 roadblocks and dozens of interviews. A young ex-rebel displayed a handless stump and described his "long sleeve" amputation by angry fellow fighters. His crime: being noisy one night in a bush camp. A tailor, he despaired of working. At a small town, Mile 91, an adopted boy, Omo George, refused to return to his distant village; he feared his family would kill him for his acts as a fighter. The fourteen-year-old had fought for three years. Another ex-rebel said he was "fighting for freedom". What is freedom? "Free food, free electricity, free housing, free schooling."

All were victims of a failed country. More precisely, of violent guerrillas led by a former army photographer, Foday Sankoh. Though he had been arrested, his rebels were pushing closer to the capital. They were in the bush as I drove north. They traded diamonds for weapons; backed by neighbouring Liberia they outgunned the Nigerian and government soldiers. Child-fighters were used by all sides; militias did their killing among civilians, villagers, farmers, those they claimed to protect.

Less than two weeks of reporting and travelling and I was exhausted – deflated by heat and humidity, worn out by never-ending tales of mutilation and torture. Nor did I know that by New Year, a few weeks later, rebels would again swarm into Freetown. Gunfire, misplaced Nigerian bombs, and rampaging soldiers would kill another 4 000 people in just a few days. A street where I bought shillings, a little up from the tree with plump fruit bats, would be flattened. A hotel that a friend had recommended was already a blackened shell; a few weeks later it was barely a crater.

But by then I wrote of Sierra Leone's renewed war from safe and distant London. One woman came to mind each time I called aid workers, diplomats, missionaries and others who still cowered in the rebel-free corners of the city, or who sheltered next door in Guinea.

Rose had found me at the very end of my trip, after several days of knocking at my hotel door in Freetown. The distant cousin of a man I had spoken to, once, by phone, in London, she wanted to tell me her story. She and her extended family of 28 had all been captured by rebels some years before. They lived with the soldiers in the jungle, dying by turn of disease and hunger. Small boys joined units to inflict violent punishments and keep discipline; small girls cooked and carried. "We were living just between the act of heaven and the act of hell. When the rebels laughed we laughed, when they sat there quietly we sat there quietly."

For several hours late into one evening, Rose, 39, described life as a slave to the rebels. She was articulate, educated and direct; her story summed up much of the war. She had a unique point of view. Literate, she got a job as a rebel cleric, issued permits and kept notes for the army, using typewriters looted from small mining offices. That usefulness kept her alive. "When captured you were asked what you had done, where you'd been. They made a list of who had been where, and if they went to attack a place they chose someone from there to lead it. If you refused to move they shot, slaughtered or beat you to death."

For two years she was bound to the moving army, keeping to the bush, never the road. All but nine of her family died; most starved. Her father was taken by another militia. Her sister fled to Liberia. Her own life was destroyed. All evening she spoke, faltering but persistent; a calm voice that sometimes fell silent in the middle of a description. For hours we sat at a dark table on the hotel veranda, the Atlantic within earshot, two warm cokes untouched on a low table, the only light a feeble gas-fired lamp. When guests passed – diamond traders, gun smugglers and aid workers in different guises – she fell defensively silent.

Her escape came after a battle; she was grabbed by government troops, jailed and beaten. Again she feared for her life, but came to Freetown for a job with a missionary caring for orphans. She saw rebel soldiers at times on

Freetown's streets, but they were in civilian clothes. Those infiltrated men would re-emerge as fighters a few weeks after our conversation, to rampage beside invading rebels.

As the evening ended Rose fell quiet. There was one more thing she would say. In the bush, on pain of being strapped high to a branch and beaten, civilians who travelled with the rebels learned by rote the Revolutionary United Front "national" anthem. Did the rebels think they fought for freedom? She began a short rendition, not a song but a rhythmic whisper, fearful someone in the hotel might hear. Without pause – she had learned it dutifully – the rebel anthem filled the gloom; chill words in the dark:

"Go and tell the president that Sierra Leone is my home; Go and tell the president my parents they see me no more; When fighting in the battlefield I'm fighting forever. Every Sierra Leonean is fighting for his land …"

It was said to have been written by lecturers from Freetown University. Its words were for children to sing; for use by an army of duped and violent rebels to justify children killing frightened peasant farmers. Rose recited the words flawlessly, yet seemed to me a model of an undaunted human. How did she think about those rebel fighters, her former captors? "I will forgive but I can't forget. Now I ask, how will we manage to climb another step? I'm still living, praise God."

Adam Roberts is the Southern Africa correspondent of _The Economist_. He has been based in Johannesburg, South Africa, since June 2001. Before that he reported on African and other developing countries for _The Economist_, from London.

He was co-editor, with Heidi Holland, of a compendium of journalist commentaries on Johannesburg, _From Jo'burg to Jozi, Stories from Africa's Infamous City_, (Penguin Books), 2002.

Brown shoes don't make it

Lukas De Vos

They were lying there neatly and inconspicuously. Red-brown like the volcanic earth and shining after the rain: two shoes with hardly used soles. Peaceful, but a strange sight in amongst the plastic trash, the withered manioc leaves, and the sharp sounds of the crickets in the afternoon heat.

For several days I had been on the road with Kasereka. He was from the Nande tribe living along the borders of the then Zaire. The Nande are traditionally traders, not fond of armies, political membership, and anything that smells of bureaucracy.

Kasereka had affiliated himself with a group of Banyarwanda who were advancing with the RPF from Uganda, along the east side of Lake Kivu, from Kisoro via Ruhengeri, Gisenyi and Kibuye. They just passed Cyangugu. I had known Kasereka for years. I called him Kas.

He had driven us in a jeep through the mountains around Uvira at night. No lights – like a bat over the small paths. In daylight you couldn't avoid the potholes or the rocks along the edge, so lights or no lights didn't make much difference. And Kas was driving, barefoot and smiling.

Sometime long before, I had climbed the Nyaragongo. It still had a bubbling lava lake, 4 000 metres high. Climbing next to me was Lucien from Bruges. Sweating like an ox. And his drinking buddy Basjier, a former sergeant (or was it colonel?) from the Syrian army. I never dared ask why he left the army. Sacked or disillusioned? But Basjier wasn't too lucky. During a game of throwing knives at his hotel room door, a knife bounced back and destroyed his eye. And a few years later some disease killed him. Bilharzia, glandular fever or AIDS. Nobody knows.

But here on the flanks of the Nyaragongo he was going strong. And Lucien was singing, which drove most of us crazy. He got his strength from the crate of Primus beer one of our guides was carrying on his shoulders. He was walking barefoot. Luckily for him the 24 one-litre bottles were emptied in a few hours, to the delight of our sherpa, as the weight on his shoulders was reduced every 150 metres or so.

I wasn't drinking any alcohol back then – silly in a country where water breeds diseases. I even drank water from a little lake where elephants came to quench their thirst. But the elephants had left the volcano some days earlier. Followed by the Pygmies; a warning sign that the volcano was about to erupt. On top of the Nyaragongo all 16 of us sought refuge in a metal cabin made for eight. That night a storm unleashed its havoc on the volcano. The wind played with the metal plates of the cabin. Temperatures dropped and the mountain rumbled like continuous mortar fire. But Lucien and Basjier just kept on joking. I was in pain, my stomach in turmoil. And every so often I had to run outside to find release behind a rock, in ice-cold rain. There on top of the mountain, it felt as though the volcano was echoing my intestinal disorders.

Whenever we entered a village there was the obligatory banana beer. How I hated the foam on top of it. Once, with a hangover and a splitting headache we continued our journey down to Lake Tanganyika.

I jumped into the lake for a refreshing swim. Kas declared me insane. "How can you swim? It's full of strange bugs, you can drown, and there are crocodiles hiding in the reed along the banks. They kill several children every year."

Sometimes I thought the locals were only afraid of three things: water, snakes and witchcraft. Wearing an amulet for protection and having been blessed with invincibility by a local magician, sometimes they get shot. This idea of invincibility seems to be linked to every civil war in Africa. From Biafra to Liberia; from Rwanda to Sudan. The child soldiers of Charles Taylor or Prince Johnston put on wigs and pyjamas over their jeans and Nikes, to flow like ghosts across barbed wire and through tanks. The savannas and mountains were full of untouchable ghosts with their Adidas sneakers, polished boots, callouses on their feet.

But if shoes lie along the road, then something's wrong. And much more is wrong when they lie there polished.

In Burundi, in 1972, the teachers had been targeted. They were ordered to gather at the army barracks. I would have run away to escape the bullet, or the machete. But the teachers arrived at the barracks the next morning in pressed pants and shirts, ties and polished shoes. "If I have to die I will wear my best clothes," one of them told me. He passed through the doors and never returned.

Shoes again made their mark in Vukovar in the former Yugoslavia. It was ruined. A ghost town. We had heard rumours of Croatian militias – "rats", they called them - climbing out of the sewers at night to cut the throats of the remaining Serbs. But we didn't see anyone. Not even a dog running around. Then, in between collapsed walls, kicked-open doors and piles of bricks, I saw it – a new shoe shop. I still do not understand why.

There were no people in the town. No customers. It was just a statement. I, the trading Serb, in the annexed parts of Croatia, do business. Where my shoes are stands my flag.

The shoes along the Ruzizi were pointing upwards, like arms spread to the air. I looked further. There were legs linked to the shoes and a big belly and flies around a large wound. The eyes were gone. The body ripped from shoulder to loin. Lower down in the curve of the river more bodies. Swollen, stuck in the grass along the water. The smell of wild honey, manure and acacias. I gag. It isn't my first body. That was a drowned cat in the canal near home. White, no hair. Swollen and stinking.

I throw some earth on the body. I cut a banana leave from a tree and put it over the unrepenting shoes.

Lukas De Vos is Senior Journalist Foreign Affairs and International Relations at VRT-RVI, World Service Radio of Flanders (Belgium). He read at the universities of Bukavu, Antwerp, Melbourne and Brussels. He has published on literature, film, economics and politics.

Katlehong, before and after

Tom Cohen

A January afternoon in Katlehong was always hot, with the sun burning down on roads of red-brown dust.

This particular day, January 8, 1995, was hotter than usual. Maybe it was the cloudless sky and a dead calm that seemed to stifle any sound or movement.

Or maybe it was something else. A year earlier, in the same place, Abdul Shariff died in an afternoon of gunfire. Memories of diving for cover and panting in the dirt jumbled together with the image of his body on a hospital gurney, his Nikon F4 dented by the lone bullet that entered his lower back and exited through the chest.

Abdul was a freelance photographer covering a visit to the township by two top African National Congress leaders a few months before South Africa's first truly democratic election. They chose Katlehong's Dikole section because of the violence – the mayhem of shootings, stabbings and other slaughter that claimed lives daily.

As the election that was certain to bring the black majority to power approached, the violence increased. It was political in nature, and only later did the suspicions of police collusion in arming Inkatha Freedom Party supporters to fight ANC loyalists get confirmed.

When ANC Secretary General Cyril Ramaphosa and Communist Party leader Joe Slovo arrived that day, they walked down the rutted roads toward a clearing separating the township houses from the Mazibuko worker's hostel full of Zulus loyal to Inkatha.

A pack of journalists trailed them, with only a few wearing the bulletproof vests that were standard equipment in working the townships. This was supposed to be a political sideshow, after all. The first shots sounded like balloons popping in the distance. In an instant, everyone was flat on the ground or ducking behind the nearest wall.

Shouts filled the air, and young township "comrades", or ANC vigilantes in Katlehong, appeared from nowhere, most with the weapon of choice – AK-47 assault rifles.

More shooting erupted, much louder as the comrades returned fire toward the hostel half a kilometre away. People piled on each other in taking cover, afraid to move because no one could tell who was firing.

Puffs of dirt or chips flying off walls showed where the bullets were striking. It took about 20 minutes for comrades to direct people from their bellies on the streets to safe cover in nearby houses.

Abdul, a small man of quiet efficiency, had worked for various newspapers and agencies, and at 31 seemed poised to propel his career forward with the upcoming election. He was known for sensitive photographs, and for getting the job done without unnecessary risk.

After the initial barrage of gunfire, Abdul followed another journalist in a dash across an open lot, probably for a better vantage point. His scream was the first indication he was hit. It was impossible to know the source of the shot.

He was dead by the time his body arrived at the nearest hospital, in Tokoza.

Friends and colleagues shouted profanities and stamped in disgust and anger, but for those living in Katlehong, it was all too familiar. One woman showed a scar on her thigh where she got shot while waiting in line for bread one day. Another told journalists taking cover near her house: "We don't walk on the street. This happens every day."

A year later, the houses and nearby worker's hostel, still housing Zulu miners, looked the same. The neighbourhood was different, though. People walked the streets, passing a yellow trailer that housed a satellite police office.

Nelson Mandela was now president, and the fighting that killed Abdul and thousands of others had ceased with the election that brought the ANC to power.

On a dusty township road, a group of young Dikole residents led two visitors toward the Mazibuko hostel. One man, Keith Dakile, said in a soft voice: "I didn't use to come this way."

He remembered the day the previous year as "very tense, man, very tense". Now there was calm, a sense of normalcy, in the unrelenting heat.

"Peace has prevailed," Dakile said.

The group approached the hostel, where several young men stood in the shadow of a doorway, out of the sun. Within minutes, the Zulu hostel dwellers and their visitors sat on darkened steps inside, passing around joints and bottles of soda.

Dikole men pointed to bullet marks in the hostel's concrete walls and laughed that maybe they fired the shots. One patiently translated a hostel dweller's Zulu.

"I'm not clear on what stopped the fighting," said Thabo Sabelelo, 29, stretching a slingshot strap around his arm. "My main concern is to find a job. I didn't like the violence."

Outside the hostel, two police reservists in blue uniforms with matching bulletproof vests patrolled a pedestrian bridge over train tracks. One of them, Joseph August, bore scars on his face and neck from fights with Inkatha when he was an ANC comrade. Now he stood where, a year earlier, he would have been killed, no questions asked.

"Those times were not like this time," August said, as Dikole and Mazibuko neighbours stood around chatting. "I'm just enjoying it."

Tom Cohen covered southern Africa for The Associated Press from 1990 until 1998.

My second dead body

Stephanie Scawen

The first dead body I ever saw was that of an old man who keeled over and died of a heart attack in the lobby of the local newspaper I worked for when I was 19.

It was a tiny office. The entrance to the editorial department was through the kitchen.

I could lean back in my chair and hit my head on the wall behind me. We still worked on typewriters with carbon sheets to make copies. I sneezed constantly from the newspaper dust and cigarette smoke. Those were the days when you could still smoke at your desk. The risk of fire never seemed to occur to us.

Some things of course never change. The advertising department's office was three times the size of ours. The number of staff five times – mostly young women – all big hair, shoulder pads and stiletto heels – who'd spend the day making coffee in the kitchen behind me gossiping about their latest date. They had company cars to drive around in. I had a clapped out Ford Fiesta, which refused to start at the first hint of cool weather.

The reception area was really just a desk with a high front. There wasn't even room for chairs for people to sit.

I'd been filing photographs behind the reception area when the old man came in. I didn't actually see him fall, just my friend Julie rushing to give him mouth to mouth. She spoke later of the death rattle he made; his final breath as he hit the floor – the air forced from his lungs by the impact.

The old man looked remarkably composed for someone who'd just exited this life in such a rapid and unexpected manner. He lay there, apparently asleep, but definitely dead.

He collapsed right in the doorway, which was unfortunate as it meant anyone who wanted to either enter or leave the newspaper offices literally had to step over the stiffening corpse. A problem compounded by the fact the ambulance crew would not move him until a doctor had pronounced him dead. A doctor had been called but would be at least 30 minutes.

'How dead do you have to be?' I wondered as I stood in the lift lobby warning new arrivals to the 4th floor, that: "We have an unfortunate incident ongoing, and perhaps Madam might like to come back in an hour or so."

Standing guard to prevent more untimely deaths from shocked old ladies who wanted to place a "For Sale" ad in my paper was not how I had envisaged my journalistic career progressing. But then I suppose part of the reason I decided to become a journalist was for its unpredictability.

It was another 13 years before I saw my second dead body. I was in East Timor with a TV current affairs crew for the Independence Referendum. The security situation had been deteriorating daily.

Food became hard to come by. Breakfast, when we'd first arrived, had been delicious Portuguese-style bread rolls, which we devoured with mugs of instant black coffee. After a week, breakfast simply failed to appear.

The streets were always dusty. It hadn't rained in Dili for years, the locals said. Small groups of men would hang around on street corners. I was never sure if they were looking for trouble or trying to avoid it. But you could tell when something bad was going to happen, even if you couldn't see it.

The militias played a wonderful mind-game. They threatened journalists with guns and machetes. They would attack this hotel, we'd hear. They'd rape the white women. The militias had already destroyed the offices of the CNRT – about 100 yards from where we were staying.

It became difficult to work, difficult to unravel fact from rumour.

A few days later we arranged an interview with Basilio Araujo – a pro-Indonesian militia spokesman. His compound was next to a church. We sat on the benches outside, facing the seafront smoking cheap Indonesian Marlboros while we waited. It was dusk and the mosquitoes were starting to bite.

For a man representing groups already accused of intimidation and violence, Araujo spoke calmly and with moderation. He wanted to bring up his kids in a time of peace, he told us. But as he spoke violence was breaking out on the other side of town around the UN compound. People were attacked. Shots were fired.

Suddenly a Catholic nun appeared and whispered to us to visit the small medical clinic behind the church. She thought we might like to see what was going on.

We wrapped up our interview and made our way to the clinic. There we discovered doctors desperately trying to save the life of a man who'd been shot through the neck.

The medics were vigorously pumping his chest – trying to restart his heart. No defibrillators here. Finally the doctors gave up trying to revive the man. He was dead, they said, from blood loss.

As I watched I remember thinking how clean the man looked considering he had just bled to death.

In the room next door a woman had just given birth.

Stephanie Scawen is an award-winning, television current affairs producer, based in Hong Kong. Her work has taken her across Asia, covering a broad range of human rights, cultural and political issues.

Everything is under control

Jeff Koinange

We find ourselves in a convoy of vehicles heading to the front line. Rebel forces had tried to march on Monrovia before government troops forced them back. A shaky truce is now in effect, awaiting an official signing by the various factions fighting for control.

The government, meanwhile, wants to show us it is in firm control of the city. President Charles Taylor has dispatched his own personal security team to guide us to the front. The team is led by Lt. Gen. Macsfarian Jibba, a 6-foot-4-inch, 300-pound, 30-year-old former child soldier. His colleagues know him by his nom-de-guerre, "Bulldog".

Today Bulldog bears the scars of the latest rebel incursion: a bandaged arm where a bullet lodged itself between his wrist and elbow. But he smiles and brags about how bravely he and his men fought to save their capital from attack.

"Monrovia is a hellhole," Bulldog says. "Anyone trying to enter our capital illegally pays the ultimate price."

Evidence of that price abounds. Dead rebel soldiers are everywhere, their bodies a reminder of the brutality of war. I count over two dozen badly decomposing bodies strewn along the roadside. Government casualties have long since been removed.

Suddenly, we hear shots in the jungle beyond. We jump into our vehicles ready to bolt back to the capital. Bulldog smiles again. "Don't worry. It's just my boys letting me know they're around."

Out of the thick bush emerge several scary individuals armed to the teeth with enough of an arsenal to level a small town. Everything from the standard issue AK-47s to rocket-propelled grenades and surface-to-air missiles.

As the men draw closer, I notice something else, two of them are wearing wigs, one blond and the other brunette, giving them a bizarre appearance that would not be unwelcome in a circus. Another has mounted a blue flashing light on his head, the kind usually found atop police vehicles. In this war, it seems fighters believe the more creative they are, the better their fighting skills.

Among the newly arrived troops, we learn, is Gen. "Cuckoo" Dennis. It is said that "Cuckoo" refers to how crazy he acts when he makes a kill.

According to legend, he likes to rip the heart out of a victim and squeeze the blood down his throat to drink down the strength of the enemy and possess his soul.

Cuckoo whips out his cell phone. Even the most hardened fighter in the jungle, it seems, has to reach out and touch a family member or two.

We move on. We're about to meet the commander of the Liberian Armed Forces, who is hunkered down with his troops at the front line. We find him holding court at Saint Paul's Bridge, the gateway into the capital. He is Lt. Gen. Benjamin Yeaten, alias "Fifty". I ask one of the soldiers why they call him Fifty and receive a blank stare in return.

Suddenly one of them breaks into song. I learn the words go something like "Anyone who says no more Taylor, we kill you like a dog". The Taylor it refers to is none other than embattled President Taylor, himself a former rebel-leader, who takes credit for starting a vicious civil war in 1989 that lasted seven years and cost over 200 000 lives.

A year after his war ended, Liberia held internationally monitored elections overwhelmingly won by Taylor. Even he has a nickname: "Chief". Bulldog tells Fifty and Cuckoo that we are here at Chief's request. We are welcomed like old friends.

Fifty looks no more than 40. He's diminutive and soft-spoken, and as I quickly surmise, commands both the fear and respect of his troops. I ask him for a status report on the latest rebel invasion. He too smiles easily.

"Everything is under control," he says. "We've managed to secure our city and drive the marauders back to where they belong ... the bush."

His men respond with an ear-piercing roar.

These guys are battle-hungry, I decide, the kind who wouldn't easily shy away from a good fire-fight.

The nation whose very name was supposed to symbolise freedom is anything but free.

Monrovia is like the set of "Mad Max," the 1979 Mel Gibson film in which everything seemed in a perpetual state of destruction or chaos. No building in sight has escaped hits by mortar fire. Gaping holes replace door frames. Forget about windows. There are none. One-time luxury apartment buildings are home to thousands of squatters seeking shelter from another brutal and vicious civil war.

When he had his turn as Organization of African Unity chairman in 1979, President William Tolbert built the Hotel Africa. So keen was he to impress his African colleagues that he built 52 European-style chalets along the beach, one for each African president and his entourage.

198

Back then the swimming pool was also a remarkable sight, built in the shape of the African continent, with a sunken liquor bar all the way from Somalia to Rwanda, with a lifeguard station high above Liberia, of course. Now, long abandoned in the rages of war, Hotel Africa is literally a shell, a carcass that no vulture would give a second glance.

One morning in April 1980, Tolbert woke to the sound of gunfire. Before he could summon help, a gun had been pointed to his head and the trigger pulled back. The man holding the gun was Master Sgt. Samuel Doe and Liberia's next president.

The country's largest sports stadium and home of the national football team, the Lone Stars, was later named for him. The same stadium is now home to thousands of refugees. The sound of cheering football fans has been replaced by the chilling cries of hungry children, exhausted and hopeless adults and mothers pleading for the world to intervene.

Doe faced his own rebellion and vowed to fight to the bitter end. He spent the last hours of his life screaming for mercy as he was tortured by rebel forces.

Charles Taylor also swore never to give up.

(Some weeks later he fled Liberia for the sanctuary of Nigeria.)

History has an uncanny and wicked sense of humour.

Jeff Koinange is Kenyan and CNN's bureau chief in Lagos, Nigeria. Before joining CNN, Koinange worked for Reuters Television from 1995 to 2001, covering most of the African continent. In 1999, Koinange was a finalist in the Prix Bayeux for his coverage of the war in Sierra Leone. He is also on the judging committee of the CNN African Journalist of the Year Award presented each year in Johannesburg.

The tuk-tuk wallah

Gilbert Ahnee

It was not very late when Robert left the party, at around 11, which was quite early for him. Although he hated walking in the countryside, he could walk for hours at night in metropolitan cities, alone, left to his thoughts and fantasies. He had done so in Paris, London, New York, even in Bombay. Nevertheless, after having left the hotel's premises, he quickly realised how imprudent it would be to venture across Colombo without really knowing where to find places of interest. He quite liberally agreed to pay 20 dollars to a *tuk-tuk wallah* for a one-hour drive to see the sites.

"Here, Colombo, very sexy girls Sir, you wishing, I take you."

The three-wheeler had not gone further than twenty yards when the driver came with that oft-made proposal. Robert said that he was not interested.

"Then, I taking you to Buddhist temple, Sir, very nice, very beautiful."

Indeed it was. Right from his arrival in Sri Lanka, Robert had been impressed by the quality of architecture, even of the most simple buildings. He was tempted to attribute that purity of line, that incredible balance and harmony to some imagined old Buddhist treatise on numbers.

"Your country, Sir?"

"Mauritius."

"Ah, Muslim, Muslim – me too Muslim, my name Nawaz, Sir."

"Allah Ackar!"

Robert felt that the man could have heard Malaysia instead of Mauritius. He was interested to know how Muslims related to others in this country. He also felt that his little knowledge of The Book might help him to see this man with more respect than one would a filthy driving pimp.

"Me taking you to Hindu temple Sir?"

"Houn … Tamize Kovil, Am'a …"

Sri Lankan Muslims spoke Tamil – a touch of Thiruvalluvar's language could also help.

The *kovil* was stunning. The *gopura* was in the purest Madurai dravidian style but the façade also had two spires, one with a clock, as if the whole thing had been inspired by early XIXth Century South Indian neo–

gothic architecture.

"You take me to the *Jummah Masjid* now."

Robert was not in a position to know whether the mosque he was taken to was really Colombo's leading one; however, the neighbourhood was predominantly Muslim.

"My house near, Sir, you come, see my family."

Visiting that man's family was, for a journalist who was staying in a five-star hotel, a unique opportunity of touching the grassest or the rootest grass-root Sri Lankan destitution. Robert felt a bit uneasy at the voyeurism that it entailed but, God, he was a journo.

After walking through a narrow passage between a tea stall and a tyre repair shop, he was finally ushered into a four-by three-metre room in which a grease-stained piece of plastic foam thrown on a ramshackle metallic bed-like structure was the only sign of comfort. From the attached kitchen came the *tuk-tuk wallah*'s wife. She must have been in her mid-40's at the most, but she bore the mark of neglect and devastation that befalls women in such living conditions.

The man had said that he had two children. In no time, a young boy appeared, saying he was 12. Robert son's also was 12. A father deprived of his son's company for nearly a week can easily become emotional when he comes across a boy of the same age. The kid's name was Naruz and his English went a bit further than his father's. He pretended to be in his last year of primary. Robert's son was in his first year of secondary. The boy said he studied IT in school, Excel and Word, Sir, and that he desperately wanted a computer. Robert felt he was touching one of this world's distressing inequalities, an emotionally loaded illustration of the digital divide.

"How much does a computer cost, here?"

"Sri Lankan Rs 25 000, Sir."

That was less than $300 US. While walking back to the *tuk-tuk*, Robert knew that his wife would once more tell him that he was naïve, that it was so much safer to give to charities – but if he charged it to one of his credit cards ... Barclays debited only 5% of the total credit each month ... it would go unnoticed ...

Surprisingly, while the man's English was totally broken, his wife was more articulate, leading Robert to think that she had had a formal education. And he wondered how come that woman had married that quite brutish chap pulling his *tuk-tuk* starter.

"Your wife is well educated, no? She speaks good English."

"You wanting me calling my wife, Sir, she going to hotel with you. "

Robert refused to construe this last maladroit assembly of semi-understood words as a further attempt at caring for his night's comfort.

When they finally reached the hotel, as it had been initially agreed, Robert gave the guy a twenty dollar note.

"Twenty dollar for one hour, Sir, more than one hour driving, Sir."

"But you took me to your place, and I gave ten dollars to your son."

That was perhaps a bit mean, but Robert felt the ride he had been taken for was quite a crooked one.

"You give my son, Sir, not me."

"How much do I owe you, then?"

"Fifty dollars, Sir, I'm a poor man, Sir."

Robert suddenly hated that man. He finally admitted that the wretched *tuk-tuk* driver had tried to sell him his wife. How could such a dark soul inhabit a human being? Being spared the time for a further argument spent in such an individual's company was certainly worth the supplementary thirty dollars he was claiming. Robert gave him his fifty bucks and left without a word.

The next day, over breakfast, Robert told a friend how betrayed he had felt, how disgusting he judged a man capable of introducing a total stranger into his family's privacy while also trying to trade his wife for a few bucks, and finally claiming an outrageously unfair charge for a single *tuk-tuk* drive.

And then, all of a sudden, it occurred to him that he had seen no phone in the room, that the man had asked the boy to give HIS phone number. It was now too clear: good massage, sexy Sri Lankan girls and beautiful Russian white women had provoked no interest from him. It may still have been unfair, but Robert felt that Nawaz must surely have concluded that with such a blasé customer at least a young boy might have been alluring.

Editor-in-Chief of *Le Mauricien* and winner of the 2000 Commonwealth Press Union's Astor Award, Gilbert Ahnee began writing in 1970. After studying in India for two years and in France for five years, he became a full-time journalist working in France and Mauritius.

Men don't cry

Barnaby Phillips

Imagine being in one of the saddest cities in the world, and meeting a man of overwhelming charm, who lights up your life. That's what happened to me in Huambo, in central Angola – a man whose home is in ruins, whose family has been killed, but a man who cannot stop smiling and laughing. Not because he is stupid – in fact he is very clever, and well educated, but because he is brave enough not to look back and knows he cannot dwell on the past. His name is Sebastiao; he is handsome, and he speaks English fluently, although it is his third, maybe his fourth, language. He is a doctor.

You might remember Huambo. In 1993 and 1994, it flickered briefly on the world's consciousness. Angola's war was in its fiercest stage, and Huambo, that elegant city in the central highlands, was in the eye of the storm. Government and rebel UNITA troops fought on the streets. UNITA pushed the Government out; then the Government pushed UNITA out. Shells and mortars crashed into Huambo's colonial buildings, and smashed the trees along its wide avenues. In the following years, the war ebbed and flowed, but Huambo never recovered. The city the Portuguese had called "Nova Lisboa" was a shadow of its former self; a city of refugees and empty factories, a city without cars or electricity, cut off from the fertile countryside, where UNITA rebels were still at large. Its railway station and its university were abandoned. Then, finally, in 2002, Angola's war came to an end. And that's when Sebastiao came back to Huambo. Because this sensitive, engaging man had been out there in the bush all those years, with those dreaded UNITA rebels.

How do I reconcile the two? I know Angola well, and I know what evil UNITA did – the torture, the rape, the burnings. I once met an old man in rags whose eyes had been gouged out by UNITA soldiers because they suspected him of being a government spy. Now he stumbles alone down the streets of Huambo, begging passers-by to take pity. Cruelty without reason; for the last ten years of the war, UNITA fought on only because of the senseless ambition of its leader, Jonas Savimbi, a man ready to drag his country down with him if he could not achieve his dream of becoming president.

I had been introduced to Sebastiao by a UN official, who said he would be a useful person to take to the demobilisation camps outside Huambo, where the UNITA soldiers were waiting to be disarmed and sent home. The UN official was spot on – Sebastiao had an easy, natural authority in the camps. It was obvious that the soldiers liked him, and respected him.

I was intrigued. "Why did you carry on fighting for so long, in such a destructive war?" Looking back, I realise it was a naïve question, the kind of question an outsider or someone with no comprehension of what a civil war is, would ask. When war breaks out in your city, and you cannot run away, you take sides in order to survive. And when that war drags on for 28 years, you are trapped by the decisions you took at the beginning of the conflict, and which side of the lines you are stuck on, and staying alive is all that matters. Maybe that's what Sebastiao might have said, if we had got to know each other better. But we only had one day together, and, instead, he laughed, and would only say, "The war was very terrible".

I wanted to know more. What was it like at the end, those last two years, when UNITA knew it was losing, but was still fighting on, and the soldiers were hungry, and running out of ammunition, but always on the move. "Remember, I am a doctor. My job was not to fight, but to try and cure the sick and the wounded. But you are right; the last months were very terrible. I had no drugs; I had no clean instruments. We did operations under the trees, using sharp knives. Often we were ambushed, we just had to keep on running. We ate the mushrooms that we found in the forest."

We were on the outskirts of Huambo, driving up a long avenue, in the shade of mature trees, to the remains of a Portuguese villa. "This was where I spent my childhood," said Sebastiao. The house was gutted, but it didn't require much imagination to picture what it once had been. The tiled roof was still intact. There was a garden full of fruit trees, with a path running through the long grass to a well. "This was my brother's room," said Sebastiao, pointing through the remains of a window frame into the shadows, "and this was my sister's. I was born here; we all grew up here together. It seems so long ago." I asked what had happened to them. "They died, both of them. My brother was a brigadier with UNITA – he was shot in 1993. And my sister died in childbirth the year before". Sebastiao led me to the bottom of the garden, and showed me a low brick structure partially covered by undergrowth. "This is the bunker, where we used to hide when the government planes flew over, and dropped bombs. By then things were bad, and we knew we had to leave this place."

The sun was low in the sky, and we were walking down the avenue back to the car. "Maybe I can rebuild this house," he mused. "How do you say in English ... where there is will, there is a way? But we need peace,

204

without peace nothing is possible. I've tried to rebuild it before, but the war always came back." I admired Sebastiao, but I still found him inscrutable, I still hadn't managed to puncture his defences. I took a punt. "I don't know how you can stop yourself from crying whenever you come back to this house, with all the memories of your family, and of what Huambo was". Sebastiao looked at me. "Men don't cry. Even if I am crying inside, outside I must smile." And he was still laughing as we got back into the car.

A BBC correspondent, Barnaby Phillips has been reporting and living in Africa for most of the past decade. He has been based in Mozambique, Angola, Nigeria and now South Africa. Originally from London, he grew up in Kenya.

Johnny Thaljieh – the friend I never met

Inigo Gilmore

The unexpected and unforgettable encounter with Johnny Thaljieh, burnt itself deeply into my mind. It occurred in October 2001, a year after the second Palestinian *intifada* erupted. Israeli troops had entered Bethlehem following the assassination of Rehavam Ze'evi, the Israeli tourism minister and the town was now a war zone. With many other journalists I went to report on a peace march, led by religious leaders, through the town of Jesus's birth, a brave yet ultimately futile appeal for an end to the madness that was now unfolding around us. In the three days prior to the peace march, 14 people had been killed in the West Bank town of Bethlehem, and there were fears many more may follow.

With crosses held aloft, priests and nuns marched through the checkpoint in a swirl of colour and soon we were walking through the cobbled streets of Beit Jala, heading toward the centre of Bethlehem. Women and children waved from the balconies amid the clamour of pealing church bells, being tolled in solidarity. For a moment the siege was almost forgotten as the marchers smiled and waved back. Then 12-year-old Sharbel Boutto somberly emerged from the throng, clutching a poster of his friend. The young boy was sad and confused.

I gazed at the poster and Johnny gazed back at me. I was looking at a young man, no more than a boy in fact, with chubby, almost angelic features. He appeared full of life, bursting with vitality. His eyes sparkled, speaking of hopes and dreams. His young friend told me Johnny wanted to be a priest, talking as if I were about to meet Johnny. It was not to be. This was a poster of Johnny "the martyr" whose wish would never be realised … He had been dead for three days, shot as he stood in a street after attending mass. He was just 17.

Through Sharbel and others I sketched the details of what had happened. The teenager had just left the Church of the Nativity, the basilica built on the site of Jesus's birth, following the late afternoon Greek Orthodox service, where he served as an altar boy. He met and talked briefly with his father in Manger Square, then ran into his cousin Elias and his toddler nephew, Michael. Johnny, as always, cheerful and smiling, flung the tiny boy playfully in the air. As he was holding Michael aloft, above his head, a single, high velocity bullet penetrated under his left armpit, piercing his heart and exiting the other side of his body. He didn't stand a chance. As he stumbled, bleeding profusely, he managed somehow to set the screaming child on the ground before he collapsed, dying minutes later as his father, who rushed to the scene, cradled him in his arms like a baby. Poignantly Johnny breathed his last just metres from the manger where Mary had once cradled the baby Jesus.

As we entered Manger Square, Sharbel pointed out the spot where Johnny had been hit, now an impromptu shrine. "Johnny and I used to play together, but now he is gone," said the tearful Sharbel, staring at me imploringly as if somehow, in some magical way, I could bring Johnny back to him. "I don't understand. Why did they do this?"

It was a question that now burdened my mind too – and one for which I had no answer. Why? Why this senseless killing? His death and the circumstances surrounding it, touched me deeply, very deeply. A few days later I went to visit Johnny's family at their house just off Manger Square. His mother, Suzan, wore the black of mourning. In the 10 months since I had been working in the Holy Land I had encountered far too many similarly appalling scenes of grief, meeting Israel and Palestinian families trying to come to terms with the loss of their loved ones.

Time and again during those encounters the families spoke of their thirst for revenge, how they lusted to avenge the killing by spilling more blood. They deluded themselves into thinking that by extracting an eye for an eye they might, somehow, ease the pain of their grief.

Not in Johnny's household though. The family told me they were aware that an Israeli sniper, positioned on a nearby hilltop, had shot Johnny dead without provocation or justification. But they did not seek his name, they levelled no anger, no abuse and no venom – and there were no calls for revenge. Before me sat a family, clearly in deep distress, whose quiet acceptance and faith in God was humbling and awe-inspiring.

Yousef, Johnny's father, stood up and moved slowly across the room. He picked up a typed letter and handed it to me … It was written in the first person as if Johnny was now there among us, reflecting on his all too brief 17 years on earth, a life cut short in the cruellest manner.

"I am the martyr Johnny Thaljieh," the letter read. "I had never been afraid of the Israeli F16 fighter planes or tanks. I was so beloved to Jesus and was always praying for peace and love between all the nations."

The letter went on to describe the circumstances of his death and then continued: "My blood is still leaking on the land of Manger Square. I pray to God that my blood will lead to peace between Palestinians and the Israeli people and to finish all the war in this Holy Land. Finally, please let this message be heard by the entire World. 'Greater love hath no man than this, that a man lay down his life for his friends. John (11:25-26).'"

As I finished reading the letter, I could hardly breathe. I was choking back tears. Here was a family so recently torn apart by such a senseless killing, bewildered and devastated by their loss in this cruel, futile war and they had the presence of mind to pen a message of peace. How? How was this possible? Where was the anger, the outrage? If this were me, I reflected, surely I would be screaming from the rooftops, crying out for divine justice for this murder. For Johnny's family though this was divine justice: if Johnny's life – and brutal death – could in some way make the world a better place, then justice had been served.

I asked Johnny's father what people could do to help, what might be a fitting tribute to his son. "We do not want any money for ourselves," he said. "We want people to invest here, to invest in the young people. We must give them a sense of hope for the future, to feel their lives are worth living. This will help build peace."

Johnny would, no doubt, have approved of such a selfless response. My encounter with Johnny Thaljieh had been unexpected and unforgettable. He may have gone but his spirit lives on, an example and inspiration to others in this sad and torn land.

Inigo Gilmore was born in London. He worked as a journalist in Africa for six years, covering South Africa's 1994 elections and reporting from more than 30 countries on the continent for *The Times* of London, *The Sunday Times* and Sky Television. He films and produces his own documentaries, which have been broadcast on BBC and Channel 4. Since 2001 he has covered the Israeli-Palestinian conflict and Iraq for print and broadcast outlets. His recent films *Behind the Fence* and *Searching for Saddam* appeared on the BBC. He is single but maintains this is only because he has not asked anyone yet.

Suburbia

Chris Booth

And then one of them starts screaming. Her peroxide hair, which has been styled with great care in spite of everything, quivers around her head like an angry halo. Spittle collects on her scarlet lipstick; each maddened accusation explodes into the cold, leaving puffs of condensation that curl slowly and dissipate in the mist.

The damp air reverberates to the lazy throb of artillery elsewhere in the city, its dull beat punctuating these hysterics. What she is saying or what we can have done to upset her is not clear. But there are many things now that are beyond understanding and very little, it seems, that can truly surprise or hurt.

So we stand in silence, catching our breath after the running, watching as her anger dissolves, as she collapses against a wall, crying into the orange and lilac velour flowers which decorate the fabric of her dirty housecoat. The others, neighbours or refugees, pay her no attention. They stare blindly into the mist, no longer flinching at the louder explosions, as though in a mesmerised vigil for the flash that will sooner or later rend the late afternoon fog and illuminate everything for the instant preceding utter darkness.

Each fat report rolls heavily around the courtyard like some beast in a pen. But there is nothing to see: the mist swirls about the walls and blows over the grey earth, the remains of cars, and the unwanted household items refugees or looters have discarded at the last moment.

From here, you cannot tell where the fighting has reached, although it appears to be growing nearer. The people in the stairwell mutter to one another between explosions, one saying it must be near the ironmongers, another disagreeing – near the library, isn't it obvious, not by the children's clinic but where Yevdokia Ivanovna lives, remember? They are silent again, pondering this. Another blast, which this time shakes the building. Someone turns to the woman in the housecoat, who is still crying and murmuring something between sobs, and snaps at her to be quiet. Then he turns to us:

"She is tired, she says you should leave. You must understand. We think you should leave; you will only bring more trouble. Switch it off and leave, please."

As though the lens itself was spewing war onto their street, chewing the pockmarks from the walls of these crumbling flats, littering shrapnel over the playground where a teenager with a bandaged head sits alone at the sandpit pissing in his trousers, talking to himself out there alone in the mist, while the explosions grow louder until you can feel them in your chest and at the back of your throat like a second heartbeat. So we turn it off.

And at some point we switch the camera back on. The people who have either chosen to remain or who have been abandoned in these buildings tell us of an elderly couple on the next stairway. He is a veteran of the Second World War and an invalid. His wife cares for him in their tidy apartment. He speaks calmly into the microphone. At length, he asks if we think the war will come to their neighbourhood; we say it surely will, and he begins to cry quiet, old man's tears.

So we suggest they leave with us. There are relatives in Kizlyar, he says. We should leave now before it grows dark.

Over an intermittent satellite line, the editor instructs us to film the rescue operation. And then to film an update later, of course. A series, no less: this could run. It would "personalise the conflict", he tells us. But we find we cannot lift the old man down three flights of stairs and keep filming at the same time. Later we find we cannot mediate between the old man and his wife without getting shot. And she will not leave, not without the carpets, which she cannot bear to abandon to the soldiers and bandits and the neighbours. But the carpets will not fit in the car. It is not a big vehicle. There is a long and exhausting argument – tempers flare, more tears are shed.

It is a while before we notice that dusk is closing over us, that the sky has already begun to pulse with the aurora borealis of evening artillery. Yet in the end the wife insists she will stay, and we depart, saying reassuring things to the veteran, trying not to make promises we cannot keep, wondering, when he quietens down, whether what we have filmed is enough to cut together, not sure how much it matters now anyway.

By turning to books about the conflict I can work out that it must have been springtime. If I really wished to know, I could find the original tapes, which I am sure Vadim would have dated and labelled. They may still exist, although a recent fire at the company where we both then worked may well have claimed them, turning tape, box and liner into unreadable polymers and vapour. At the end of the war, Vadim would have taken a dub when he found he was to be made redundant. But this only occurs to me now. I hadn't thought much about him until someone told me, as I began to write this, that he is dead. He was killed in a car crash earlier this year. I had no idea: we hadn't kept in touch. I can picture his happy moon face, hear his irritating nasal voice, his snorts of derision at how inexpertly I drove the jeep over potholes and rubble on the roads. I can remember how much I hated him for that. But I can't remember for sure if it was spring or winter, or the name of the veteran, still less those of his wife and relatives in Kizlyar. I think his name may have been Nikolai, though I would not swear to it. The fact is I do not know if I care as much as I probably should. Sometimes this worries me.

It is not always clear what is truly remembered and what the mind chooses to call memory for reasons of its own. Such as to find meaning in one's role in events. Or in order that the stories one tells of them later might sound more engaging.

It must have been spring. Some of the trees in the courtyard would have been coming into bud. Others would have been sketched in charcoal against the grey mist, their branches cauterised by shell blasts and unlikely to produce leaves, fruit or seeds in that season.

Along with Vadim Allakhverdiev, and many others, Chris Booth covered the first war in Chechnya. The second war attracts less attention – which may be among the reasons it has yet to end.

Nairobi, August 1998

Sam Dhillon

On an ordinary August day in 1998, Kenya's capital city, Nairobi, was rocked by a thunderous explosion. I was sitting behind my desk in the office. The rumble shook the things on my desk. Having covered stories in other war zones like Somalia, I immediately recognised that this was a huge explosion and not just a tyre blowout on the highway. I whipped up my camera and on instinct headed for the big smoke plume I could see in the middle of the city. Arriving on the scene within minutes of the blast I realised that the US Embassy in Nairobi was the target. Through my camera lens I saw images of utter carnage.

Debris was littered everywhere and there were people in all sorts of condition being rushed around. There was mass panic and hysteria as severely injured people wandered aimlessly in shock while others tried to help them. A whole seven-storey building adjacent to the US Embassy had collapsed and you could hear the screams from those trapped under the rubble.

The air was filled with the smell of sulphur, dust and charred human flesh. Bodies burnt beyond recognition littered the immediate area lying amongst shattered glass and plaster. There were upturned and burning vehicles in the immediate area.

As I picked my way through the devastation, my eye to my viewfinder, I saw images which to this day disturb me. I had seen death and destruction before but this was different. These were my people on my turf lying in agony, buried under big concrete pieces, wandering around with half their bodies shredded by the blast.

The questions that kept shooting through my mind were "Why here? Why our people? Who was responsible?". A major part of me wanted to just put down my camera and help anybody I could. I wanted to claw at the rubble and help people out. The other part of me held me back so that I could capture these horrific images and show the world how the innocent are the ones who suffer at the hands of such cowardly terrorists.

What one sees through a viewfinder and actually films is much more graphic than the images which are finally aired. These are more intense and leave an imprint on the mind. Many times during the next three to four days of covering the issue round the clock, my vision was blurred not because of the smoke and dust, but from the tears that flooded my eyes as I saw lifeless bodies being pulled from the rubble.

There is also a constant fear, in covering such stories, of a further or secondary explosion taking place. At one point I found myself stepping only inches away from a live, unexploded bomb cartridge.

Adrenalin keeps one going in such a situation, helping to shut out certain events. I remember vividly that when I got home after three exhausting days and nights on the site, I sat back and the whole grizzly event kept playing again and again in my head. I needed sleep badly but when I lay down and shut my eyes little nightmares kept jolting me awake.

The memories of that day always linger in the back of my mind. I am sure even the most hardened of us cameramen have similar incidents lurking in our consciousness.

Sam Dhillon has been in the film production industry since 1989. After his studies he followed in his father's footsteps, those of world-renowned cameraman, Mohinder Dhillon. Father and son run a news and documentary production company in Nairobi.

Faith

Charlayne Hunter-Gault

The pouring rains had come and gone, but not the devastation they had brought to Mozambique and its people. I had come to see just how bad it was after the worst was over and I found a family living in a temporary shelter provided by a church. They had fled their town – some two hours away – in search of higher ground. Father, mother and four children. The wife was pregnant when the sudden rushing waters forced them to flee their home in the cold dead of night. They made it out of the neighbourhood just before it was completely engulfed in water, the relentless rising tide following them.

They took shelter on the roof of a house, huddling together as the rains continued beating down. The wife went into labour and soon gave birth to a baby girl. And then another baby came. It was also a girl.

It was three days before the rains slackened and the waters receded enough for them to climb down from the roof. By this time, one of the twin girls was dead.

The image I had in my mind's eye was that of thousands of poor men, women and children clinging to what few possessions they had left, or staring silently into a distance too far for any of us who had not been there to see.

After listening to this family's incredible story, I turned to the father. He was, like my late father and grandfather, a minister. So I asked him what this awful time had done to his faith in God. To my amazement, he said it had made it stronger.

"God could have taken all of my children," he said softly, "Instead, He took only one."

Faith like that is bound to take the edge off even the most cynical souls. It reminded me that I am different from my computer. Their faith fuelled my passion to tell their story with unapologetic compassion.

A year later, I received a gift from that family. They had had another daughter and tracked me down in the US to ask my permission to name her Charlayne. I gladly consented, hopeful that her father's faith and her mother's courage would become hers, too.

Charlayne Hunter-Gault is Johannesburg Bureau Chief and Correspondent, CNN. She was previously Chief Africa Correspondent for US-based National Public Radio, following more than 30 years with US broadcasting and print media. She is the author of *In My Place*, about her role in the American Civil Rights Movement as the first black woman to attend under court order the previously all-white University of Georgia.

Rhino

Mike Cadman

In the chill of an early winter's evening, high-tower spotlights cast their orange glow over the 18-wheel pantechnicons, heavily laden pick-up trucks, officials and the usual mix of travellers bustling through the Oshoek border post between South Africa and Swaziland.

The border post is undergoing major reconstruction and Mike Jamieson, an animal rehabilitation specialist from Wildcare Africa in Pretoria, and myself wander around the piles of fine building sand, stacks of unpainted steel window frames and patches of newly laid concrete, trying to familiarise ourselves with still un-signposted offices.

A young woman, and judging by her dress and attitude, a lady of the night attracted by the flow of lone men with some money and a little time, looks at Mike who stands 1,90 metres (6 foot 4 inches) tall, smiles and comments, "Nice body!"

We burst out laughing in surprise. We're here to pick up a baby rhino, not to have women pick us up.

I'm with Mike as part of my research into a book about Wildcare Africa and have joined him on a mission to collect a two-day-old baby White Rhino (*Ceratotherium simum*) that has been abandoned by its mother after an altercation with male rhino at the Hlane Game Sanctuary in Swaziland. Without its mother the animal has little chance of survival in the bush so Wildcare, experts at hand-raising baby rhinos, has been asked to take care of the animal with a view to returning it to the sanctuary in two years' time when it is big enough to look after itself.

We link up with the South African veterinary services officer who has been in touch with his Swazi counterparts. We show everyone all the relevant veterinary and CITES permits – CITES is the Convention on Trade in Endangered Species, a World Conservation Union (IUCN) agreement that regulates trade in endangered species.

The officer talks with customs officials on both sides of the border and generally paves the way for the "swap" to take place. I also chat with the officials on both sides of the border trying to impress upon everyone the urgency of getting the unusual animal from one vehicle to the other as quickly as possible.

The Hlane game rangers and the owners of the rhino arrive at the border post with their 25 kg charge warmly secure and asleep under blankets piled on top of a bed of hay in the back of their off-road vehicle. The orange spotlights create deep shadows and in the eerie light the whole procedure slowly begins to take on an air of intrigue.

At the red and white boom gate a few doubtful Swazi border officials and policemen peer under the dark canopy of the vehicle to establish if I've been talking nonsense.

"What's that thing? Is it a pig?" a uniformed policeman asks as the rhino, about the size of a fat Labrador dog, wriggles and wakes up. The spectators all know what is going on and laugh at their silly colleague.

The officials are helpful and the vehicle is shepherded through to where Mike waits in the "no-man's land" between border posts. After greetings are completed, Mike examines the rhino and, together with the game scout who has cared for the rhino on its long journey, prepares a milk formula in a large plastic bottle.

Mike towers over his small newfound colleague but they both display equal gentleness towards the tired and confused small animal. As the hungry rhino noisily sucks the milk from the bottle she folds her ears back along her neck and rolls her eyes in pleasure.

A crowd of curious, and some incredulous, onlookers gather. "What are you going to do with it?" people want to know. Someone else, who has been listening to Mike answering all the questions spots an opportunity and asks if there are any jobs going at Wildcare. "I'm good with animals – I'll come and work for you," he offers.

I'm left to help sort out the paperwork and together with the rhino's owner we set about getting the correct stamps and approvals. Things go fairly smoothly, but there is a minor hiccup at the South African customs office "You have to have a CCA1," an official says and sends me to the relevant office.

It turns out that this is the all-important "The Declaration Of Goods In The Southern Africa Common Customs Area". I ask where I can get one.

"Depends what you are importing," an official says.

"A rhino," I tell her. It's already eight o'clock, it's cold and she's clearly impatient to go home and not at all impressed by what she takes to be a feeble joke.

A brief conversation in siSwati ensues amongst the officials and one man points to a picture of a fearsome charging Black Rhino on a 2003 calendar.

"You didn't tell me it's a dangerous animal," the woman accuses.

Things are beginning to unravel so, anxious to make it clear that I only have a baby White Rhino, that it is not at all dangerous – not a 2 000 kg adult – I invite her to come and have a look. Most of the office traipses out with us and, sure enough, the baby rhino magic works. Her attitude changes instantly and the CCA1 is completed and stamped. "GOODS – one rhino, *Ceratotherium simum*".

As Mike and I climb into our vehicle to leave, cheerful soldiers carrying assault rifles and a few policemen warn us to be careful because the road from Oshoek is well-known as a car hijacking hot spot. "You don't want to lose your rhino – have a good trip!"

The journey back to Pretoria is relatively uneventful, if driving an orphaned Swazi white rhino through the night can be considered an uneventful event. Sometime around midnight we stop to feed the rhino at the Ultra City petrol station in Middelburg. Opening the back of the vehicle I'm greeted by the strong smell of rhino, an unshaven and tired but cheerful Mike who has been travelling with the rhino, and a curious look from two tiny bewildered brown eyes fringed by long eyelashes peering out from under a warm blanket. "What now?" the eyes seem to ask.

It's cold and most of the garage workers are huddled indoors so nobody seems to notice when the little rhino squirts about five litres of milky pee out of the back of the vehicle.

We arrive at Wildcare in the early hours of the morning and immediately shepherd the tiny animal into a heated room that will act as her nursery for the next few weeks. If everything goes well she will make the return journey to Swaziland in two years' – with absolutely no chance of being mistaken for a pig.

Mike Cadman is a veteran South African journalist, foreign correspondent and television producer. He is the author of *Wildcare* published by Jacana in 2003.

Return to Auschwitz

Kim Barnes

Arbeit Macht Frei – work makes you free. The over-used image of Auschwitz still hangs, threateningly, over the entrance.

We were there to work, to mark the fiftieth anniversary of its liberation. Thousands of journalists, more than I'd ever seen in one place – all seeking accreditation, all of them, it seemed, queuing at the same time as me, for the plastic pass which would validate us and our purpose.

This was concentration camp as theme park, and we crawled all over it, with cameras and notepads, seeking the story. But the place itself was the story. A nondescript, bleak part of Poland, incredibly just a few miles from Kracow, a city of extraordinary beauty, and of learning.

It didn't seem real. It seemed unfair to mark any sort of anniversary here. Who could want that – not the Poles, ashamed it had happened here. But – how can this be? It's now a "tourist attraction". It's in the guidebooks, on the maps, on the European trail.

The throng gathered around the president of Israel, the microphones in his face. What would he say, what could he say that would have any meaning? The tenuous yet iron-strong link between this place and Israel. A link wrought from misery and pain. Why come back? Why would anyone ever want to come back?

And then I met Arieh. A kindly face, crinkly grey hair, a warm scarf. He'd been here. Been here? And survived? Not only survived, but apparently strengthened by the experience. Now he spent his time bringing groups of teenagers from Israel to Auschwitz, so that they could see. What did they see, and what was it they should understand?

Arieh led us away from the crowd. Most of the barracks of Auschwitz have been razed, and rightly so. But a token shed remains, and that was the one. He remembered the iron ring, intended to tether horses, that remained in the room. I slept there, he said. I turned my head to the wooden bench, and tried to imagine this gentle, quiet man enduring the desperate Polish winters here, when there was ice inside and nothing to eat and human beings shrivelling and dying every day. How could he not be consumed by bitterness? How could he bear to look at it again? How could he have a found a reason, any reason, to carry on and have any space in his heart for the needs of others? Wouldn't anyone turn away from humanity, lose himself in pain and loss? What kind of person is able to transcend that?

Just the three of us in that dark, damp shed. The bright spring sunlight outside shone in defiance of what that place seemed to represent. We found a timeless, strange peace, the pack of people lost to us. Now there was an urgent reality in what had seemed surreal. Our deadline, or a "line" for a story was meaningless.

And so I saw Auschwitz through another pair of eyes – always the priceless privilege of the journalist, but here, it was shattering. An imaginative leap was possible, to a glimpse of unthinkable pain, and then an understanding of the redemptive power ... not of forgiveness, how could he forgive? But of finding the strength to make another life, a good life, in itself the ultimate transcendence of evil. And the power of one life. If he made one more, ten more, one hundred more people see and feel the same as I did, hadn't he already rubbed out some of the madness and made his own indelible mark, which would survive and endure beyond his one life?

Kim Barnes is a freelance reporter, currently working mainly for the BBC in London. She's also a partner in a small production company, producing features from the UK and abroad.

Silver tapes

Tony Headley

The story of the sinking of the Achille Lauro – eight years after its storming by Palestinian militants made it a household word – started for me in APTV's Norwich Street newsroom in London. Nigel Hancock, then the head of news, jolted when the story hit the wire. Frenzy soon took hold of the entire newsroom.

It was November 1994 and Associated Press Television had been in existence for only a month or so. We all had the same thought at once: if we did things right, this was the story that could put us on the map. Sitting on the planning desk, I was trying to figure how to get myself onto the story. The South Africa-bound ocean liner had left Genoa with 1 090 passengers and crew on board and was ablaze somewhere close to Somalia. She was going down in the middle of the ocean and we had no idea where to go to meet the survivors. Bets were open.

One of the news editors was adamant that the Seychelles was the right destination and promptly disappeared to collect his bathing suit.

At Hancock's request, I was desperately trying to charter a plane to take a crew somewhere in the vicinity of the ship. Having been given nearly all the possible flight plans to the area, I started getting the costs, which I still remember not understanding fully; there were too many zeros involved for me. That soon led me to come up with a cheaper option that would immediately exclude most of my colleagues: Djibouti. I was one of the few people at APTV who spoke French.

I booked myself on a flight from Paris to Nairobi for that same evening, wandered into Nigel's office and outlined my plan. I would fly to Nairobi, pick up a cameraman, get us to Djibouti by charter and see if the French navy was going to get involved. Perhaps they could take us to survivors.

Nigel spoke a particular kind of British to my American ears – posh but muffled – and I was never quite sure if he was agreeing with me or not. But this time, his answer was quite clear: "Yes, go, but get me those tapes, get me those tapes or you don't get Paris."

Nigel had unilaterally decided that someone on the ship must have shot pictures of the vessel's sinking and those shots were going to be ours and they would be bigger news than the sinking of the Titanic. As for Paris, there had been talk of opening a bureau there, but nothing had been decided. Having grown up in France, I was pushing hard for the creation of a Paris bureau and I wanted to run it.

So off I went with a large wad of cash in my pocket and the mission to find some of the sinking liner's surviving passengers in the hope that success would earn me the job in Paris – my first posting as a senior producer, all this at 27 years old.

Nairobi, early morning.

The overnight flights from Europe always end up the same in Africa: you get in having only slept a few hours and the humid muggy heat wraps you up in a hazy cocoon.

Wilson airfield is exactly what you dream an African airport should be like: a road lined with small wooden houses leading up to an array of hangars and a tarmac with Pipers parked everywhere. The cameraman appeared out of nowhere and made me immediately panic about what I was supposed to do next, as he seemed not to have the slightest clue.

I'd brought with me the names of a few charter companies, and I was going to have to choose one to fly us to Djibouti. I immediately drew a blank. What did I know about airplanes? Nevertheless, one came through and I offloaded some of the dollar bills I was hugging to my body. The pilot was a tall lanky Ethiopian who, as he was showing me his plane, pointed to another TV crew just walking into his office: Reuters TV, the opposition!

I asked him how we could get to Djibouti before them. Easy, he answered. Take a half tank of kerosene and fly higher, faster and out of the flight path. "Okay," I said, "let's go!" Next thing I knew, I was sitting in the co-pilot's seat wondering what could be more fun than this. We flew between the clouds, diving in and out of African cumulus. It was a glorious sight. Soon, we were descending and I asked if we were already approaching Djibouti. "No," we were just off on a low altitude flight over his farmland in Ethiopia. "This is not good," I was thinking.

As we prepared to land at Ambouli, I realised again that I needed a plan. I decided to concentrate on slowing down the opposition. I asked the pilot for some tips on how to put the most time between us and the Reuters' crew in the plane not far behind.

The pilot had a smart idea: by midday, fresh qat would be in the market. When we landed, we distributed cash among the taxi drivers waiting at the airport. Soon they had all left to go get their daily fix. The Reuters crew would not find a single taxi.

My next destination was the port of Djibouti. An Air France stewardess had told me about a French guy there who owned high-speed boats, which I thought might be useful to get out to an incoming boat with survivors. Negotiations were difficult because the usual clutch of Air France crew members would be arriving the next day for a two-day lay-over and would want to hire the boats for an outing to a nearby island. My trusty, yet thinning wad of cash proved useful once again and I landed a deal to rent a boat. But I was starting to worry; it was the only money I could count on.

I approached the French navy, which has a Djibouti base, but was told that at that point they were not involved in bringing survivors back to land. I should call back, a spokesman told me. I then met with an official, who promised to let me know as soon as there was news from any of the ships that had gone to the Achille Lauro's rescue. I filled my cameraman in on my latest plan: wait until a ship nears the coast, speed out to sea and hope to board the vessel and … well that was good enough for now. The Reuters crew was just checking in to the hotel; it was time for a drink.

We spent the next day waiting. APTV producer Sahm Venter had flown to Mombasa from South Africa to try and grab interviews with some Achille Lauro passengers who were due there. Meanwhile, an army of doctors, nurses and psychologists had descended upon Djibouti's Hotel Meridien, waiting to participate in the rescue effort. The Air France crew had arrived for their lay-over but couldn't leave for their island cruise as I had block-rented the speed boats. So everyone milled around the hotel lobby and bar, awaiting the Achille Lauro survivors. News was that three people had died in the blaze, while all the others had been rescued by ships heading towards the east coast of Africa – but we were not sure at which port they would dock. Karaoke became the main source of entertainment and the French stewardesses were the star singers.

The next day, the port authorities finally gave the call. There was a mad dash to the port. I soon found myself speeding out to sea, with a smaller boat trailing behind: my Djibouti contact was on board and so was the Reuters crew!

Still we were ahead, and when I approached the cargo ship a wooden ladder had been dropped down its side. The cameraman refused to climb up the frail planks of wood for fear of dropping the camera. So off I went with the Betacam hanging across my back.

Only a few surviving passengers were sitting on the deck of the rusty cargo. They were happy to see land and be alive.

The first person I interviewed turned out to be the gold mine I was hoping for. He had been working as a musician on board the Achille Lauro, had just happened to have an Hi-8 camera with him ... and, as a matter of fact, had shot pictures of the sinking liner. Now I finally had a plan: keep this man as close to me as possible, do not let the Reuters crew near him, get off the ship, aim for the satellite feed point and have a look at his footage to see if it's worth buying. The only hitch was that my providential man, who had already been through a ship sinking once before and had sold footage of it, knew how much his pictures would be worth to an international news agency.

When we got back to port, I was first off the ship with the musician. Reuters, in sending around the world the first pictures of Achille Lauro survivors arriving on land, had included in their edit, shots of me walking off the ship. London was furious. Why wasn't I at the port getting pictures of the survivors reaching land?

Arriving at the local TV station with the musician, we saw the Reuters producer on the phone with his office in London. I asked to speak to his editor, hoping to ask him to call the people at APTV in London and tell them to call me. I had to let my colleagues in London know that I had pictures of the sinking, but this was still before the advent of the mobile phone and we were not allowed to dial out – only incoming calls were permitted. It was a long shot after the pranks I had been playing and as the Reuters producer handed me the receiver, he hung up the phone with his other hand. It was a cheap trick, but hey, he was getting back at me. The musician witnessed the whole exchange. Back at the hotel, as he was being cared for by rescue workers, he agreed to give me right of first refusal on his pictures. Meanwhile, ITN had flown in, and they soon became a useful ally in my endeavour. Like all networks they had come with a full crew and a tape editor.

When I first saw the pictures I knew I had a scoop. Speed of delivery became a must. Further negotiations with the musician were under way, but he hadn't committed yet. I suggested he go hear the Reuters offer. The Meridien was buzzing with stories about his footage. Before letting him go I reminded him of how the Reuters man had behaved at the TV station. I was brokering a deal in which he would sell the British rights to ITN and world rights to APTV while retaining all the archive rights after initial usage.

At last he agreed, turning down the others. It was late, he went to bed and we sat down to trim down the footage with the editor, before a late feed to London. We slid the first tape into the edit machine and hit the play button. Horror hit us. The tapes no longer showed the strong drama of a ship sinking, only black and white flashes. There were no pictures. I had just spent a huge amount of money on blank tapes. The editor came up with the theory that the musician had been at sea for several days with his tapes and a layer of salt must have set on the magnetic band. We needed to remove it. But how?

This time the editor came up with a plan. Dollar bills contain silver and silver will do the trick, he said.

We spent the entire night using what was left of my money to rub down the tape ribbon. The pictures still did not appear. London was getting frantic. I saw my hopes of running the Paris bureau grow dimmer. Finally, at around 7 a.m., the musician walked in. "Sorry guys, I handed you the wrong tapes last night. You must have the blank ones!"

As a producer for APTN, French television and CBS News, Anthony Headley has covered conflicts throughout Africa, the Balkans and the Middle East and has run APTN's operations in Russia and CIS. A freelance TV journalist/producer, he now lives in Paris with his wife and two children.

The monster gaining

Jimmie Briggs

"She's dead isn't she?" I asked no-one in particular, slowly walking toward the figure lying by the side of the road. A small form, covered with a patterned wool blanket rested on a bamboo stretcher. I assumed the refugee was a woman but given the expression on what remained of a face, I couldn't be sure. It was the tall, lanky soundman who turned and whispered, "She's alive".

At that moment, I heard the moan. The cameraman and a stills photographer leaned in to capture their images. I moved in for a closer look. "Uuunh," came the sound again. The colour was already leaving the body, giving her skin a greyish cast. She didn't move once and that scared me the most. The only audible sounds were the constant moaning and nervous shifting of our feet. The jungle gave us nothing to hear. It didn't have to.

Through its most vicious minions it had begun processing its claim on her. Hundreds of ants and flies were taking advantage of the open orifices to venture in and out of the deaf ears, sightless eyes and unmoving mouth. Standing on that muddy stretch of road in the largest country in Africa, I understood that the most violent things done to the human body are by the earth's smallest creatures.

A refugee from her own nation's genocide several years before, the Rwandan woman was stranded, along with thousands of her compatriots, by a civil war in Zaire. At worst 200 refugees were dying each day, from starvation, cholera or murder. The road leading from Kisangani really wasn't a road at all but rather a muddied, washed-out path lined with mud-brick homes, huts and lean-tos. The tattered clothing, bare feet and emaciated forms blended together, making women and men, young and old, indistinguishable. There were no graves. The dead and the living shared the same ground. The line between the two states was blurred.

Were we going to take her somewhere? How much longer did she have? Should we kill her? These were the questions none of us spoke aloud, but I'm sure we all thought them. Never having watched someone literally be "eaten alive", I fought back stubborn tears. The others wouldn't see my weakness.

The next few minutes seemed like hours.

One by one we turned and walked back to the truck. The decision had been made without any real discussion. We were going to leave her to die. A few steps ahead of the others, I found my lips involuntarily forming the words to the Lord's Prayer. It wasn't a conscious action and if anyone had told me they'd done the same thing elsewhere, I wouldn't have believed them. My insides were hollow for having witnessed what I had and walking away, becoming a silent partner in the decision to let another person die that day. I felt ashamed.

Slamming the doors shut we focused our eyes on a point beyond comprehension. The vehicle lurched forward. The moaning continued and slowly grew distant. As we retreated from the jungle, I could only feel remorse. A man in a cleric's collar came up to us and asked if I would help his ailing wife and children. Watching them play on a strip of railroad track all I could do was smile and say, "We're journalists but we'll be back. There's nothing to give now." Saying it I knew I would never see him again. By the look on his face, so did he.

I still wonder if that woman alongside the road kept moaning after we'd gone and if she did, weather there was anyone to hear. Maybe she died soon afterwards. Maybe no-one heard my prayer for that matter. There is no God in Hell.

I sometimes wake up at night, screaming with the belief that I killed her. Just as sure as if my hand put a bullet in the head or a knife through the heart, hers is the face that rouses me, desperate for escape. Now and then, it comes during those furtive moments walking along a buzzing avenue when breaks in thought emerge. She is a reminder of every housing project, drug hangout or emergency room I ever entered and left without a backward glance. Her fate and those of countless others are the justification of my life. There but for the grace of God go I …

I had gone to the central African nation of Congo, then known as Zaire, with the intention of reporting on a civil war. Instead, I discovered the unshakable guilt borne by all survivors or witnesses of human tragedy.

"Don't look back," baseball legend Satchel Paige once said, "because the monster might be gaining". The tattered image of that anonymous face comes in successively focused snapshots. The "monster" is inside my head now, and I have nowhere to run.

A former reporter with LIFE, Jimmie Briggs has been reporting on child soldiers and the impact of war on children over the last five years. His book will be published in late 2004 by Basic Books.

Twenty-one years

Elizabeth Rubin

In March of 2003, I was in northern Iraq writing for a weekly American magazine. I had a Wednesday deadline, and as you know, besides getting a story, deadlines are a journalist's number one duty. Wednesday came and there were twelve hours left to Bush's 48-hour ultimatum to Saddam Hussein. Everyone knew war was imminent and so I and a few other journalists went down to the border between the autonomous zone of Kurdish-controlled Iraq and Saddam-controlled Iraq. A steady stream of young men and women were walking along the road escaping from Kirkuk. I was just about to leave because I still hadn't written that week's dispatch when I saw three Kurdish men crossing the checkpoint, who were somehow different than the rest – older, and dressed in grey suits. The Kurdish fighters nearby said they were prisoners of war returning from Iran, leftovers from the forgotten eight-year war between Iraq and Iran. "Twenty years in prison," I heard someone say. I was astounded. The return of Martin Guerre I thought.

"Twenty years?" I asked the tallest of the three.

"Twenty one," he said, and he couldn't stop smiling, said he felt like he was just born and had stepped out of a graveyard. He also looked a little lost. Where would he go? He had no idea if his family was alive, if they'd survived all the wars and Saddam's chemical attacks. He'd had a wife and five kids and another on the way when he was conscripted to fight Iran back in 1982. I had no time to be helping him search for his home, his family, his past. I was going to miss my deadline. But I couldn't resist.

I opened the computer and started writing my dispatch in the back of the car, writing Mohammad's search as it unfolded. No luck at the first house we stopped at. At the second we were told his family had just packed up the day before. "They left for the village," one shouted. "To escape the war," said another. Neighbours were swarming and pawing him now, stunned that this man had returned from the dead. Stay for tea, talk, they insisted. But Mohammad had no time. He was too anxious to even think, and we bounded off out into the mountains. Despite his anxiety, he managed to tell a few stories about his 21 years in prison: how he tried to escape, one time digging a tunnel with an iron bedpost; how he kept his brain alive without the benefit of TV, radio or books, by writing with ink made of soot and water and syringes stolen from the clinic.

Finally we arrived in a tiny village, and pulled up in front of a stone wall and green corrugated metal door. Mohammad was going to wait outside, while his friend warned the family. (Mohammad had heard stories of wives going into cardiac arrest when their prisoner-of-war husbands returned out of the blue, and he wasn't taking any chances.) But his friend was so excited he shouted out the news as soon as he reached the door.

A thin woman in a blue and black gypsy dress peered out at Mohammad, screamed and threw her arms around his neck. It was his cousin.

He hugged her, and then stepped up the stone path towards a short woman in a green dress and baggy pants. It was his wife Aatia. She stood so calm, gazing at him bemusedly. Her Mohammad was dead. She had his death certificate from the Iraqi government. Perhaps this was just another one of her dreams. She kept staring up at this man twice her height, and then she said softly, "Thank God I found you." He touched her hair and they smiled at one another, so much felt and not said, but you could see her eyes shining. All around them was chaos.

Up the yard a young woman was sliding down the stone wall of the house, weeping, screaming, beating the ground with her fists. "Tell that car to take this strange man away. My father is dead," she wailed. It was Mohammad's youngest daughter. She was only three months in her mother's womb when Mohammad went to war. She pushed him away as the ever-smiling Mohammad tried to embrace her. "Take him away," she shrieked. "This is just another dream. My father is dead." And she crumpled into herself.

Mohammad teased a little two-year-old racing around the yard. "Who's this?" he asked. "It's Sargul's child." His daughter Sargul was five the last time he saw her. Now Sargul was 26 with a family and a beauty salon of her own. "Oh no, who did you marry?" Mohammad joked. Sargul broke down in tears. Neighbours streaming in were crying. Everyone was crying. I was crying. Lynsey the photographer, who was travelling with me, was clicking away and crying.

And Mohammad was laughing. "Cheer up everyone," he said. "You should be happy! Why are you all crying?"

By now it was getting dark. Inside a room packed with dozens of adults and kids Mohammad told awful stories about how the Iranians had tortured him – that's why he had such a charming lisp, they'd broken his jaw. So many wasted decades of suffering, and Mohammad didn't even know at that time what his family had endured – climbing for days through the mountains several times over the years to escape Saddam's army.

Yet every time the atmosphere in the room grew sad, Mohammad waved it away with a laugh. He was the most resilient, optimistic man I'd ever seen, in love with life, with music, with laughter. He made jokes and tickled his new-found daughters. He and Aatia were slipping back into banter. Someone suggested they get Mohammad a second wife, and Aatia balked – she'd kick anyone new out of the house. But then she changed her mind. "If we're not killed by chemical weapons," she said. "We'll talk about another wife in the morning."

I finished my dispatch several hours late that day, and a few hours after midnight the war began.

Elizabeth Rubin is an independent journalist who has written about the Middle East, Africa, Russia, the Caucasus and the Balkans. Her articles have appeared in *The New York Times Magazine*, *The New Republic*, *The Atlantic Monthly*, *The New Yorker*, and *Harper's*. Rubin was one of two journalists who received the 2003 Kurt Schork Award in International Journalism.

If we were meant to fly, we'd have wings

Karen Sloan

Flying is one of the occupational hazards of the roving reporter.

It's especially problematic for me, since I'm prone to motion sickness, particularly when travelling with the military. I've been sick on every military plane and chopper going. Sometimes if I'm travelling with a group of colleagues they mention me if they're writing a colour story about the journey. If I'm lucky they don't use my name.

Nothing seemed to work to keep the nausea at bay, until one day I got fed up and marched myself down to sick bay on an aircraft carrier and demanded they give me whatever they hand out to seasick sailors. Bless those little pills ... they were magic!

I've never had much trouble that way on big commercial airliners, luckily. But you do get your share of other kinds of adventures.

There was the time I flew to Kazakhstan with a bunch of journalists on an Aeroflot charter flight. We were heading down to see a space launch from Baikonur. The plane needed to make a refuelling stop somewhere in deepest central Asia. As we began our descent the flight attendants made their usual announcement about seatbacks and tray tables. The only problem was, they'd forgotten to collect our food trays. I think the plane divided itself in two – passengers who just left the tray on the table, and the ones who decided to pick up the tray and hold it during landing.

When we finally arrived in Kazakhstan, there were no ground crews available to unload the luggage. So we all formed a human chain and tossed the bags down from the cargo bay across the tarmac to the bus. On the way back we had to reverse the process. There were a lot of network TV crews in the group. The cameramen and engineers took the lead in actually stowing the bags. I'm sure the ground crew in Moscow had never seen such neatly packed cargo.

It was pretty much an adventure flying around Central America in the mid-1980s. TAN, LACSA, TACA: we made jokes (some politically incorrect) about what the airlines' initials stood for. I seemed to fly the Salvadoran carrier TACA (we called it Take A Chance Airlines) most often. They NEVER got me to my chosen destination within 24 hours of the time I was supposed to arrive.

The most disconcerting thing was when I ended up in the wrong city. I think the problem was that the airline had a hub in San Salvador. If the fighting there was too heavy at the time, when you landed they'd throw you on the next available plane heading vaguely in the direction you were trying to travel. They wouldn't let you hang around at all, and there was no arguing with them.

So if I wanted to go to Tegucigalpa I'd end up in Guatemala City. If I wanted to go to New Orleans, I'd end up in Miami (you try to scramble for last-minute onward connections at the end of Spring Break).

But my favorite TACA story involved a stop in Belize one day. I hadn't been aware the flight to Miami stopped in Belize until we were on the ground there. But once we landed, we never took off again. After a while, I looked out the window and saw mechanics taking apart one of the engines of the new-ish 767, laying the pieces out on the runway in rows. This went on for hours. Inside they were re-running a reel of Disney cartoons over and over again. Authorities in Belize wouldn't let us off the plane.

Eventually the mechanics started trying to put the engine back together. They'd put a piece back in, peer at it, shake their heads, and pull the piece out again. This went on for more hours.

Finally they let us off the plane, and we stormed the terminal to make phone calls. I tried to hitch a ride on another plane that had landed, but no-one would let me board.

Darkness fell, and someone drove a jeep up and shone its headlights at the wing of the TACA jet, so the mechanics could continue trying to put the engine back together. There was still a lot of head shaking going on.

Finally after 10 o'clock at night they seemed to be making good progress. I got back on board the plane and waited in my seat. But then one of the flight crew came onto the PA system and asked the passengers if they had seen a missing part! They really seemed to think that one of us had stolen it, which I felt was pretty outrageous, given the circumstances.

Anyway, that was the straw that broke the camel's back, and TACA had to take us off the plane and bus us to Belize City for the night. They brought us back the next morning, hustled us on board the same plane, and we took off. When the flight attendant came around to serve drinks, I inquired what they had done about the missing part.

"We made one," replied the stewardess. Now I was sorry I'd asked. But we did land successfully in Miami, if a day late. I couldn't make up my mind whether to join the general applause as we touched down on the runway.

A friend of mine back at my office gave me a turbine blade as a memento of the experience. I don't know where he got it from, but it makes a good paperweight.

Karen Sloan has been AP Radio's main foreign correspondent since 1989, covering wars, the Olympics and the fall of the Berlin Wall, among other stories. And she's still flying.

El Salvador

Susanne Ramirez de Arellano

We were all gathered in the back of a church, in a dusty, hot town in El Salvador, where the Devil screamed three times and no-one heard him. We had been called to cover yet another God-awful story.

A representative from the Salvadoran human rights group Tutela Legal had arrived at my apartment at 8 a.m. and knocked loudly on the door. Bleary-eyed and hung over after a night of dominos, tequila and various chemicals, I opened it and stood there as she told me that all of the foreign press were invited to an exhumation. Most of the international media had been at the house all night – we were not that many – and were really in no condition to witness anything.

But we piled into taxis and began the long journey to town, which was on the outskirts of the capital. The story was this – ten townspeople had been executed in an attack. The FMLN rebels claimed that the military had done it – that they had rounded them all up and opened fire and lobbed hand grenades at the group – until they killed them all. The military claimed that the rebels had done it – in much the same way. The villagers had been interred for more than a week and Tutela Legal had obtained permission to exhume the bodies to try and ascertain what had really happened.

And this is when the Fellini part starts. El Salvador was always a strange place – with a stench of pure evil covering everything like the fine mist of dust that was ever present. What happened next was the farce that mirrored the true horror of this nasty civil war funded by Washington.

The exhumation was being done by the two town drunks – bottles in hand as they dug the bodies out. The bodies had been in the ground for more than ten days and the smell was overpowering. It was a sickly, sweet, pungent smell that attacked the nostrils and permeated your clothes. The drunks tried to place the bodies in an old wheelbarrow – but because they were so inebriated they kept on tipping the barrow over and the bodies would flop out. It was worse than Keystone Cops. They kept on slipping on the ground and falling all over the cadavers. All of them were wrapped in what looked like bed covers in bright colours – which as they fell to the ground would open to reveal grotesque death masks – many missing limbs and parts of their faces.

As the bodies were placed one next to the other – the "forensic experts" were called in. These "experts" came dressed in some semi-medical green garb and armed with scissors and knives in order to butcher the delicate operation that would determine how these poor people died. As they began their task, I could hear a veteran journalist vomiting in the back of the church.

This process took hours – under the hot, sweltering Salvadoran midday sun. This made things worse because the brightness made everything stark and clear. The townspeople who were there refused to say what they had seen. If they blamed the military, the soldiers would extract revenge. And if they blamed the rebels, they could expect the same kind of treatment. They were trapped between the two – the real victims of the conflict.

Among them was one woman whom I have stamped in my memory. To this day she represents in my eyes the strength and dignity of the Salvadoran peasant. She looked quite old – haggard, lined, tight face – very thin with a kerchief covering her hair. The thing is in El Salvador women aged very fast – so she could have been any age. She sat in the same spot for hours – smoking a thin cigar and just staring at the bodies and the grave. Not batting an eyelid, no expression on her face. I approached her and asked why she had not moved since the exhumation started. She turned her head and looked up at me with the saddest expression I have ever seen – "My husband and my three sons are in there. I am not leaving until they are all out and I can bury them as God would want me to."

And she did just that – with the elegance of her silent grief.

At the end of the day – the press piled back into the taxis – outgunning each other to try and get there first to tell the story. The conclusion of the experts – the military had done it. Now that was a first. As our car approached San Salvador, I thought of that woman. We – the press – choose to be in a story for whatever reasons we care to explain to ourselves. But she could not leave that hellhole that was El Salvador at war.

El Salvador is now America's forgotten war. They came to this small Central American nation to correct the mistakes of Vietnam and to hold the *rojos* at bay.

Someone needs to go back and tell the world what really happened and let the bones finally have their say.

Susanne Ramirez de Arellano is a London-based freelance television producer and print reporter. She previously worked as APTN's senior editor for Latin America and assignment editor for ABC News in New York. In El Salvador, she was UPI's bureau chief.

Waiting for a bomb

Raymond Louw

The Jaffa Road had been cut almost in half to prepare for a new transport system so the congestion of traffic and people was much more overwhelming than usual. Shoppers bustled on the pavements while buses and cars jostled for headway in what was left of the narrow street. It was nearing midday and warm.

Then our guide, senior writer Daniel Ben Simon, on the staff of Israel's remarkable independent newspaper, *Ha'aretz*, motioned to me.

"Have you seen the soldiers on the pavement?" he asked, gesturing towards two young soldiers chatting together as they cradled their guns in their arms a few metres from our Mercedes–Benz Sprinter bus. With so many soldiers about in Israel I confessed that I hadn't noticed.

"Well," he said casually, "they're trying to spot the suicide bomber. We received a warning last night that a bomber would be making his way into Israel this morning and the soldiers have been called out on patrol."

"What are they supposed to do?" I asked. "Keep their eyes open for anyone acting suspiciously or who looks like the bomber," he responded.

The soldiers didn't seem to be doing anything special at all. They appeared relaxed as they chatted, idly glancing at passers-by. Over the road from them, the shoppers, too, scurried around, apparently the next purchase the only thing bothering them. The journalist followed my train of thought: "Yes, they would have heard the warning, too. It was broadcast. We don't know much, just that a bomber is expected to cross into Israel today; we have no idea where or at what time."

We were stuck in the traffic. Ahead of us were several articulated municipal buses snaking along the street towards us, one after the other. Involuntarily, I tensed; my senses seemed to have become forensically acute. Here we were in the main street of Jerusalem with people and buses all around. How many times had one read of attacks on buses or of suicide bombers blowing themselves and others to smithereens in just such crowded market places?

My thoughts were starkly ominous: "And why not here today?" I wondered what thoughts were passing through the minds of the bus drivers as they wrestled their clumsy vehicles through the throng. But whatever they were thinking it was clear that it was not causing them to

236

falter in their urging of their buses along the street. I marvelled at their courage. They were prime targets and they must have known it.

Daniel said, "People are used to it, so they carry on as if they have not heard the warning. What else is there to do?" Had we been anywhere else, say, in the country, I have no doubt that I, too, would have been able to mirror their apparent unconcern. But not here in this seething street – a known target area. My awareness was hypersensitive.

Our small bus lurched forward and a few minutes later, (and I was surprised to discover that I felt a sense of relief), we were meeting up with colleagues in the foreign Press corps.

We were a small visiting delegation from the International Press Institute on a mission to see what aid we could give the foreign media in Jerusalem who were in dispute with the Israeli government over the employment of video cameramen, sound engineers and Palestinian translators.

The foreign correspondents had been telling us their troubles for some 45 minutes when someone answered a phone and the room suddenly erupted. "Suicide bomber – in Netanya," (a city some 75 km north-west of Jerusalem where a policeman and three people were killed and a score of others wounded). The bomber was a young woman who had been stopped by the policeman as she was walking into a store and detonated the bomb.

The foreign correspondents rushed off and we returned to our bus, heading for our next meeting. It struck me that Daniel Ben Simon was now more relaxed. I guessed that his earlier casualness had been covering an inner tension. He nodded smilingly when I remarked, "so, everyone's relieved now that the bomb has gone off and, as the bombers operate individually, there's not likely to be another one today. That is, of course, apart from those victims who were caught up in today's awful tragedy".

He nodded: "That is the way it goes."

Raymond Louw is editor and publisher of the weekly current affairs newsletter, *Southern Africa Report*.

Footnote from Raymond Louw:
Ha'aretz is the only newspaper in Israel which tries to report the situation evenhandedly by giving the Palestinian side of the story as well as the Israeli one. One of its journalists, Amira Hass, was chosen by the International Press Institute in 2001 as one of its 50 press heroes for her coverage of the Palestinian cause from a West Bank city.

Video me

Romuald Luyindula

The villagers down in Escavos were angry.

Pregnant women already in labour were forced to clamber aboard a little canoe and cross the many rivers of the Warri Delta to reach a clinic far from their homes … in time for their babies' arrival.

They were angry because their villages built around the complexes of international oil companies like Chevron and Shell, saw no benefit from the wealth reaped from the river of black gold streaming through their areas.

They wanted a better life, basic social conditions like improved maternity facilities, schools for their children, hospitals.

A "hostage-taking" was how it was described, and why I travelled to southern Nigeria. Some Chevron employees, Americans and Brits were stuck in the refinery, prevented from leaving by disgruntled locals.

Strong, angry women, whom I called, with increasing respect, "The Nigerian Amazons of Warri," were blockading the oil company. Nobody was allowed in or out of the Chevron plant.

It was like a hostage situation.

Moving from one blockade to another, I began filming the demonstration. Some women were cool, others more upset.

And then there was one woman who really didn't like my camera. She threw herself onto me, trying to separate me from my television equipment. As I was fighting her off, a group of local men and some of my media colleagues came to the rescue.

But before I could be saved, the Amazon managed to get in a few hearty slaps across my face. My rescue team arrived just as she let go of me and walked away. I did briefly think about slapping her back, but that would have ignited an already semi-volatile situation. And I also didn't want to end up as one of the hostages.

Some minutes later another agitated woman approached me yelling "Hey you, cameraman! Video me! Video me! Hey! Video me now!"

That's when I remembered the slapping I just got. I honestly wasn't ready for another Amazon's special treatment. So I decided not to react to her loud demands – just as if I hadn't heard her.

But the woman in denim shorts and a white T-shirt kept on harassing me and yelling "Video me! Video me!"

Fleeing might have been an option. But I would have missed filming the sideshow and – even worse – all the women would have made fun of me.

"Video me! Video me!" the screaming continued. Stopping just long enough to remove her T-shirt, the woman stood there in her bra and shorts, still yelling her demands that I capture her on film.

The other protestors had begun laughing, mainly at the situation, but also at me. She just kept shouting.

I asked myself if this was another trap which would end with me falling victim to another series of slaps. Or was it a choice between physical assault or filming an Amazon in her bra?

The first argument was more persuasive. So I took the risk.

I pointed my camera at her and hit the record button. I keep rolling for three to four minutes. All the while she was frantically moving around in her bra while delivering her plea: "Video me! Video me!"

The onlookers began laughing even harder. It crossed my mind to conduct a little interview with her about the basis of her unhappiness with Chevron. But before I could form the words she snapped. "Shut up! Don't you think what you have is enough?"

That time I got away without the slapping punishment.

So, if you ever go down to the Delta, please watch out for the Amazons.

Romuald "Romeo" Luyindula is a DRC-born cameraman/ producer currently based in Ivory Coast for Associated Press Television News from where he covers West Africa. Before Abidjan he was based in his hometown, Kinshasa.

The damp squib wedding

Emmanuel Tenoh-Tumanjong

In impoverished Cameroon, situated in the heart of Africa's equatorial rainforest, soccer surfaces as the leading pastime. Sex and alcoholism jointly follow as the few pleasures in this country whose inhabitants fondly describe it as "Africa in miniature".

On 4 October 2003, over 250 guests who had turned out to blissfully seal the conjugal bonds of Jackie E. and Robert A. at the latter's residence, instead met with what an eyewitness described as a "monumental and life disappointment".

After one of the six Yaounde mayors declared Jackie and Robert married, they went to receive a blessing at the conspicuous Our Lady of Victory Cathedral, the biggest Catholic church in Yaounde. The just-wedded couple was then ushered to the groom's luxurious and spacious residence, a four-storey building in the Elig Esono neighbourhood in the northern part of Yaounde, by a convoy of over 40 cars. The opulence and pride of Robert's father were sufficient an invitation for nearby needy neighbours who know that the retired worker with the country's Ministry of Economy and Finance had acquired more than enough wealth to keep his family comfortable even after his death. And for Robert, his third of eleven sons, the only one he had introduced into business, it was the opportune time to exhibit the acquired wealth and haughtiness.

Neighbours, who share the sumptuous building as tenants, were part of the anxious crowd that had thronged to the ostentatious residence to eat, drink, dance and celebrate with the new husband and his wasp-shaped wife. The bride's long, dark hair and softly muffled walk painted her with a mermaid's incredibly dangerous beauty and charm. In his dark suit, Robert's height, lanky look and serenity, gave him a mannequin's sinewy charm that every woman would want from a man.

Darkness drew nearer. Then eating and drinking entered higher gear, while servants started preparing the dancing floor. After pieces of advice from the elderly guests and close friends of the couple, dancing started. Clicks of beer and wine bottles could be heard from all corners. Real heavy discotheque beat the waves and wooed the guests to shake their bodies in bliss to welcome Jackie and Robert into the complex marriage kingdom.

About three quarters of an hour into the dancing and heated ambiance that had engulfed the house, the bride requested permission from the groom and climbed to the third storey of the building reserved for them – to "change her wedding dress and wear something lighter", according to Essomba Gérald, a friend to Robert and special guest at the ceremony.

More than half an hour had gone by, but Jackie was still absent, and the uxorious Robert who had had his hand around Jackie throughout the occasion would not stay without his newly wedded wife. Apparently caught in a telepathic frisson, Robert held his calm and for a while padded around the bungalow floor of the building, in front of which the occasion was being held.

He began getting irate and "wondered why Jackie should stay away for such a long time at such a very important ceremony of their life," recounted Cécile Atangana, a niece to Jackie and confidant to Robert.

"Shortly after I left him, he gently climbed the building," Atangana narrated. "Downstairs, gripped with consternation when we heard a male squeal from the third floor, the crowd began drifting to the staircase and into their apartment". Pandemonium and hysteria caught the crowd, drowning out the music and transforming the atmosphere into utter confusion.

Fretfully confused, Robert, 36, had started crying before the crowd reached him. According to Gérald Essomba, "Robert had sorrowfully caught his newly-wedded wife enjoying sex with her former boyfriend inside their very sleeping room". Describing the scene, Essomba said Robert had been combing the entire apartment looking for her, but Jackie had gone and closed herself inside the sleeping room where special drinks and foodstuffs were reserved to be shared with guests in the later part of the occasion.

"Since the door was not bolted, Robert surprised them, bursting in on his new wife who was being taken from behind by the boyfriend. Her wedding gown that she had gone to change out of was lifted and thrown over her head. The boyfriend's jeans pants were lowered to his knees, and he was glued to Jackie's buttocks, and both of them were enveloped in carnal joy and ecstasy".

Infuriated, Robert pounced on his wife, and just as he bundled her up to throw out of an open window, he was arrested by the crowd that came in from below.

Meantime, Jackie's boyfriend managed to sneak away, disguised within the crowd, and dashed out of the locality.

"I had noted that Jackie was always dancing with that boy. I quietly suspected that the boy was not a simple guest at this occasion. I'm sure that there is some witchcraft involved in this incident," said André Olomo, an uncle to Robert who said he was going to consult a soothsayer "to explain this mystery to me".

Meanwhile, Robert's father immediately sued for divorce and is claiming recompense from Jackie's family through a Yaounde court – he wants them to reimburse Robert for the more than CFA8 million he spent for bride price and the entertainment.

Jackie, 24, is a sophomore of the Law Faculty at Yaounde University II, somewhere in the northeastern outskirts of Yaounde. She returned to her small room at school without remorse. It is whispered that despite Robert's handsomeness, he is frigid and proud.

"Adultery is common these days, but it shouldn't be done by someone on his or her wedding day," lamented Olomo, and swore it was "witchcraft".

Emmanuel Tenoh-Tumanjong has been the Cameroon correspondent for The Associated Press since 1995 and Dow Jones Newswires since 2000. Born in 1969 in Bamenda in Cameroon's North-West province, he speaks both English and French. He has also reported for *The Herald, Cameroon Post, UMI Today, Weekly Post, Africa Today, NewsAfrica,* and *Business In Africa.*

Peace ... barely

Chris Burns

May 2001. It all seems too good to be true – a hopeful spring day for peace with Albanian rebels in southern Serbia pulling out of rugged areas along the Kosovo border that they had so fiercely defended. Giving up their weapons to NATO.

Our 4X4 negotiates steep, muddy roads to witness the handover. Through sun-drenched mountain valleys we travel, where the loudest sound isn't gunfire anymore, but the river.

My notebook full of material and our camera full of pictures, we begin to head back to the hotel to cut the piece. We used far more fuel than we expected, driving through the rough terrain, so we have to find a shortcut. We were told that in one direction there were probably mines, in the other, rebels. As the day's events appear promising, the latter seems the best bet.

After more beautiful, lush mountain landscapes, we come upon a deserted checkpoint, the coffee cups still full. Strange.

We drive on, and see youths darting into the bushes as we approach. Something's up, but what? The dirt road becomes quiet as a graveyard.

We get to the first town and we're met by a crowd standing in silence, blocking the road. We learn that a rebel commander had just been shot and killed by the Serbs. Cornered and unable to go further, we have no choice but to park outside a house used by the rebels. Adil, the cameraman, begins to film the crowd, and we ask for more details of what happened.

Then another commander arrives, crying, hysterical, blood on his clothes. He witnessed the shooting, the circumstances as yet unclear. But to the rebels, it was a plain and clear assassination.

Capturing the emotional moment, Adil keeps the camera rolling, next to a stills photographer who clicks away. The commander, deciding to vent his anger, grabs the stills camera and smashes it, then goes for Adil's camera. Adil initially resists and is aided by an assistant. The commander stands back and pulls his pistol. All of us in the crew turn and dart for cover, and the commander grabs the camera and he and his comrades smash it to bits with their AK-47s.

I run inside a farmhouse and hide, while the shouting continues. Thankfully no gunfire, but the fear and tension are electric. Will they go after us? Will they shoot? Will the crowd turn on us?

We regroup in a house not far from our jeep, where a family offers us refuge. I manage to get Atlanta on our satellite phone to explain the situation. The commander decides we can't leave until a US monitor comes to explain what had happened. In effect, we were hostages.

As the minutes wear on, as the men with guns and the angry crowd wait outside, the anxiety intensifies. We decide to lie low.

Then the *deus ex machina*. A local who speaks English and objects to our captivity contacts the local mayor, who persuades the rebels to release us.

But the commander wants Adil's smashed camera, to keep the pictures of the incident. Despite our assurances that the thing was useless, he insists. As we wait in the house, Adil manages to salvage the damaged videotape from it, so we hand over the rest of the wreckage to the commander.

It was an eerie, anxious moment, as some of the rebels boarded our vehicle to escort us past the rest of the rebels and through the angry crowd. At the edge of town they jump out, and we're on our way.

Back at the hotel, we pop the video in the SX machine. Not only did we get away with our lives, but we had pictures for a story.

Barely.

Chris Burns, Frankfurt Bureau Chief for the international news network, CNN.

My old charmer

Nicola Byrne

There's something about airports which make them ripe for romantic encounters. Humphrey Bogart and Ingrid Bergman were to learn this lesson in the film *Casablanca,* and it was to be repeated for me at Cape Town Airport on a Monday morning in March, 1996.

Most Africa correspondents get a Mandela story and eighteen months into my stint there, I was to have my brief but memorable meeting with the great man.

It happened in the airport VIP lounge, where the media had assembled for the arrival of the former Irish president, Mary Robinson. Mr Mandela, who was there to greet her, had agreed to a short interview and, having answered questions briskly, he rose to go before spying me at the back of the room, whereupon a definite glint came into his eye.

"Young lady come here," he said.

I marched forward.

"Are you married?" he asked.

"No," I squeaked.

He stopped and smiled broadly. "Ah well, you see I ..."

The attendant reporters waited, eager for a reference for his divorce from Winnie which had happened only five days previously. He checked himself, still smiling and put out his hand to me.

"Well, if you were to ask me to marry you, I would consider the request very favourably."

Overcome, I managed to say nothing and bustled on by a flurry of aides, he departed. Cursing myself for my inarticulateness, I set off on another job and thought no more of it, until later that day when my mum phoned from Ireland.

Arriving home, she had been greeted by a neighbour who ran from her house to tell her that Ireland's main TV station, RTE, had run a humorous story on their one o'clock news about how her daughter had been propositioned by Nelson Mandela. By the following day, the South African papers had picked up the tale and when I visited Robben Island the next morning on another assignment, I took a barrage of phone calls from newspapers and radio stations.

Waiting for some foreign dignitary to arrive, I had a souvenir photograph taken on the bed in Mandela's former cell. While posing, a photographer from a local paper rushed in and started snapping furiously. "I don't think that was very wise," another foreign correspondent remarked to me.

"Mandela's new girl," said the headline on the front page of the Johannesburg *Star* the next day, followed by a lot of made-up quotes which told of a young Irish woman who was charmed, flattered and "gobsmacked".

By the end of the week the stories had abated, leaving me a little mortified in their wake.

Some years later and back in the greyness of the northern hemisphere, the *Sunday Tribune* newspaper in Dublin phoned me to ask me to review a copy of Anthony Sampson's biography of Madiba.

Having collected the book from their office a few days later, I got caught in a rain shower and stepped into a phone box to shelter. Thumbing through the index as I waited for the weather to comply, I was a little shocked and pleased to see, in Sampson's book, just under Mangosuthu Buthelezi's name, Byrne, Nicola, p 546.

Fumbling through the pages, I found the relevant one, a reference to the above episode, but with this epilogue. Sampson wrote: "But the 'proposal' looked less flattering when Mandela later appeared to mistake another reporter, Alexandra Zavis of the Associated Press for Byrne."

I slipped the tome into my bag and reflected on what I'd always really known. He may be the world's greatest statesman, an icon of the twentieth century and hero to millions, but as any woman who's ever met him knows, he's also just an old charmer.

Nicola Byrne is a freelance journalist who worked in Africa from 1994 until 1998, contributing to *The Australian*, *The Scotsman* and *The Boston Globe*. She now writes for *The Observer* from Dublin.

The take-off

Tom Sampson

We had an uneventful flight from Nairobi to Lokichokio. It was the standard boring trip, and we arrived in Loki at about eight thirty in the morning. The air had already started to heat up for the day ahead.

Martin Dawes of the BBC and I were there to fly into Southern Sudan on another of what felt like a never-ending series of trips to find more victims of the famine. This was to be the fourth trip there in less than three weeks. It was all becoming pretty routine, fly in for a day or maybe an overnight or two, and then back to Loki or Nairobi for the editing and then back on the plane again for another round to find more of the same.

We walked over to the charter company that would fly us into South Sudan. Martin had asked about a new location in Jonglei province, called Duk Faiwill. We had heard they had just received a large influx of people running from the fighting. We thought that these people might be in pretty bad shape.

The pilot had received information that the locals had repaired the airstrip so an aircraft could land and so the decision was made that we would try it. Our aircraft was to be a trusty Cessna Caravan, the real workhorse of planes flying into the difficult airstrips of Southern Sudan. We decided to fly to the town of Bor to collect our Sudan Relief and Rehabilitation Association (SRRA) minder. We were going to a location where there were no SRRA officials, so we had to get one from somewhere else and the closest location was the riverside town of Bor.

The gear was loaded onboard and off we went. I usually enjoy the trip into Southern Sudan, although there is very little that is happening that you can see from about 3 000 or 4 000 metres, but every now and then you see a town and you know where you are. After such an early start from my house in Nairobi I can usually get a bit more sleep.

The arrival in Bor was fine. We collected the SRRA minder, and then it was a short flight to Duk Faiwill. The minder assured us that the airstrip had been repaired for the imminent arrival of aid flights. The pilot told us that he would over-fly the strip to assess the condition of it and if he felt it was okay he would land.

As we over-flew the strip at treetop level, we could see a large numbers of locals who had stopped there after fleeing from the fighting.

The pilot told us everything looked fine and he would circle around and land on the next approach. A few minutes later we were on the ground and the pilot said we had one-and-a-half hours in which to get back to Loki before dark.

Off we went to see what was going on and get the footage to tell the story of what had happened to these people. After an hour of filming, we pretty much had what we needed of these poor, hungry refugees. It was another situation where the non-combatants had drawn the short straw. They had to flee their homes with very little and were now stuck just behind the front line and maybe had to get up and run again at any minute; we were happy that we had our plane to get us out of there.

A local came up to us and told us the pilot had asked us to come back to the aircraft. Martin and I wondered what was up. We walked back over to the plane and he told us that in fact the airstrip was in very poor shape. It had been covered with a layer of sand and dirt so there wasn't any hard base to it. Due to its short length it was going to be an interesting take-off. Great, all in a day's work. He said that he had placed a stick about 100 meters from the end of the airstrip so he knew that if we were not airborne by then he would have to throttle back, and we would have to lighten our load.

As I sat in the co-pilot's seat, I heard the engine revving loudly. Off we went for attempt one. At the cutoff point he throttled back quickly, saying, "too heavy". We taxied back to our starting point and he shut down the engine. We all knew what was about to happen. The pilot told the SRRA minder that he was going to have to walk back to Bor. To say he was unhappy about this is a major understatement, but eventually he got the fact that this is the only way he would get back home. So off he headed – mind you, it was a two-day walk and all he had were the clothes he started out in. We gave him our bottled water and the snacks we had brought along and wished him luck. By this time a crowd of about 500 semi-clad locals, many holding automatic weapons, had gathered. We had the soldiers, we had the boys, we had the shy young girls, we had crying babies; there were also a few chickens and a lonely cow. In this village, this was high entertainment.

About 70 kilos lighter, we tried again. This time way before the takeoff stick the pilot throttled back and said "too heavy". Back at the start of the airstrip, he said we were going to have to off-load some of the fuel as it was the only thing left that we could dump. We asked around for some containers for the fuel. It's Jet A-1, basically very refined kerosene and very useful in Southern Sudan for cooking. But all we could find was a broken gourd and a half a plastic bucket sewn together with cotton thread; they each held about three litres.

The pilot got out a tool used to siphon small amounts of fuel. He started the process of draining the fuel into the gourd and bucket and told us he would try to empty out about 100 litres. One of the biggest hassles was that the wing was about 2,5 metres in the air and there was nothing to stand on, so he had to stand on his tippy toes. He didn't want the fuel dumped near the aircraft so we carried the containers to the side of the airstrip and dumped it there. After about 30 minutes he was getting pretty tired and was soaked in Jet A-1. We worked out that he had only drained 50 litres. "Argh," I say, "hey, I'll have a go for a while." Well it's very unpleasant to stand on your tippy toes with your arms stretched over your head and be showered in Jet A-1.

"Hurray," he says, "let's try again." So we board and all the locals were watching to see if we crashed in a ball of flames. Off we went with full power, I was dreaming about a cold beer and a hot shower back in Loki, then I saw him reaching for the throttle and I thought "noooooooo!".

Back to emptying more fuel. This time it was another 100 litres, and I was starting to itch. The pilot kindly informed me that most people break out in a rash after being covered in Jet A-1. Lovely. To the east, the afternoon thunderclouds were starting to gather. No one said anything. We all knew that if it rained we would be there for the night and most likely longer as the airstrip would never dry out.

Draining the fuel then became a lot more urgent. After about 20 minutes it was all aboard for the fourth attempt. Argh ... no luck. Lots of noise, and lots and lots of dust, but still no take-off.

The weather was really starting to close in and so we tried again. My rash was really uncomfortable. I had taken off my shirt and the fuel now more or less ran off my body and onto the ground. The pilot decided that we needed to drain more fuel. We still had enough on board to make the one hour 45 minute flight back to Loki. He said there was a fuel dump at a village about 35 minutes' flying time to the west across the Nile River, where we could refuel for the flight back to Loki.

We had a good system going, and even a few locals were helping. They were doing more laughing than work so we took over. Back in the plane, seat belts tightened we were off for attempt five. But we were still too heavy. The pilot was starting to look worried. I did not want to sleep in the village. The last time I got stuck in a place like this was in Rwanda where I got a bad case of malaria – not fun.

We were all back out under that damn wing having our Jet A-1 shower and having off-loaded something like 1 000 litres of fuel, most of which felt like it had soaked into my hair and skin. The pilot – he was pretty confident of success. Yeah right.

All aboard, doors closed, I took my co-pilot's seat, watched him crank up the engines and off we went for attempt six. I could hear the locals yelling from the side of the airstrip. I watched the pilot's every move to see if he would throttle back, but no, he went for it, we were airborne. We cleared the trees at the end of the airstrip by all of a gourd's worth of Jet A-1 and gained height quickly. In the distance I saw the Nile River and thought, "time for a beer soon".

Tom Sampson has lived in Africa as a freelance cameraman since 1988 and has worked for the best and the worst in that time. He currently lives in Ethiopia with his wife, Angela, and son, Myles.

Jerusalem

Benjamin Pogrund

He was powerful-looking, of medium height with broad shoulders, a light-brown face that looked tanned, a shiny bald head and a neat goatee beard. Dressed in the white uniform of an orderly, he had come to fetch me from the X-Ray department in the Hadassah Mount Scopus Hospital in Jerusalem, where I had undergone yet another examination after surgery for stomach cancer.

He did not say a word as he took hold of my bed and pushed it towards the lifts. He's a Russian immigrant, I thought to myself, and doesn't speak English. We passed a woman, her head covered according to Muslim tradition, and he broke into an animated, laughing conversation with her in Arabic. Ah, I thought, he's an Arab. A few minutes later, as he pushed me into a lift, there was a woman with her head covered according to Jewish Orthodox tradition. He broke into an animated, laughing conversation with her in Hebrew. Ah, I thought, this is quite a guy.

On the third floor he pushed the bed out of the lift, along the corridor and into my room. He locked the bed in position and then said to me, in English, "Now you must get better."

I was astonished. His job was to push beds around the hospital. He had never seen me, had no idea who I was, yet he took the trouble to wish me well. It was a simple human contact and it took me close to tears. Perhaps in my weakened state I was especially vulnerable and emotional. Yet it also confirmed what I had been seeing during the previous four weeks as I watched the bustle and routine of the surgical ward.

The Hadassah Mount Scopus Hospital is in East Jerusalem, which is the area of the city populated mainly by Arabs. About half the patients are Jewish, and half are Arabs. The chief surgeon, a Jew, who operated on me, had been recommended to me as the best there was. He chose my anaesthetist, an Arab. It seemed to me that both Jews and Arabs, mainly the former (I wasn't always sure who was what), made up the doctors who did the daily rounds checking me and taking blood samples. One of them, an Arab, told me he had very recently been accepted as a surgical intern. I complimented him on the skilful way in which he drew blood – by that time it had been done so often that it was a painful experience for me – and he laughed and asked me to be sure to tell the chief surgeon.

Most of the nurses who treated me were Jews; some were Arabs. I watched them together, the relaxed interplay between them, the shared concern and caring for me and other patients.

I was in hospital over the Jewish Passover festival. Gideon, my youngest son, and his wife, Elisha, are religiously observant and do not travel on festivals. They came to spend the night to look after me. They laid a table in a waiting-room and celebrated the *seder* – the ritual meal and prayers. Only Arab nurses were on duty that night – and they opened a ward to give Elisha a bed for the night.

Knowing the history of the hospital made me even more aware of the beauty of the relationships that I was seeing and benefiting from. Mount Scopus was built in the 1930s with funds collected by the American Jewish women's Hadassah Organisation, named after its founder. They still work for it: hospital walls are lined with metal plaques recording the generous money donations made by Jews around the world.

But in 1948 the hospital was caught in the Jewish-Arab conflict. In November the previous year the United Nations had voted to partition Palestine between Jews and Arabs. Fighting broke out and the hospital, and the Hebrew University neighbouring it, was in Arab-controlled East Jerusalem. The hospital kept working. Each week a convoy of buses and trucks, guarded by armoured cars, ferried doctors, nurses and patients a few kilometres from Jewish-controlled West Jerusalem.

On 13 April, Arabs attacked the convoy. Some 77 Jews died in the hours-long barrage of bullets and firebombs. Only a half-dozen survived.

The hospital died. It was unused for the next 19 years. Then came the 1967 war. Israel conquered the West Bank, including East Jerusalem. It united West and East Jerusalem. Hadassah Mount Scopus again came under Jewish control. It was renovated and re-opened, even though in the meantime another bigger Hadassah hospital had been built on the opposite, western edge of Jerusalem.

Driving now to Mount Scopus there's a simple stone memorial at the side of the road marking the site of the massacre: it lists the names of the victims.

This is a blood-drenched part of the world. The Israeli-Palestinian struggle continues. When I came to live in Jerusalem in 1997 hopes were high for peace. Six years later, the prospects are bleak. There is much hatred, fear and rejection on both sides. That is why my hospital experience affected me so deeply: it was a reminder that Jew and Arab still do reach out to each other; that a common humanity binds them.

252

Benjamin Pogrund was deputy editor of the *Rand Daily Mail*, Johannesburg, when the newspaper was closed in 1985. He is founding director of Yakar's Center for Social Concern in Jerusalem. He has written books about Robert Mangaliso Sobukwe, Nelson Mandela, and the Press under apartheid.

The drama with pictures

Bruno Beeckman

I must have slept through the knock at the door at the Eurovision feed point. When I opened my eyes on that cold January morning in Khassavyurt on the Chechen-Dagestani border, I was confronted by three unmistakably Russian women who were holding paper parcels and starting to introduce themselves.

Nadezhda Pavlovna had come all the way from the Siberian city of Irkutsk and she presented me with an authentic Irkutsk sausage. Irina Vladimirovna had travelled for one-and-a-half weeks from the Sakhalin Islands and she presented me with local cheese. Marina Alexandovna had travelled for a week from the city of Saratov before she presented me with some delicious pickled cucumbers from her own garden.

I was, by then, used to unusual things happening. In fact, I was used to them from the day that we deployed our satellite dish in Grozny. It was December 6 1994 and, four hours later, Russian troops invaded Chechnya to present history with the first Chechen War. We had to leave Grozny two weeks later when the conflict spun out of control and planes were dropping flares and bombs two hundred metres from our feed point.

Forty-eight hours later we made it through the Caucasus Mountains to arrive in the Dagestani border town of Khassavyurt, where we found a new place to stay at the Sports Centre of Alikhan, a Chechen wrestler. Alikhan was respected by everyone in the town, whether Russian, Chechen or Dagestani, as it was he who had lifted the Soviet Wrestling Federation to new heights. It was a time when no journalist had heard the expression "to be embedded". Since we were the exclusive satellite feeding facility from the start of the war, the sports camp was turned into the main press centre overnight, where correspondents could live and work in the wooden barracks next to Chechen and Russian refugees who had fled the merciless brutality near their homes.

As I blearily struggled out of bed that morning in my long johns and ushered the three women into the next room (the actual feed point), I was asking myself what had prompted them to present me with a sausage, some cheese and pickles.

While making tea, their story emerged. The three women had come all the way to Khassavyurt to get news of their three sons who had been sent to Chechnya by the Russians. No more had been heard of them. Meanwhile, in the two months since their departure, Russian broadcasters, who had had unprecedented access to the front line, that is to say they were not hampered by censorship, had been showing the nation pictures of dead Russian soldiers and prisoners of war on a daily basis.

Simultaneously, an organisation called "Soldiers' Mothers" had sprung into existence in Moscow. Their main goal was to provide information to the mothers of Russian soldiers who had been fobbed off by the Russian Defence Ministry since the conflict began, especially since the ministry had not proven to be the walkover the authorities had predicted.

"You are our last hope," said Nadezhda Pavlovna. "The ONLY thing we want to know is whether our sons are still alive." She continued, "we know you have all the pictures as all the journalists pass through your facilities. Now we want to see them ourselves, and may God help us, maybe we can find our sons among the many pictures you keep here".

I was looking at the dozens of master tapes that had been left behind by correspondents in the edit suite and started to pick them up, still trying to grasp the unimaginable.

Fifty minutes into the silent process of scrolling through tapes of POWs with the three women standing behind me, holding onto my shoulder, Irina Vladimirovna shrieked and collapsed to the floor. She was helped to her feet by the other two women and stammered that she had just seen her son Dima on the tape. Dima, as it turned out, was a POW in a city not too far away from where we were.

It was then that Alikhan walked in. He stood there, watching silently and left after ten minutes while we continued looking for the other two boys. Half an hour later we located Marina Alexandovna's son Andrei, who had been filmed alive and well four days ago in a POW camp in the Chechen town of Shali.

When we had gone through all the tapes, I got up and told Nadezhda Pavlovna that I would check with correspondents whether they had not come across her son, Sergey. Her face turned to stone. "Show me the other tapes, the ones with the bodies."

I told her I could not do this. But the three mothers implored me to change my mind. "We are mothers, Bruno, mothers, and this is the only way to know the truth. And the truth, however hard, will eventually calm us down. It's the not knowing which hurts.

I dreaded it.

Ten minutes into the tape with the dead Russian soldiers, Nadezhda

Pavlovna knew. She was carried out of our barracks by Marina and Irina. I will never forget this image. It has stuck in my mind ever since.

Through Alikhan, on that January morning, Andrei and Dima were reunited with their mothers one week after their arrival in Kassavuyrt.

Bruno Beeckman has been a Eurovision News producer since 1993. From 1993 till 2001 he was based in Moscow, since then in Geneva. His work has brought him across the CIS (the former Soviet Union) – including Chechnya and Siberia – the former Yugoslavia, China, Afghanistan, Cuba, the USA and Iraq. He is married with two children.

Hitchhiking home

Gaby Neujahr

April 1999, Morina/Kukes, Border Albania/Kosovo

It was 4:30 in the morning when my ugly cellphone did the only thing of use in Albania in those days: it woke us up (photographer Thomas Hegenbarth, our driver/translator Apollon and myself).

We camped in the living room of an Albanian family in the tiny village of Kukes, close to the Kosovan Border for $400 US a week – a little extra income in terrible times. No coffee, no shower, we jumped into the car while chewing another round of muesli-bars washed down with far too sweet orange Fanta.

It was the same procedure every day. Each day of the last week we had travelled along the border to document the cruel exodus from Kosovo of hundreds of thousands Kosovars forced by Serb militias to flee their country.

A gigantic trek of people walked or squeezed into old buses or rode old tractors to flee the militias. Never before in my life had I seen such a large, seemingly never-ending number of devastated people. Day after day the same scene in Morina, a border-post between Albania and the Serb Kosovo: one tractor lined up behind the next as far as the eye could see. All were packed with women, old men and kids who had sheer horror written all over their gaunt faces. For weeks Serb militias has been systematically forcing them from their native country, and nearly half a million refugees had swept into the neighbouring countries, especially into bitterly poor Albania.

Nato had been bombing suspected Serb posts in Kosovo for two weeks. Their jets thundered over our heads to release their deadly load only a few kilometres away and Serb snipers across the border occasionally shot into the fleeing crowds or in our direction just for the fun of it.

But then, all of a sudden, from one day to the next, it fell silent. All paths and streets were deserted. Overnight the Serbs had closed the border and planted mines. A ghostly silence had taken over. Well, we had our story and the deadline was in two days' time.

We had a deal with the German Bundeswehr – that we could get home to Germany in one of their planes which flew aid to Albania's capital,

Tirana, every day. We had to get to Tirana as soon as possible. Our best chance was at the provisional helicopter landing spot of the French legionnaires in Kukes.

It was eight in the morning. Armed with big smiles and loads of charm we managed to talk the French into offering us two seats on the next incoming machine. Just two hours later we were in an army helicopter to Tirana. As soon as we landed we went in search of the Germans, but were disappointed: "Today no German plane will arrive. Maybe tomorrow", we were told.

We reluctantly accepted, hired a taxi and went to the only international hotel in Tirana. There we hoped to get a shower (after spending a week in the dirt) and we could make contact with our colleagues in Germany. But there was another blow: the Hotel Rogner was booked out. Hundreds of journalists from all over the world had taken over the place.

At least we were able to use the phone to call our editor and our families. Tired and smelly, we nestled into chairs in the hotel bar and drowned our frustration with beer. Finally a receptionist was sympathetic – mainly because of how we smelled, I suppose. She offered us a shower in the room of a British TV crew who were going to be out the whole day. With a broad smile she gave us the key and some towels – we were jubilant. An hour later we approached the reception and the same woman ushered us into a small conference room. While we were showering the hotel crew had set up two provisional beds – what a relief! We had just stored our meagre luggage when we were called to the phone. A German officer quickly informed us that a Trans-All, a military transport plane, would land in Tirana in two hours. We grabbed our luggage and left the Rogner, boarded another taxi and sped back to the airport. But there was no hint of the Germans. Our taxi driver simply drove his old blue Mercedes onto the runway to check for incoming planes. No one knew anything about a German plane. Finally the guys in the tower informed us that the Germans would not come because of "technical problems".

Luckily one of the guys in the tower mentioned that a French Trans-All was due to arrive later and that another plane was waiting to fly the Czech prime minister back to Prague. Our patient and caring driver took us for another ride on the runway. When we approached the Czech plane some deeply irritated security guards scanned our rotten Mercedes and its occupants with obvious disgust. We tried to explain that we urgently had to get to Western Europe; that the Germans hadn't shown up; that Prague would be ideal and if they could please be so kind as to give us a lift "tonight". Sheer astonishment crossed their faces and they refused – "for security reasons".

We sped to the French. Night had fallen and while our driver again raced down the runway I tried to suppress my giggles at the bizarre scenario. In the French camp a young soldier patiently listened to our litany, left us for a few minutes and came back with the responsible officer. "*Pas de problème*, you could fly with us, our plane will land in 30 minutes and will fly back to Marseilles tonight," said the officer. I could have kissed that guy! Minutes later we heard the sound of a heavy cargo plane. The officer ushered us into a jeep, we waved goodbye to our fearless driver and again raced down the runway.

Before entering the French cargo plane, the officer took me aside: "You better pee here before we start. There is no 'Ladies' on board ..." I looked around. No bush, no tree, nothing except tar and lawn. But who cares – I did as recommended. But it was not enough as I discovered three hours later. I managed to abuse a plastic can – much to the amusement of Thomas, my colleague. The urinals were too high for me to aim at and it was all I could find.

We landed at a deserted military base 60 kilometres outside Marseilles just after 1 a.m. The gentle French quartered us in their officers' dormitory and left us with the phone numbers of local taxi companies. And while Thomas booked our flights for the next morning, I could not raise a taxi driver to drive us to Marseilles airport – people in the French countryside seem to head for bed early.

We finally found a taxi and were fetched at 6 a.m. and raced to the airport, stormed through the departure hall, picked up our tickets and ran to the plane. We were the last passengers to arrive and the plane took off while we were fastening our seatbelts.

Eighteen hours later, our report about the exodus from Kosovo went into print.

Gaby Neujahr is a German-born journalist who has worked for various publications including the news magazine, *Focus*, as international politics reporter and later deputy foreign editor. Since January 2002 she has run the sub-Saharan Africa media project for the Konrad-Adenauer-Stiftung, Berlin.

Vultures

Ben de Pear

"It's a challenge, mate, that's what it is, a challenge," said Martin, neatly encapsulating the near-impossible in a bite-size phrase. "Once we're across the minefield we just shimmy up those hills."

"They're mountains, Martin."

"Alright, those mountains," he conceded, running his thick fingers further down the map.

"Then it's six or seven days, bivvy bag it during the day in the snow, nice and snug, hiding up with a bit of Gucci gear and then yipping it during the night. Then we follow these rivers down the contours to the nearest friendly village, and then 'opefully get one of the locals to give us some donkeys to make it to Arbil. It'll be great. We can't hang around here all war like spare pricks. We came here to do something and we've got to do it."

The thought of it made me feel nauseous, and there was in fact a growing knot of pain in my stomach. We were ten days into our recce around the outside borders of Northern Iraq, trying to find a way in through either Turkey or Syria, without permission from either country. We had started in Istanbul, flown to the border town of Silopi, and there met the usual people who will smuggle you across borders: local gangsters, "freedom fighters", and "fixers", all of whom had shaken their heads and laughed – they couldn't help us. Anyway why did we want to go?

In Syria we had met similar characters, but the border there was fairly flat, and it was crucial to know which part had friendly Kurds on the other side and which the unfriendly Iraqi army. We put our names on a list in Damascus, a process that may have borne fruit within a month or so, but we did not have a month, it was February and nobody knew when the war would start. So we headed back to Turkey, whose border with Saddam's unfriendly Iraq was better for sneaking across, said Martin.

Martin thought I was "up for it" and had listened to my small number of conflict stories with rapt attention, even embellishing them slightly when telling them back to me later and trying to convince me I was the man he was. He hadn't convinced me.

That day our flight from Damascus was so early that we had arrived at 06h00, hadn't slept, and after final desperate visits to political offices, embassies, and some local TV stations, we resolved that our last option, trekking illegally through the heavily fortified border, was now our only one. The more we talked of the plan, the more we drank, and the sicker I felt. By midnight the pain was excruciating and I went to bed – Martin thinking that I had "the squits".

By 4 a.m. and after hours of watching BBC World without sleeping, a near impossible feat, the hotel called a doctor. By 6 I was in a hospital with another doctor scanning my belly with ultrasound, and repeating the word "happindix". I had been undressed, smocked and was on a trolley in a lift, going up. I had yet to hear a word of English.

At the sixth floor I was wheeled out into what appeared to be a surgical ante-chamber. On about five or six trolleys other similarly besmocked patients lay in different states of consciousness, two marked with felt tip crosses as surgical signposts, one above an eye and the other near an ear. A nurse came and gave me a pill, a drip was fitted into my arm. One by one the patients were taken into theatre until I was alone and feeling drowsy. As each new surgical team emerged I had taken to rubbing my stomach and repeating "appendix, appendix", hoping that when it came to be my turn they would know what to look for.

"Binjamin, hello."

Leaning over me was a doctor with a finely manicured beard.

"Hello."

"I am your surgeon. Your appendix is swollen and we must remove it. You have been given a sedative and soon the anaesthetist will make you sleep. Do you understand?"

"Yes."

"You are English, yes?"

"Yes."

"What are doing in our country?"

"I am working."

"What work do you do, Binjamin?"

"I am a journalist."

"You are here because of the war", he snapped. "The war is a very bad thing. You must not attack our Muslim brothers. You being here makes the situation much, much worse. Journalists are not needed in this country to heat the situation."

"No you don't understand, if we tell the truth, maybe there will be no war, anyway my appendix …"

"Binjamin understand me. The war will happen with or without you.

They have decided. This will be a catastrophe," he said, now visibly angry. "You journalists are like vultures. Nobody is inviting you."

A woman was now sticking a needle into the drip – the anaesthesia. I had seconds in which to convince the man who was about to slice open my belly that I was a good egg. It was too late. I awoke facing a window with whirling snowflakes skidding down it.

"Hello, mate! Nice one – you must 'ave been killing but you never said a thing. Here you go, I've brought you a present," said Martin, pouring the contents of his mini bar in my lap. Miniature bottles of vodka and whisky clinked against each other whilst crisps and peanuts lay uninvitingly against my bloodied bandage.

"Let's have a look then."

"No."

"Come on, get it out."

I unwrapped what looked like the bloody and enormous top of a Cornish pasty, running vertically downwards for ten or so inches next to my belly button.

"Fuckin' hell, mate, they've taken everything. They've bayoneted you," said Martin, roaring with laughter. "Anyway, I'm no good at this sort of thing, I'm off. I'll see you later."

• • •

When it happens first it is very loud and then it goes deathly quiet. It was close, closer than any before; this time the building really shook. Then from down the hall comes the sound of screaming, chilling and distant at first and then urgent and close.

"Get a doctor, are you a doctor?" someone screams at me as we rush into the corridor.

At its end and coming towards us is a mattress containing a body. It's so raw it's shocking but for some reason I'm shocked into calmness; my first unstoppable thought is "thank God this is not me, or someone I know," although it's hard to recognise the bundled shape of blood and body prone on the mattress as anyone. My second thought is, "there is nothing I can do for this person, it is beyond me". The man is still screaming in my face and I don't know what to do other than get the lift. We're on the 14th floor. They'll need a lift.

Downstairs there's real outrage. Nobody invited any of us here, but we all came anyway. Now that we're here and really taking part everyone is appalled. And an American tank, one we'd watched all morning – after waking up shocked to see it – and others were on the other side of the river. We all watched through binoculars from our balconies as they and American A-10 bomber planes strafed and destroyed the ministries opposite, a fantastic but frightening show we were here to observe but not, we hoped, take part in.

Downstairs in the lobby there's pandemonium as they try to get the injured into cars and get them to some place that still functions. All the hospitals are full. But nobody invited us. We are vultures.

Ben de Pear is Sky's Africa News Editor and has worked extensively for Sky across four continents. He was the producer for Sky's coverage of the entry of NATO troops into Kosovo in 1999, and for the last week of the recent Iraq war in Baghdad.

The last word from Kerem

John Lawton

The last time I talked to my son, Kerem, he spoke bitterly of the "assholes" in London, who were making "up to five phone calls a day" demanding "more spicy", "close-up, not long-shot" coverage of fighting in Macedonia. Three days later he was dead; a victim as much of this pressure as from the shell that slammed into his car and killed him.

This is clear from Kerem's comments to colleagues who argued against getting too close to the fighting. He said, "at least it would stop the phone calls from London", one told me later.

When those responsible for making the phone calls were named in my presence in London, APTN executives declined to comment. While news managers confronted with the same names sat in embarrassed silence.

Ironically, the person largely responsible for making the calls took more time off work to recover from a nervous disorder (guilt, I suspect) than Kerem's widow Elida, also an APTN producer, was given to recover from his death – and give birth to his baby.

The person responsible for instigating the calls was put in charge of "safety decisions on day-to-day operational deployment" of APTN employees in conflict zones. The somewhat twisted logic of putting the arsonist in charge of the fire brigade, seems to have worked: Kerem's colleagues, who I meet regularly in the field, say the pressures from London have eased significantly since Kerem's death.

This is good. So too was AP's decision to triple life insurance for staffers like Kerem (although they refuse to pay it to his dependents), and their introduction of Safety Guidelines for war correspondents (embraced by AP and other media giants meeting in Barcelona before Kerem's death – but not announced by APTN until nearly one year later). Chief among these guidelines is: no pressure will be exerted on any employee or freelancer to go on assignments to a hostile area regardless of competitive or external considerations.

Too late for Kerem – how else could he satisfy repeated requests of "close up" coverage without going into a hostile area? And too late too for APTN cameraman Miguel Gil Moreno de Mora, who died a year earlier in Sierra Leone because of pressure of competition; he followed competitors into an ambush after being reprimanded by APTN editors in London for being beaten by them on an earlier story.

There has always been, and always will be, competition among journalists. But it should not be fuelled by irresponsible editors, many of whom have little experience in conflict zones. Nor by ambitious news managers eager to please existing clients or win new ones for their news gathering services.

The APTN team covering the fighting between the Macedonian army and Albanian insurgents were, in fact, besting their competitors. But the so-called "silly coverage requests" continued because, by then, pressure from the London news desk had become endemic. It was even suggested that Kerem's then-pregnant wife, who speaks Albanian, enter the conflict zone to interview guerrilla leaders.

Much anger at APTN editors was expressed in private at Kerem's funeral, by which time APTN had lost three men in two years. And management was bluntly advised, in my presence, that unless things changed, we shall lose even more. Once again, no comment.

Journalists frequently complain to each other about the pressure from headquarters. But few go public for fear of losing their jobs. While those who work within their organisations to improve understanding between desk and field are usually frustrated. "It is something I tried to get APTN to deal with," one of Kerem's colleagues told me. "I suggested that when people come to London, they should be allowed space to talk to desk people about pressure and how they needed to be treated in the field." "Oh, good idea," was the general response, but nothing ever happened.

The safety of journalists is one of the top priorities of World Press Freedom Day – to which, in part, this book is dedicated. And many individuals and organisations work year-round to protect journalists from threats from external sources. But threats to their safety from within are frequently glossed over. It is a darker side of our profession that few of us like to discuss openly. But it is just as important that journalists working in conflict areas be protected from their managers, as it is they are safeguarded from combatants.

Both can be lethal.

John Lawton is a freelance journalist, father of Kerem Lawton and grandfather of Tara Lawton.

I didn't bring a suit

Claude Colart

The calendar in my flat near Brussels must have been open at October or November 1997. It had been a busy year but it wasn't over yet.

Fundamentalists in Algeria were waging a violent campaign and journalists were one of their favourite throat-slicing targets. So it wasn't with great joy that I took the call-of-duty from the editor in London who wanted to see if I "wouldn't mind" going to the former French colony to cover the elections.

I knew that my good friend and colleague Dominique "Hombre" Mollard was part of the deal. A Frenchman living in Madrid and expert on Algeria, he had been there many times. I had never set foot in Algeria, which made it more attractive to me.

I also needed an emotional escape and what better place to go than purgatory for an adrenaline rush?

My dad had just left my mom and I had trouble dealing with it. I needed fresh air and told my family I was going to Kenya. I couldn't tell them my true destination; too many "unpleasant" pictures from Algeria had been on TV recently, and my mom liked following stories of where I was.

Heavy-hearted, I left Belgium.

Our visas were ready in London so Hombre and I decided to hook up across the Channel. At Heathrow we stocked up on spirits, cigarettes and perfume.

"Necessary for persuasion," Dominique claimed.

The woman behind the till at the duty free shop looked amazed.

"Are you travelling within Europe?" If so, we had to put 99% back.

As we filled the backpack with Marlboro, Jack Daniels, Hugo Boss and other goodies, a businessman sitting a few chairs from us waiting for his boarding call looked strangely at this funny scene: two men pushing all this duty free into a backpack. Obviously we were not tourists escaping rainy Europe for the Canary Islands. Maybe we were planning a big party? But it was probably our TV camera that said we weren't in search of a tan.

Minutes later we were sitting at an airport bar eating salmon and drinking white wine.

"It's good to have an excellent meal before dying," Dominique joked. My mind was shifting between Algiers and my mother.

A few hours later we touched down on North African soil. As we were standing in the passport queue, several gentlemen in suits walked towards us.

"Monsieur Mollard et Monsieur Colart?" one of them asked politely. Welcome to Big Brother Algeria. The embassy in London must have sent our passport photographs ahead of our arrival and the omni-present state security was waiting for us. It felt awkward. But we had no choice. We followed the men as they led us through passport control and into waiting cars and then to the El-Aurassi Hotel. The few international journalists covering the elections all had to stay in the same hotel overlooking the harbour.

At least we weren't stopped at customs. That would have been an interesting conversation.

Algiers – a stressed city with an uncertain future. Dominique called around his contacts. We hooked up with Said, a local fixer. Every time we wanted to leave the hotel we had to tell the state security agents who had set up a desk in the lobby. They wanted to know where we were going and gave us two minders. The bodyguards, who were more like Big Brothers, drove ahead of us in an unmarked white French car.

Soon it was clear that we had to use "tricks from the old book" to convince our minders we wanted to go to places they didn't like very much. Officially their objections were for security reasons, but it felt more like polite censorship.

But this is where our Heathrow bounty came into its own. Dominique handed a few packets of Marlboro and a bottle of whiskey to one of our regular minders. He smiled as though he had received a birthday present for the first time in his life.

As we walked towards the exit door to go to our "unwanted" location, a senior state security officer stopped us. With a big smile on his face he said he saw that we had given one of his officers some interesting presents.

With his typical wit and a large smile, Dominique said: "I can't give this to you because you are a good Muslim, isn't it?"

The officer laughed but was speechless. And off we went to the Kasbah. The old part of Algiers with its small streets was a breeding ground for extremism, especially since the banning of the FIS party.

Hundreds of eyes were on us as we stepped out of our cars accompanied by four secret agents. Two of them stayed near the cars while two others walked with us into the Kasbah. The Marlboro and booze must have come as a welcome gift as the agents let us go ahead and into the office of a pro–FIS lawyer. They politely stayed outside. No Big Brother eyes and ears during our interview.

The story was building up. There had been some killings and demonstrations. Tensions were running high.

"Don't use the phone inside your room", Dominique warned. "It's probably bugged, especially now that our FIS interview has gone around the world." For a moment I wanted to pick up the phone and tell a dirty joke to whoever was eavesdropping.

Two days before polling day several organisations had planned a large demonstration in central Algiers. The pro–government local media and our contacts warned that the GIA might use the occasion to plant bombs and create a bloodbath in an attempt to derail the elections.

My heart was pumping fast. Would this be a day from hell? Would we die today here on the streets of Algiers, while back home everybody thought I was on a smooth trip to Kenya? But the adrenaline rush took over. We knew we couldn't nor did we want to miss this.

"You've got to do what you've got to do," I told myself.

As we walked towards the glass rotating doors of the hotel, the same senior officer asked us to fill in his papers to say where we were going today. The usual routine.

"The demo of course," I told him.

He asked me with a smile: "Why didn't you put on your best suit then?" Always that same intriguing smile. I looked surprised. Before I could respond, he continued. "Because today the terrorists might use the occasion and explode some bombs. And then it's better to be in your best suit if you are going to die."

What do you say to that? It just makes your heart go an extra beat. The minders were also extra touchy. They didn't really fancy going to town today. It was clear from their behaviour that their superior's joke contained at least some truth.

But off we went. We covered the thousands of people walking through the streets of Algiers. The minders were so close behind us that you could feel their breath on your neck. But the day passed without bombs. No bloodshed.

That evening it was "decompression" time. Escapism in the form of Jack Daniels and Van Morrison. Sitting on the balcony floor, Hombre, Said and myself. Brothers–in–arms in a hellish place. A glass of JD in our hands and the mind smoothed by Van's "The Healing Game".

Months later I told my family I hadn't been in Kenya after all.

Claude Colart is a Belgian, freelance TV producer and journalist living in Johannesburg where he runs be_africa Productions. He was previously Senior Producer and Deputy Managing Editor for Associated Press Television News.

San Giuliano's twenty-six little angels

Trisha Thomas

The sun beat down on the dozens of cameramen, producers and correspondents perched like vultures on the edge of an olive grove as the funeral procession crawled up the road before us.

Twenty-six small white coffins were passing. They called them the "Little Angels of San Giuliano of Puglia". Twenty-six school children from the Italian village of San Giuliano were crushed in their classrooms when an earthquake hit and their school collapsed on top of them. The mini coffins were covered with white flowers, stuffed-animal puppies, teddy bears, and dolls.

The lengthy procession snaked its way up the hill towards the cemetery. Policemen, firefighters and paramedics shouldered the tiny coffins as the families trudged slowly forward leaning heavily on one another. The mothers' eyes were dark and swollen, and their lips look dried and cracked. Some gripped pictures of their children in one hand. Others murmured softly – prayers? Their child's name?

My sunglasses fogged up. I turned and slipped away – back in the olive grove I crouched by the knobbly trunk of an ancient olive tree. Tears rolled down my cheeks and I rustled around in my bag searching for a kleenex and loudly blew my nose. My cell phone vibrated, I had it on "silent".

"Yes," I whispered into the phone, trying to conceal the sadness in my voice. But it was my husband, not the news desk.

"Are you okay?" he asked. I burst into silent, heaving sobs.

"No, I'm not."

"I'm sorry," he said, "No mother should have to cover this story."

"I can't talk to you or I'll cry," I snivelled, "I've got to pull it together or I won't be able to get through this."

I hung up, pulled out my notebook and pen and went back to stand next to the cameraman. He didn't look at me. He was crying too.

The earthquake hit at 11:32 on October 31st 2002. In the hillside town of San Giuliano the roof of the schoolhouse came crashing down, trapping the children inside. It took time for rescue workers to wind their way up the narrow, steep roads to reach the town. I was standing in St. Peter's Square when I got the call and I knew I would have to go. Early reports said there were 50 children trapped in a school. Hours later, as we were speeding up the dark roads, my boss called, urging the cameraman and me to rush, that he needed pictures – that we had to beat the competition.

When we arrived a frantic rescue operation was underway. Firefighters were desperately trying to get to children who were still trapped under the rubble. Anguished parents stood nearby. The operation was painfully slow.

"We have to work slowly," a fireman told me. "It is like a house of cards, pull out the wrong one and everything will collapse. There are still children alive in there."

I thought of my own three small children at home in bed ... then I pushed the thought out of my mind. We watched as firefighters picked their way through the rubble. They carefully placed a dust-covered Pokemon bag, a pink and yellow Barbie knapsack, and brightly coloured notebooks in a pile on a low wall.

At four in the morning, rescuers pulled the last survivor out from under the rubble ... it was a nine-year-old boy named Angelo. As the stretcher passed before me, I caught a glimpse of Angelo under the blankets. He looked like my son, snug in bed at home. Again, I pushed the thought from my mind. I would not cry.

At dawn we walked around the town. Old ladies wandered aimlessly through the streets, blankets wrapped around their shoulders, crying helplessly. Their homes were wrecked; they had nowhere to go. I stood near the cameraman as he filmed a home whose front wall had collapsed. It was as though it has been sheared off and we were looking at a doll's house with an open front.

Standing on the street you could see the second floor bedroom, the double bed with the crucifix hanging over it. Behind us we heard desperate sobbing ... a couple was walking down the street away from the school leaning on each other, both of them crying uncontrollably. Their dead child had just been pulled out from under the rubble.

The cameraman discretely filmed their backs as they disappeared down the street. I turned away, ashamed.

Trisha Thomas has been working for Associated Press Television since 1994 covering Italy and the Vatican. An American, she lives in Rome with her husband, Gustavo, and their three children, Niccolo, Caterina and Chiara.

Grozny tale

Peter Dejong

I don't remember much about who was with me then, but I know I was with other photographers. We never travelled alone.

A cold and crisp winter morning, the sun was breaking through the clouds and snow masked most of the traces and scars.

It could have been a beautiful day. Maybe it was but few noticed anything but the war. We had gone out because there was a lull in the fighting, although it was hardly a fight, more like the mathematical destruction of a city, sector by sector. Besides a few Chechen fighters holed up in bombed-out buildings, the city centre of Grozny was deserted, destroyed, its heart ripped out.

On the periphery of this war residents tried to keep up their routine and normality. It's weird how little things can give one a sense of normality. Finding firewood, cooking, making bread, even washing cars. It may seem absurd to the outsider, but it deflects, routine is normality, routine is an escape. Taking pictures in a high-rise from the ground floor, looking up, counting the holes in nine floors where a penetration bomb had gone through, I felt dust and grit fall on my face. Two floors up, a woman was sweeping the floor.

We returned to a spot where a mortar had exploded in a crowd the day before, a wide open field where people queued for the one water point around, on the same assumption that there was a lull in fighting, or bombing. I had seen the images shot by a photographer minutes after the attack, injured people evacuated on a sled, dismembered.

What makes people stay in a city under a daily barrage of hellfire? Why was it that all we saw were old people?

As I milled around I saw a lone man make his way up the road heading out of the city, limping on a crutch, a small knapsack slung around his shoulders. I focused my camera, getting ready to make an image as he headed towards me. I waited for something to happen, something which makes a picture come together, the undefined. Instead he gestured, winked, he wanted me to come over. He halted, leaning on his crutch, and as I approached he slung the knapsack around and began rummaging. A piece of bread came out first, but he kept feeling around till he produced a red booklet, which he gave to me. "Afghanistan" he mumbled, "Afghanistan" he repeated.

He started talking and only very few words made sense to me. "War" I understood, "soldier" and "Afghanistan".

I pointed at him and asked, *"Russki?"*

He nodded.

The red booklet was a military passport of a man, a Russian soldier who fought in the Afghanistan war, for the Russians. It all flashed through my head, and with my very limited Russian I tried to ask him a question. I gestured, pointing at his leg.

"War, you were a soldier, your leg?"

Again he nodded.

Then his weathered face turned skywards, his hand pointing, he said "Russians bombing". As I looked up he turned away, trying to hide his tears as he limped off.

I never made a picture, and I have never regretted not taking one. Till this day I feel his sadness, his anger over getting forced out of a city he lived in, by his own army, the army he fought for in Afghanistan, the army and country he lost a leg for, only to get bombed, shot at, chased from his home a few decades later.

The shelling got worse, and closer, fewer breaks in between, closer all the time, a house we slept in just a few days ago was reduced to rubble the night before. We came to check on the people who gave us shelter – three or four of us, all photographers. A woman was weeping as she held on to a pole that once supported the roof.

"What if we had stayed?"

My thoughts get mixed sometimes, flashes intermingle, and scenes connect, but I think we decided soon after that there were not enough people in this ghost city to make us stay. Leaving the city under heavy shelling, senses heightened, analysing as you go, working your way out of the city.

Minutka Square meant we were half-way, the worst was behind us, the noise of a raging fire of a bombed gas pipeline our exit gate out of this inferno. A sense of relief came as we passed that landmark, but the shelling was still going on, thuds and thumps shattering the silence that accompanied us.

A bit further on I saw a woman taking cover alongside a wall. We all saw her and made our way towards her in spurts, the first living soul in a day, except for the four or five of us. Stuck out against an odd, light green metal gate a woman with golden teeth cried – she cried, she could not stop crying. She cried in shock. Her teeth, golden teeth and a green background and her crying. Sometimes the brain holds the oddest details. This time I took pictures but I stopped not long after. There were too many of us. I remember holding her and being annoyed that one of my colleagues was taking my picture. Weird, now *I* felt invaded.

She wanted to go into the city, back to her flat, to search for her daughter's diplomas. She was focused on a job, a future for her child. She needed the papers. She was willing to go into the heart of darkness for a piece of paper, a job for her child. We had to take her back out of the city. Her apartment was in an area under heavy shelling; we would not let her go.

It's odd how certain images stick to you, how they find a place in your brain and pop up when you least expect it. I call it my luggage, it's the suitcase I carry with me after 14 years of travel. I'm proud of it, proud to carry the weight, even for the images and memories that haunt me, for it reminds me I'm not made out of stone, it tells me I feel, I absorb and I filter.

P.S. A lot of Russians transmigrated to Grozny decades ago. Most of the Chechens fled the city to go and live with family in the countryside. The ones who got stuck in the city were the ones without relatives, mostly Russians and the elderly who did not want to move.

Peter Dejong has been a photographer with The Associated Press for 14 years in Europe, the former Soviet Republic, Middle East, Asia, Africa, North and South America. He lives in Amsterdam.

Close to death? Come closer to Allah!

Khaled Kazziha

Saddam has just been toppled; "down with Saddam" was the mood on the streets. Baghdad was still smoldering as hoards of looters were scavenging for whatever they could get their hands on. The US Marines with their terminator sunglasses looked ready to kill anybody who was remotely suspicious, save for the handful of women and children who deceptively appeared to be welcoming the US as "liberators".

I spent three surreal weeks in Iraq filming breaking news to soft features, but at the end of these agonising weeks I still couldn't put my finger on what really was going on here. The more I searched for the truth the more I realised I was only scratching the surface. It was time for me to leave. The level of hypocrisy and deception on the streets was doing my head in, and frankly speaking I wanted to be with my girlfriend back home in Kenya. However going home was going to be a mission on its own.

The road from Baghdad to Amman was supposed to be relatively safe, most of the incoming and outgoing journalists said so. However my news agency had to follow strict safety guidelines imposed on us by our insurance company after the deaths of Myles Tierney and Miguel Gil Moreno. Two exceptional journalists and sorely missed friends who were gunned down on the treacherous roads of Sierra Leone.

I was under the impression that these insurance companies would not dish out anymore life insurance to grieving families unless they could dictate to us how we could get in and out of Baghdad. I would be required to travel in a bulletproof 4X4 with tinted windows and a risk management specialist and former British soldier named Matt Briggs along with Tom Szypulski, an American producer working with me.

That night Matt explained us our exit strategy. "We will need to move by 06.00. That means we should all meet in the lobby at 05.30. Clear?" "Yes" we responded simultaneously. "We will be taking extra fuel and will have two spare tyres Because our bullet-proof car is heavy and can only travel at 100 kilometres an hour we will need to travel alone and not in a convoy, but not to worry by the time we get to Ramadi the press convoy will have caught up with us. I will drop you off at the border with Jordan and spend the night with the US military, then return the following morning to Baghdad. Any questions?" I had one. I wanted to know if Matt was going to be taking any weapons with him. He said he wouldn't because our company has strict rules against that.

I had a sleepless night, worry and fear gripped me. Being an Arab traveling with Tom, an American, and Matt who looked like a mercenary on a deserted highway to Jordan could be hazardous to my health. My preferred exit strategy, as was Tom's, would be to go out alone in an inconspicuous car. But I had no choice. Besides my fate was sealed and if I am meant to die so be it; I was ready to go home either way.

Before the crack of dawn we were loading up our bullet-proof Land Cruiser. Matt started the car and we were on our way. We missed our first exit and after getting lost we managed to find the highway to Jordan.

As Matt drove I noticed how deserted the road to Jordan was. A worrying emptiness. Nobody said anything. Oddly on the front dashboard there was a kind of walkie talkie. I asked what it was, feeling a bit like a little boy asking too many questions in a very silent car. "I don't know but try talking into it." said Matt. I pushed the side clip down and said "hello". My voice was amplified. It was a loud speaker, not a radio, and could be used to address people outside our bulletproof car in the event that we needed to speak to people outside without opening our bulletproof doors.

We continued to drive; the silence was making me feel uncomfortable. There was a CD deck in the car and I offered them my Buddha Bar CD, a collection of calming music. I laid down on the back seat using my jacket as a pillow. I slowly started dozing off when suddenly I was abruptly awoken by Tom screaming "Oh no please, oh no!". Matt slammed the brakes and I slipped off the back seat onto the back floor. We collided into another vehicle and started skidding. I struggled to get off the floor as Matt struggled to keep the car on the road. I peaked out of the window and saw a car with three men in it, the man in the back seat was pointing a pistol at us while the man in the front passenger seat had a walkie talkie on his lap. Matt tried to run them off the road as Tom pleaded, "Please don't do that, you'll make them mad and they'll kill us!" The gunmen's car was now just a few meters behind us. And they were no longer pointing a pistol but an AK-47. They fired a round into the back door. Then they drove up to us and fired into the front passenger door. I could see them pointing their rifle at our window. We all knew that if they fired at our glass window it would only take four or five bullets before the bullet-proof windows would come crashing down leaving us fully exposed.

"Give me the speaker" I said. I addressed the gunmen in Arabic. "We are journalists, please don't shoot". But they fired again, this time at the front passenger door. "I beg you please don't fire, we are journalists, we have nothing, I beg you, please." I kept repeating this as the gunmen's vehicle sped ahead of our car while firing at our wheels. Suddenly they were ahead of us and shooting directly into our engine. Matt made a ninety degree turn off the deserted highway straight into the desert. Our Land Cruiser was bouncing over the mounds of sand, our heads where bouncing off our shoulders and crashing into the ceiling as Matt struggled to keep our vehicle from flipping over.

"Please don't drive into the desert, they will come after us and kill us and nobody will find our bodies." I pleaded with Matt. We were all panicking. Suddenly Matt stopped. "I want to assess the car" he said. Matt was frantically running around the car, then looked at me in absolute horror "We have two flat tires!" A plume of smoke was heading towards us, the gunmen were coming after us into the desert. We quickly jumped into the car and Matt made a direct turn heading straight for the highway. The car was out of balance and rocking from side to side like a boat on a stormy sea. We managed to get on the road, the gunmen were not far behind us. Suddenly a press convoy of about eight vehicles with TV stickers splattered over them, appeared. Our car was on the road with two flat tyres and a leaking radiator, but they zoomed right passed us. They did not even slow down.

"We are going to die!!" Tom screamed. Neither of us doubted it. Matt asked me to open the top of his black bag and hand him a gun that he was not supposed to have. "Do any of you guys know how to use a gun?" Both Tom and I said "No".

Instead I grabbed the speaker one last time in an attempt to beg for our lives, but all that came out of my mouth was a prayer from the Holy Qur'aan. It is a verse that is called "The Throne" and Muslims believe it has the power to protect those who pronounce it from danger: "He, the Living the Self-Subsisting, Eternal. No slumber can seize Him nor sleep. His are all things in the heavens and on earth. Who is there can intercede in His presence except as He permitted? He knows what appears to his creatures as Before or After or Behind them nor shall they compass aught of His knowledge except as He will. His Throne doth extend over the heavens and the earth and He feels no fatigue in guarding and preserving them for He is the Most High, the Supreme in glory." (Qura'aan 2:255)

I had just finished reading the verse, mesmerised by the situation, but blind to the world around me when suddenly I could hear Matt calling out from the world of the living "By God you have done it!" I looked out of the window to see where our killers where but the gunmen had simply vanished.

On this fateful day I witnessed the power of the spoken Qur'aan.

The rest of this nearly tragic event was spent begging locals to drive us back to Baghdad and recovering our shot up Land Cruiser. A couple of hours later we were safe and sound in Baghdad.

Matt Briggs was dismissed from his job for concealing a weapon. Tom Szypulski went back to Argentina where he is based for APTN. I went back home to Nairobi and ended up in Baghdad again a few months later.

Khaled Kazziha, wrote this story in Amman after completing another rotation in Iraq for Associated Press Television News. Khaled lives in Nairobi where he is senior producer and cameraman for APTN.

Did you enjoy this book? Email or write to us and tell us
what we should be publishing, or send us your story.

marketing@jacana.co.za

Jacana Media
PO Box 2004
Houghton
2041